They and We

Consulting Editor:
CHARLES H. PAGE
University of Massachusetts

PETER I. ROSE

Smith College

They and We

Racial and Ethnic Relations in the United States

Second Edition

 Random House, New York

Second Edition

98765432

Library of Congress Cataloging in Publication Data

Rose, Peter Isaac, 1933-
 They and we; racial and ethnic relations in the United States.
 Bibliography: p.
 1. Minorities—United States. 2. United States—Race question. 3. Discrimination
—United States.
 I. Title.
E184.A1R72 1974   301.45′1′0973   73-12793
ISBN 0-394-31804-8

Manufactured in the United States of America. Composed by Cherry Hill Composition, Pennsauken, N.J. Printed and bound by Halliday Lithograph Corp., West
Hanover, Mass.

Design by Charlotte Staub

PHOTO CREDITS:
P. 171: Michael Abramson from Black Star Publishing Co., Inc.; p. 42:
Shareen Brysac; p. 106: Bruce Davidson from Magnum Photos, Inc.;
p. 79: Jules Feiffer from Robert Lantz—Candida Donadio Literary
Agency, Inc.; p. 162: Charles Gatewood; pp. 87, 208: Hiroji Kubota
from Magnum Photos, Inc.; pp. 10, 51, 226: Shelly Rusten; p. 153:
Burk Uzzle from Magnum Photos, Inc.

For Hedy

PREFACE

The first edition of *They and We* was written in 1962 and 1963 and published shortly after the famous March on Washington. 1963 was the year when the civil rights movement reached its zenith. Black Power was but a hushed whisper then. Indeed, few who listened to Reverend Martin Luther King addressing a quarter of a million black and white Americans on the steps of the Lincoln Memorial realized that he and his people and their allies in the struggle—and their enemies—were about to enter a new era. Few of those listeners had any inkling that the whisper was to become a roar.

Those days, a mere decade ago, now seem light-years away. In the period immediately before the march, thousands participated in a movement marked by an admixture of love and hope, righteousness and perseverance, liberal faith and Christian principles, and a great deal of confidence in the American system. It was oriented primarily toward forcing the country to honor its own vaunted ideals and to win for all the rights most (white) Americans took for granted. But by 1964 the tone and temper and orientation had changed. The code words were not "Love" or "Brotherhood" but "Power" and "Brother" (and "Sister," too). Many whites were eased or pushed from positions of leadership, and many blacks (and brown and red Americans in their fashion) eschewed the rhetoric of integration for the rhetoric of revolution. And, in many ways, the rhetoric was reified. In a real sense there was a revolution.

First of all, the members of the dominant white majority

were told over and over that they, all of them, were racists. A spate of books hammered home the theme "Look Out, Whitey, Black Power's Goin' Get Yer Momma." Second, many black people who, for any number of reasons, had not organized themselves before began to "get their thing together" and to add action to their verbal assaults. Demands were made, met, escalated, and often met again. The litany began where the old civil rights leaders had left off. *Equality. Freedom Now. We Shall Overcome.* Then came the call for recompense, for special treatment. Ultimately, in what many saw as justified and others saw as racism-in-reverse, the plea for admission and fairness became a cry for affirmative action, even for favoritism. Third, as the demands, especially of college students, were beginning to be responded to by frightened faculties and baffled administrators (often liberal and therefore highly vulnerable to the accusations of the young), more conservative organizations began making their own concessions. For example, large industries increased the level of tokenism to include more black and brown workers, especially in places where they would be seen. Television networks and local stations began to employ them too. (It is interesting to note how many minority people were available as potential freshmen in Ivy League colleges, as workers in various companies, as announcers and commentators, when the threat of disruption loomed on the horizon.) Fourth, as the disaffected members of the civil rights movement began to organize their troops for these assaults on the academy and the factory, the people in the streets became involved too— some in organized fashion, others more spontaneously. Dozens of urban riots flared up in cities as different as New York and Detroit and Cleveland and Los Angeles as poor folks (though not always the poorest) joined in the burning and looting and pillaging in a frenzied expression of frustration, bitterness, and, for some, short-lived pleasure as Whitey seemed to be getting his come-uppance. Other people engaged in more political activities, many of them centering on the issue of community control, especially of schools. Still others simply took renewed pride in who they were, if not in where they found themselves.

All this—the rhetoric, the organizing, the planned assaults upon the system and the spontaneous outbursts—had their effects. Many Americans reeled in disbelief—and then they reacted.

Part of the reaction came from the traditional right-wing whose preeminent theme was "we told you so." But more significant, and far greater in the numbers involved, was the reaction of what had come to be called Middle America. White, working-class or lower middle-class, not infrequently but a generation or two from ghetto living themselves, they began to feel that they more than anyone else were being asked to pay for the sins of other peoples' fathers. Backlash became a reality, though it tended to be far less blatant on the one hand and far more widespread on the other than many, including many social scientists, had predicted. Parallel to the growing resistance to the pressures being exerted by black and brown and other minority Americans was a reexamination of their own place in this society, and their own history as well. Indeed, as several have suggested, the Black Power movement was responsible for ethnic communalism becoming legitimated, then institutionalized, in a manner unprecedented in our history. By the end of the decade (1963 to 1973) the bookstores had another section to add to the one that shelved Angelou, Baldwin, Cleaver, Donaldson, Ellison, Fanon, and on through the rest of the alphabet of black writers or writers on black themes. The new shelf (not yet so long) includes Louise Howe's *The White Majority*, Andrew M. Greeley's *Why Can't They Be Like Us?*, Peter Schrag's *Out of Place in America*, Michael Novak's *The Rise of the Unmeltable Ethnics*, Murray Friedman's *Overcoming Middle Class Rage*, and many more, all concerned with the theme of reaction.

It was quite a decade on the ethnic front.

Still, certain things seem to have been unaltered by time and, in my view, certain basic assumptions about the nature of prejudice, the pattern of discrimination, and the past experiences of the multifarious American people remained as they were when the first edition of this book was published. Consequently, much of what I said ten years ago seems, to me at least, still to hold.

Keeping in mind both the apparent changes (including new issues like "Black Ethnogenesis" and the "New Pluralism") and the seeming constants, I have attempted to put some new wine in the old bottle. The format remains essentially the same (though there are two new chapters). The first chapter, which spells out those working concepts that, I feel, best help one to analyze racial and ethnic relations in the United States, is but a slightly edited copy of the original. The second chapter, on the history of America's ethnic groups, is similar in form to what it was before, but quite different in content. What was thumbnail history has become somewhat less sketchy and an attempt is made to include considerably more material on certain groups unintentionally slighted in the first go-round. The third chapter deals with patterns of adjustment and adaptation, and, once again, the issues of assimilation, amalgamation, and accommodation are examined and illustrated. This time, however, considerably more space is devoted to the controversy over the meaning of assimilation itself, a theme to which I return in a later chapter. Chapter Four, on Prejudice, is expanded. Chapter Five, on Discrimination, is entirely rewritten. What was to have been a final chapter has also been rewritten and divided into three chapters. Chapter Six deals with aspects of minority status in the United States. In Chapter Seven particular attention is paid to the last three decades—the one that began with the formation of the Chicago Committee Against Racial Discrimination (the forerunner of CORE) and ended with the Supreme Court Decision of 1954, ruling separate schools unequal; the one that began in the wake of that monumental decision and ended with the rise of the Black Power movement; and the decade which I briefly sketched out above.

The last chapter of this new edition brings the reader up to the present—and to confrontation with present-day concerns.

The title speaks to the topic: "The Resurgence of Ethnicity."

There is no real conclusion for racial and ethnic relations do not "end" in a society like ours (if in any) nor are all issues resolved either on paper or in fact.

Like the first edition, *They and We* is not a blueprint for change. It is, however, a guide for study and reflection. As I wrote in the Preface to the original volume:

While the organized efforts to bring about a reduction in racial and ethnic tension represent an important part of contemporary American life, and the tactics and strategies employed are a matter of great concern to many social scientists (including the author), they cannot be discussed within the compass of this small book. It is hoped, however, that the facts presented here will help to replace some of the popular misconceptions of the problems discussed and will thus serve as a basis for understanding—the first step toward change.

Brief passages in this edition of *They and We* have appeared in somewhat different form in several of my other writings, including *The Subject Is Race* (New York: Oxford University Press, 1968); in the Foreword to Lewis M. Killian's *The Impossible Revolution?* (New York: Random House, 1969); and in a review essay of Andrew Greeley's *Why Can't They Be Like Us?* and Michael Novak's *The Rise of the Unmeltable Ethnics*, (*Contemporary Sociology*, January 1973). Moreover, part of Chapter Seven originally appeared as an essay, "The Black Experience: Issues and Images," published in the *Social Science Quarterly*, 50, September 1969, pp. 286–297. Permission to use this material here is gratefully acknowledged.

Prefaces usually end with words of appreciation for friends, colleagues, editors, secretaries, spouses and children. Mine is no exception. I, too, wish to thank people in each of these categories: first, friends, teachers and students, American and those from the twenty-odd countries I have visited in the last decade, who have helped me to better feel what I have long tried to understand; second, my friend, consultant, and personal gadfly, Charles H. Page, who has been trying to teach me to write—and rewrite—ever since I came to him with the first rough draft of *They and We*; third, professional colleagues (who are also friends), in particular Ely Chinoy, Bill Wilson, Everett Hughes, Robin Williams, Oscar Cohen, the late John Dean, and the late Ed Suchman, who encouraged, criticized and sometimes found support for my own work in the field we used to call "intergroup relations." Fourth, loyal secretaries Agnes Shannon and Norma Lepine, who have been with this book almost as long as I have and have typed and retyped various sections almost as often as I.

I also want to thank various editors who have seen this book from conception (Charles Lieber) to birth (Ted Caris) to rebirth (Dave Bartlett). Midwives are important, too, especially to me. Lynne Farber is the best in the business.

But most important of all is my wife, Hedy, to whom this book is dedicated. She knows best what has been involved. And, this time around, so do Lies and Dan.

Peter I. Rose

South Wellfleet, Massachusetts
June 1973

Contents

They
and
We

ONE

RACE, ETHNICITY, AND THE SOCIOLOGICAL PERSPECTIVE

Introduction

Since the first edition of *They and We* was published in 1964, I have spent part of almost every year traveling and sometimes staying for extended periods in Europe, Africa, Asia, and the Pacific. In countries as different as Japan and Israel, England and Korea, Singapore and Sweden, Indonesia and Australia, I have met with politicians and journalists, businessmen, labor leaders, social workers, and, mostly, university professors and students. In almost every initial conversation the subject of contemporary American society seemed to come up. Often questions posed would be prefaced with, "As a sociologist, how do you explain . . ." The reader can fill in the blank because many, many aspects of our social life were under scrutiny. However, given my special interests it is not surprising that the interrogative sentence usually ended with phrases like, ". . . the failure of your civil rights movement?," ". . . the backlash?," or ". . . the meaning of Black Power?"

If I was not asked about America directly, I was asked indirectly. "What do you think about the fact that the Black Power movement is being adapted to the struggle of *our*

3

aborigines?" "Do you think that we will ever attain the degree of cultural integration that exists in your country?" "Why are Americans so extreme in everything they do? Those young people who come here have no respect for our traditions."

In view of what has happened during the past decade, it should not be surprising to report that many of the people to whom I spoke, especially younger people, were not very sympathetic to the American way of life as they had heard about it. Many others, including those who wanted to like America and Americans, were disturbed by what they saw and read. Since I agreed with many of the criticisms of foreign adventures and domestic problems it would have been easy to say, "Yes, America is . . . ." But the more I listened, the more I realized how little most of those to whom I spoke actually knew or understood about the matters that concerned us both.

Thus, time and again, my response to most queries was an explanatory one. I tried to place the subject in its historical, political, or social context, showing, for example, how one cannot understand Black Power without having a sense of the meaning of White Power in America; one cannot adequately deal with the seeming "retribalization" among various Catholic ethnic groups without knowing about the character of immigration and the relationship of various newcomers to both white Protestants and black ones; one cannot really comprehend such developments or ideas as community control, school crises, affirmative action, compensatory programming, even "benign neglect," without knowing something of the background and the political and social complexities involved in each of these headline-grabbing issues.

These matters, of course, must also be raised when one talks with fellow Americans about the same sorts of problems. Like many foreigners, many Americans often express the attitude, "My mind is made up; don't confuse me with the facts." These people exist too, thousands of them, in every part of America.

The fact is that very few people—here or abroad—know or understand very much about the contradictory and complex relations that actually exist on the "racial scene." This book is an attempt to provide both a framework and a foundation for greater understanding of racial and ethnic relations in the United States.

Events (and personal experiences) have altered some of the views expressed in the first edition. These changes reflect in part, at least, the conspicuous fact that the subject matter of this book is highly dynamic. Intergroup relations are constantly being altered and ours are surely no exception. In another decade I will have to look back, once again, and ask myself what I have left out, what has changed, what, if any, underlying themes still remain intact.

In redoing this book, originally addressed to American college students, I have tried to expand its scope while keeping in mind the dual function it was always intended to serve: to introduce the sociology of intergroup relations in the United States, and to familiarize others—those students, other fellow citizens, and now more than ever, foreigners too—with the subject of that sociology. In planning this new edition I decided to be at once more descriptive and more critical—descriptive to the extent that (at least in many places) I would try to go beyond the definition of terms and other conventional textbook ploys and put more meat on the bare bones; critical in that I would attempt to offer more clearly than before conflicting views of what I am trying to describe and analyze.

As before, the Study begins with a discussion of the sociological perspective on racial and ethnic relations.[1]

The Sociologist and Intergroup Relations

The sociologist is primarily an investigator, a social scientist concerned with the study of social relationships and variegated patterns of social behavior. He shares with other scientists the fundamental view that only through the systematic accumulation of empirical evidence and rigorous analysis can the realities of the physical and social world be revealed. His commitment is to the investigation, description, and analysis of what is, not what ought to be. Nevertheless, in seeking to uncover the complexities of social life, there is the ever-present conviction that man may benefit from greater knowledge of himself. Scientific research may thus serve a dual purpose: science for the sake of understanding, and understanding for the sake of providing solutions to problems.

Not infrequently the issues upon which the sociologist focuses his attention are those aspects of behavior that are considered by many people to be detrimental to the functioning of society or injurious to some or all of its members. In examining such phenomena as crime and delinquency, political upheaval, family disorganization, or race relations, it is a difficult but necessary task to maintain the criterion of scientific objectivity. It is difficult because such aspects of social life are studied precisely because they are considered problems; it is necessary for, as the late Robert M. MacIver observed, "A moral judgment—no matter how much we may agree with it, cannot be a substitute for the proper study of causes."[2]

Few problems of contemporary life are more in need of continuous sociological investigation than the tensions and cleavages that exist between racial and ethnic groupings. One need look no further than the pages of a daily newspaper or a television screen to see glaring evidence of this fact. In America the persistence of racism, manifest most clearly in continued segregation of black people in both northern and southern areas, is only the most blatant case. Puerto Ricans, Mexican-Americans, people from Asia, native Americans and other nonwhites are frequently singled out for discriminatory treatment. So, too, are members of certain religious groups (and—at least at one time—atheists) as well as political dissenters and dissidents and, of course, women in every ethnic and religious and racial category. Sometimes even members of old immigrant groups, the so-called "white ethnics," face abuse and discrimination, especially by those who engage in what one person has called "respectable bigotry" and another describes as the proclivity of certain members of the elite to play missionaries to the heathens.[3]

While examples of the overt manifestations of racial, religious, and ethnic intolerance are readily observed, the forces that serve to create, maintain, perpetuate, or alleviate intergroup tensions are highly complex. For many years sociologists concerned with the study of racial and ethnic relations have been investigating the causes and consequences of intergroup conflict. A growing body of confirmed knowledge and theory now provides important insights into the dynamics of prejudice and discrimination.

This study introduces the reader to some of the principal methods and findings of these researchers. It contains the definition and explication of several relevant sociological concepts. Chapters Two and Three are concerned with a brief summary of the history of immigration in the United States and an evaluation and critique of the theories and processes of adjustment and assimilation. In three succeeding chapters the nature of prejudice, the varied ways in which ethnic minorities have been treated in this society, and the minority communities themselves are considered. The last two chapters deal with Black Power and the resurgence of ethnicity, respectively, and the problem and promise of using the future as a guide to the past.

Differentiation and Discrimination

In all societies individuals are differentiated by biological and social criteria. People are ranked in hierarchical fashion, as superior or inferior, according to those attributes that are considered important. Even in the simplest, most isolated societies—where subsistence is apt to be the primary concern —distinctions are made on the basis of age groupings, sex roles, family and kinship ties, and essentially economic and political divisions of labor. More advanced societies are divided into distinct social classes, and those higher on the scale have access to greater opportunities for wealth, prestige, and social control. The discrepancy between those in superior or subordinate positions is clearly evident. There is an obvious disparity in the style of life enjoyed by the peasant and the lord, the yeoman and the gentleman, the worker and the owner. Such variations often account for intense feelings of intraclass identification and interclass rivalry. The rich and powerful seek to maintain their positions; subordinates often desire to raise themselves in the status hierarchy.

The opportunities for improving one's position largely depend upon a socially defined system of social stratification. Where a rigid *caste system* exists there is little hope for individual advancement, for status is fixed by birth and marriage is endogamous (within the caste group). In societies with a feudal social structure, placement is determined largely by heredity; the *estate system*, however, does provide limited channels for mobility and individuals are sometimes able to change their estate by royal decree, by marrying someone of higher status, by entering the clergy or military service, or by becoming artisans or tradesmen. The estate system is most prevalent in agricultural societies, where status is directly related to the ownership and use of land. In agricultural societies with socialist governments heredity is largely replaced as a basis for status, but not without upheaval. One thinks of recent changes in China, beginning with the civil war and the ouster of the Kuomintang, the development of the communist regime, and the cultural revolution, all designed to rid the society of its feudal character.

In industrial societies, where land tenure is relatively unimportant, wealth and income become the relevant measures of social position. In such societies a *class system* prevails. Ideally, every individual should be able to gain recognition based upon personal ability and performance, regardless of birth or previous condition of inequality.[4] While greater opportunities do exist for movement up and down the ladder of social mobility within a class system, there is no society where individual merit is the sole criterion for determining status. In the United States, for example, several factors serve to inhibit full realization of the traditional ideal of equal opportunity; not the least of these factors is membership in a particular "minority" group. Foreign-born persons, members of certain religious groups, individuals with dubious political affiliations, and, especially, those with darker skins are often handicapped in their attempts to advance on the basis of personal ability. Many members of such groups are categorically denied the right to fulfill their own potentialities in the "pursuit of happiness." In fact, as Kurt Mayer has said, "If the absence of estate-like characteristics makes the American class system unique, it is likewise true that the intrusion of racial caste-like features is almost without parallel in modern Western experience."[5] Thus, a critical aspect of placement in the status hierarchy of American society is that of ethnic and racial group membership.

Race and Culture

Culture and race are two words that are widely misused and often misunderstood. *Culture* refers to the way people live, the rules they set for themselves, the general ideas around which they organize their lives, the things they feel are good or bad, right or wrong, pleasurable or painful. Cultural "norms" are learned from those around us: parents, teachers, friends. We often speak of "Western culture" as the principal source of the American heritage. And this concept is quite accurate for, despite many modifications, our society is largely a product of European values and attitudes, including certain prejudices about the relationship between "looks" and "outlooks," between physiognomy and culture.

From ancient times to the present people in the so-called Western World have tended to divide the human species into separate and visually distinct "races," as "black," "white," "red," "yellow," and, sometimes, when referring to persons of certain mixtures such as "white" Spaniards and "red"

Indians, as "brown." If one wants to divide humans into statistical categories, it is not illogical to group them according to gross similarities and not surprising that such external criteria as skin color, head form, facial features (like broad or narrow noses), stature, and color, texture, and distribution of body hair are used as variables. Indeed, some anthropologists would define a *race* as a statistical aggregate of persons who share a composite of physically transmissible physical traits.[6] Without spelling it out, most Americans would agree.

It would not be difficult for any of us to pick out an "Asian," a "Caucasian," or a "Negro" on a crowded street in San Francisco or New York; a set of criteria is associated with each category. A person with brownish-yellow skin, straight black hair, almond-shaped eyes, and a nose that seemed to lack a pronounced bridge would, most likely, be considered Asian or Oriental or "yellow." A person with whitish, pinkish, or ruddy skin, blond or brunette, wavy or straight hair, blue or green eyes, a straight, hooked, or pug nose would fall in the category "white." A person with dark brown or brown skin, kinky black hair, brown eyes, a rather broad nose, and thick lips undoubtedly would be seen as a "Negro" or "Black."

Of course, it is harder to categorize someone who has a straight high-bridged nose, dark wavy hair, and a dark brown complexion. In the United States, most people would probably say such an individual "must be Negro." Why? Because in this society, like many others, racial designations are *not merely* simple ways of classifying people according to their genetic make-up. Rather, "race" is used for locating or placing people according to culturally defined social positions—and vice versa.[7]

American history is filled with instances of "race mixing." Mexican-Americans are largely the children of Spanish and Indian parentage; Puerto Ricans are the offspring of white and black as well as Indian ancestors; and many people whom we call "black" are actually very white indeed. In fact, to find pure-Negroid types is very difficult in this country (as compared with almost any place in sub-Saharan Africa). Even so, until 1960, the United States Census Bureau gave instructions to its enumerators to include the following criteria for designating Negroes:

In addition to persons of Negro and mixed Negro and white descent, this category includes persons of mixed American-Indian and Negro descent, unless the Indian ancestry very definitely predominates or unless the individual is regarded as an Indian in the community.[8]

Many so-called nonwhite Americans long have been aware of the fact that racial labels mean something special.

If you're white, you're right,
If you're brown, hang aroun'
But if you're black, brother,
Get back, get back, get back.

If no cultural value were placed upon ancestry—whether "pure" or "mixed"—it would matter very little what one was called or in which pigeonhole one was placed, but in a race-conscious society like the United States, those who are "colored" (as opposed to "white") have generally been put in inferior positions and treated accordingly. In almost every American town and city there is and long has been a close connection between the tasks people perform and the place in which they live, and the color of their skin. Menial work is disproportionately the province of "colored" citizens, the shabbier neighborhoods being their domain. White people have tended to have a greater percentage of better and more varied jobs and, in many instances, finer homes in better neighborhoods.

The sociological importance of such a correlation lies in the fact that it is culturally, not biologically, determined. There is nothing in their nature that predisposes colored citizens to a life of inferior status. There is much, however, in the social image of their nature, which largely determines their place in the social structure. In the words of some Americans:

> A black-type person and a white-type person, they ain't alike. Now the black-type person, all they think about is fighting and having a good time and you know what. Now the white-type person is more the American-type. . . . [9]

As W. I. Thomas has written, "If men define situations as real, they are real in their consequences." When they are given inferior positions in the social order, individuals often reflect in their attitudes and behavior the status imposed upon them.[10] Shingoro Takaishi, the Japanese writer, discussing the subordinate status of Japanese women, illustrates this self-fulfilling prophecy:

> The education of our women was neglected, and her intelligence became more and more narrow owing to there being little or no chance for her to see things in the outer world. The next thing which was bound to happen was man's contempt and disdain for her narrow-mindedness and stupidity.[11]

In similar fashion, certain people considered by many

to have lower potentialities than others are given lowly jobs and denied equal opportunities for achievement. Excluded and often embittered, lacking in advantages and limited in their access to employment and schooling, they may in fact reflect in their behavior and attitudes the stereotypes held by those in dominant positions.[12]

Ethnic Groups

It has been said that "man is separated from man, not only by real or assumed physiological traits, but by differences of group traditions, national or regional or religious, that may or may not be associated with biological distinctions."[13] Groups whose members share a unique social and cultural heritage passed on from one generation to the next are known as *ethnic groups.*[14] Ethnic groups are frequently identified by distinctive patterns of family life, language, recreation, religion, and other customs that cause them to be differentiated from others. They often live—by choice or because of the requirements of others—in their own enclaves, ghettos, or neighborhoods. Above all else, members of such groups feel a consciousness of kind[15] and an "interdependence of fate"[16] with those who share the customs of the ethnic tradition. Members of different ethnic groups may look very much alike (think of the Catholics and Protestants in Northern Ireland or the Arabs and Jews in Jerusalem) but have very different views of the world and of their roles in it.

In America, members of some ethnic groups or their ancestors may have come from the same country, as in the case of Italian-, Irish-, and Mexican-Americans. Such groups are often referred to as "nationalities." Some ethnic-group members, however, like Jews or Gypsies, are joined by common traditions and experiences that cut across political boundaries; they are frequently known as "peoples."

In some societies distinctions are even more complicated. In Israel nationality officially denotes ethnic background. An Israeli citizen may be an Arab or a Jew by nationality; an Arab may be a Moslem or a Christian by religion. However, it is argued that Judaism is the only religion whose adherents belong to a single "nation" and Jews are the only "nation" with a single religion; some say that Jews *anywhere* belong to one nation while holding citizenship in a particular country like Israel or the United States or the Soviet Union.

In a society made up of many cultural groups, like the United States, the intensity of ethnic identity or *ethnicity* is apt to be determined by the attitude of the members of the "host" society toward the "strangers" in their midst. This attitude, in turn, is often dependent upon how closely the ethnic group approximates the culture of the dominant society. Acceptance may loosen the bonds of ethnic identity, as in the case of Scottish and German immigrants to America; rejection and subordination may strengthen them,[17] as among Mexican-Americans today.

The relationship between membership in an ethnic group and social acceptance has been studied by many sociologists. They concur in the conclusion that "when the combined cultural and biological traits [of the ethnic group] are highly divergent from those of the host society the subordination of the group will be very great, their sub-system strong, the period of assimilation long, and the processes slow and usually painful."[18] (It should be noted that this widely expressed view is based on the assumption that "assimilation" is the goal of most minority peoples. As we shall point out, many voices recently have been raised seriously questioning the ideology that underlies what the critics would see as a classic case of liberal dogma.[19])

Minorities

In 1932, Donald Young, writing about group relations in the United States, stated: "There is, unfortunately, no word in the English language which can . . . be applied to all these groups which are distinguished by biological features, alike national traits, or a combination of both."[20] He proposed "minority," a term that had been used in a related but different context. Earlier, "minority group" had been applied to sub-segments of European societies inhabited by conquered persons or those incorporated by annexation to another national group. The multifarious peoples of the Soviet Union and many Western European countries represent such minorities.

Since Young's adoption, the term *minority* has been used by sociologists to refer to those groups whose members share certain racial or ethnic similarities that are considered to be different from or inferior to the traits of the dominant group and who are thereby "singled out for differential and unequal treatment."[21]

Statistical underrepresentation does not, in itself, account for a group being considered a minority in the sociological sense. It is not even a necessary condition. In the Republic of South Africa, for example, the Bantu-speaking black minority far outnumbers the white rulers. Prior to independence in Algeria the community of *colons* was very small compared with the native "minority" group. Until recently, a limited number of Europeans dominated "minority" peoples in the Dutch East Indies (now Indonesia), in the Belgian Congo (now the Republic of Zaïre), and in the tiny Portuguese outpost of Goa on the western coast of the Indian subcontinent. In many towns in the southern states of this country, black people constitute the largest ethnic element in the population but remain a sociological minority.

Moreover, minority status is neither fixed nor immutable. A minority in one country may be a dominant group in another. Compare the position of the Jews in the Soviet Union with that of their coreligionists in Israel. Or compare the status of French-Canadians living in New England with those for whom the city of Quebec is home.

In most western societies the power-holding group is made up of persons having "white" skins and professing a belief in Christianity. In the United States the dominant group consists largely of white individuals of North European background who belong to one of the Protestant denominations. This "majority group" has traditionally been the determining element in public policy. In language, customs, and moral codes, these descendants of early settlers have set the standards for American behavior. Moreover, these so-called Americans have generally determined which groups are to be considered minorities and how each shall be treated.

The American Case

There is good reason for choosing the United States as the focal point for our study of racial and ethnic relations. Few nations can match the heterogeneous quality of American society. No other modern society can claim a history characterized so markedly by the importation of foreign ways and ideologies. All Americans (including the Indians) are of immigrant origin. In Walt Whitman's terms, America is "a nation of nations."

The history of this country bears witness to the fact that the accommodation of many racial and ethnic groups has been an essential element in developing and perpetuating the spirit of democracy. It is true that the customs of a hundred culture systems have contributed to the richness of American life.[22] The late Ralph Linton described the extent of foreign influence when he wrote: "Our solid American citizen . . . reads the news of the day, imprinted in characters invented by the ancient Semites upon a material invented in China by a process invented in Germany . . . and as he absorbs the accounts of foreign troubles he will, if he is a good conservative citizen, thank a Hebrew deity in an Indo-European language that he is 100 per cent American."[23]

The influence of European (and, to a lesser extent, Asian and African) culture on America is easy to recognize. This is, however, but one side of the picture, for the very presence of newcomers has, in each generation, often provoked the resentment and suspicion of those already here. America has not been immune from group hatred and discrimination. Throughout its history there have been those who have persisted in denying their fellow citizens the right to full participation in American life, who wished to maintain a society where the "right" skin color or religious preference or cultural heritage was considered to be an essential requisite to acceptance on an equal basis.

Gunnar Myrdal, the Swedish social scientist, thus characterized the United States as a nation possessing a wide gulf between the democratic ideal of brotherhood and the overt manifestations of intergroup conflict.[24] The American creed of freedom and equality of opportunity for all has been, and continues to be, violated by the acts of many citizens of this country. This "American dilemma" is self-evident; but the problems that beset minorities in this country are far more complex than the simple discrepancy between the national ethos and individual behavior. As sociologist Robert K. Merton has suggested, the failure to recognize the intricacies of these problems tends so "to simplify the relations between creed and conduct as to be seriously misleading both for social policy and for social science."[25]

Between the prescriptions set forth in the Preamble to the Constitution and the Bill of Rights and the actual behavior of many people there exists a wide range of standards for behavior, which vary markedly from group to group, from place to place, and from time to time. The formal and informal policies of a region, state, and local community; the social, economic, religious, and political groups to which one belongs; the attitudes of parents, teachers, and peers; and the demands of particular intergroup and interpersonal situations of interaction, all greatly influence the ways in which individuals act toward others. Some of these complexities are analyzed in the following chapters.

NOTES

1. For a summary of the history of studies in the field see Peter I. Rose, The Subject Is Race (New York: Oxford University Press, 1968), pp. 3-80. See also Michael Banton, Race Relations (New York: Basic Books, 1967), pp. 1-77 ff.
2. Robert M. MacIver, Social Causation (Boston: Ginn, 1942), p. 148.
3. Michael Lerner, "Respectable Bigotry," American Scholar (Au-

gust 1969), and John McDermott, "Laying On of Culture," *The Nation* (March 10, 1969).

4. For a good summary of varied systems of social stratification, see Kurt B. Mayer and Walter Buckley, *Class and Society*, 3rd ed. (New York: Random House, 1970), Chaps. 1 and 20.

5. Kurt B. Mayer, *Class and Society*, rev. ed. (New York: Random House, 1955), p. 30.

6. See, for example, Douglas G. Haring, "Racial Differences and Human Resemblances," in M. L. Barron (ed.), *American Minorities* (New York: Knopf), pp. 33-39.

7. For some further views on the use of the term "race" see Ashley Montagu, "The Concept of Race," *American Anthropologist*, 64 (October 1962), 919-928; Juan Comas, "Scientific Racism Again?," *Current Anthropology*, 2 (October 1961), 303-340; Manning Nash, "Race and the Ideology of Race," *Current Anthropology*, 3 (June 1962), 285; and Marvin Harris, "Race," in *International Encyclopedia of the Social Sciences* (New York: Macmillan, 1968), Vol. XIII, p. 263.

8. U.S. Bureau of the Census, *1960 Census of Population, Supplementary Reports*, PC (S1)-10, Washington, D.C., September 7, 1962, p. 2.

9. Robert Penn Warren, quoting a Nashville taxi driver, in *Segregation: The Inner Conflict in the South* (New York: Random House, 1956), p. 11. See also Ruth Landes, "Biracialism in American Society," *American Anthropologist*, 57 (December 1955), 1253-1263.

10. See Robert K. Merton, "The Self-Fulfilling Prophecy," *The Antioch Review*, 8 (Summer, 1948), 192-210. Merton says that "the public definitions of a situation (prophecies and predictions) become an integral part of the situation and thus affect subsequent developments."

11. The original source of this quotation appears in the Introduction to Kaibara Ekken, *Greater Learning for Women*, and appears in David and Vera Mace, *Marriage East and West* (New York: Doubleday, 1960), p. 78.

12. The effect of this situation on the development of anti-Negro sentiments is, in part, the basis of Norman Podhoretz's controversial essay, "My Negro Problem—And Ours," *Commentary*, 35 (February 1963), pp. 93-101. Also see "Letters from Readers," *Commentary*, 35 (April 1963), pp. 338-347.

13. Robert M. MacIver and Charles H. Page, *Society: An Introductory Analysis* (New York: Rinehart, 1949), p. 386.

14. See Robin M. Williams, Jr., *The Reduction of Intergroup Ten-*

sions (New York: The Social Science Research Council, 1947), p. 42.

15. See Andrew M. Greeley, *Why Can't They Be Like Us?* (New York: Dutton, 1971), pp. 120-121.

16. See Kurt Lewin, *Resolving Social Conflicts* (New York: Harper, 1948), Chaps. 10 to 12.

17. See, for example, J. Milton Yinger, "Social Forces Involved in Group Identification and Withdrawal," *Daedalus*, 90 (Spring, 1961), 247-262; and Charles F. Marden and Gladys Meyer, *Minorities in American Society*, 2nd ed. (New York: American Book Company, 1962), p. 26.

18. Lloyd Warner and Leo Srole, *The Social System of American Ethnic Groups* (New Haven: Yale University Press, 1954), p. 286.

19. See L. Paul Metzger, "American Sociology and Black Assimilation: Conflicting Perspectives," *American Journal of Sociology*, 76 (January 1971), 627-647.

20. Donald Young, *American Minority Peoples* (New York: Harper, 1932), p. xiii.

21. Louis Wirth, "The Problems of Minority Groups," in Ralph Linton (ed.), *The Science of Man in the World Crisis* (New York: Columbia University Press, 1945), pp. 3-7. MacIver and Page state that "even when mere recognition of difference is all that marks the relationship between groups—an inevitable situation in complex society—there is a necessary antithesis between the 'they' and the 'we,' between in-group and out-group." See MacIver and Page, *op. cit.*, p. 387.

22. See, for example, Oscar Handlin, "Historical Perspectives on the American Ethnic Group," *Daedalus*, 90 (Spring, 1961), 220-232.

23. Ralph Linton, *The Study of Man* (New York: Appleton-Century-Crofts, 1936), pp. 326-327.

24. Gunnar Myrdal, *An American Dilemma* (New York: Harper, 1944), Chap. I.

25. Robert K. Merton, "Discrimination and the American Creed," in Robert M. MacIver (ed.), *Discrimination and National Welfare* (New York: Harper, 1949), p. 99. See also Ernest Q. Campbell, "Moral Discomfort and Racial Segregation—An Examination of the Myrdal Hypothesis," *Social Forces*, 39 (March 1961), 228-234; and Nahum Z. Medalia, "Assumptions on Race Relations: A Conceptual Commentary," *Social Forces*, 40 (March 1962), 223-227.

TWO

A NATION OF IMMIGRANTS

Origins

While a detailed description of the origins of the American people is not an aim of this volume,[1] a brief review of American racial and ethnic history and the kaleidoscopic changes that have occurred since the days of the first settlement should help to provide a baseline for analysis of the contemporary scene. This chapter presents brief résumés of the experiences of American Indians, European colonists, Africans, and the more recent immigrant groups from across the Atlantic, the Pacific, and the Rio Grande.

Native Americans

All Americans are of immigrant stock, including the "indigenous" Indian population. The ancestors of today's American Indians were Mongolian migrants who crossed over from Asia and began to disperse in a southward and southeastward direction about 20,000 years ago. For many centuries they were the sole inhabitants of the land taken over and, in time, overrun by Europeans.

It is estimated that in the days before the conquests began 1,500,000 Indians occupied the territory now comprising the United States and Canada and that as many as 30 to 40 million

Indians were living in the Western Hemisphere.[2] Hundreds of different tribal groups speaking many different tongues inhabited the forests, plains, deserts, and mountain ranges of the Americas. A wide range of culture patterns marked their differing social structures, and their political organizations were as divergent as those of modern industrial societies.[3] There never was a characteristic or single Indian culture of the kind frequently fictionalized by novelists and scenario writers.

The vast majority of Indians did, however, share in common the fact that the conquering whites—who often treated them as one people (misnamed by Columbus, who thought he was somewhere else)—markedly influenced their customary ways, and many tribes suffered the humiliation of being dispossessed from their traditional areas of domain. From almost the first excursions to the New World, many tribal groups were mistreated and abused by whites—first by Spaniards seeking to extort riches from them and to convert them to Christianity, later by North Europeans who initially placated and then coerced them into retreating from their lands.

In the early days of Dutch and British colonial rule, each community of settlers dealt with the Indians in its own way. Some tried to make treaties, others established trade relationships, and still others fought to maintain their holdings in Indian territory. In 1754 a general policy was established by the British Crown that took decision and jurisdiction away from local communities and from the various colonial administrations. The tribes were to be recognized as "independent nations under the protection of the Crown; Indian lands were inalienable except through voluntary surrender to the Crown; any attempt by an individual or group, subject to the Crown, or by a foreign state, to buy or seize lands from Indians, was illegal."[4] Attempts to implement this new policy met with strong resistance from many settlers. Some writers, reviewing the situation, have suggested that this conflict indirectly contributed to the Revolution itself.[5]

As the frontier moved westward, the policies of the new American government vacillated between attempts at bilateral negotiations with the members of the so-called sovereign Indian nations and outright massacre and removal. What could not be accomplished by treaty was accomplished by military force. In the first half of the nineteenth century, thousands of Indians from eastern states were transported, often under brutal conditions, to the territories of the West. It is reported that one-third of the Cherokees, who in 1838 were driven from their homes in North Carolina and Georgia, died en route to Oklahoma. Their route is still referred to as the Trail of Tears.

Pierre van den Berghe reminds us that "the California gold rush was the final phase of the territorial expansion of the United States by a process of land encroachment and frontier wars between white settlers and a small number of Indian groups. It took several more decades to beat the last remnants of the indigenous population into total submission and to reduce the last Indian lands to the status of human zoos for the amusement of tourists and the delight of anthropologists."[6] Van den Berghe's bitter reflection suggests that few were any longer interested in the fate of the original Americans, save for their own selfish motives. This is an exaggeration—but only a slight one.

After the Civil War attempts were made to resolve the "Indian problem" by means of government reservations established for the alleged purpose of assimilating the now subdued and severely depressed Indians. In 1871 Congress ruled that henceforth no Indian tribe would be recognized as an independent power. All Indians became wards of the federal government. To ease the transition, federal agents were to help the tribes adjust to reservation life and to farming. Yet, as should have been foreseen, adjustment proved difficult since both land ownership and agriculture were foreign ideas to a number of Indian peoples. Moreover, the programs to educate them to efficient land utilization were woefully inadequate. The provisions of the General Allotment Act of 1887 gave every Indian the right to a tract of land (40 to 160 acres) to be kept in possession and not sold for 25 years. Because the property was to be divided equally among his heirs upon the death of the landholder, however, each succeeding generation necessarily would have less and less land to till. This situation provoked the comment: "Indians sometimes live a long time, and when Old Charlie Yellowtail dies at the age of ninety-nine, the number of heirs may be something little less than astronomical. Forty acres of land divided among, say 120 heirs, gives each just about enough room to pitch a tepee."[7]

Reservation life created many problems of adjustment—and sheer survival—for the Indian residents. Moreover, their removal from the mainstream of life had other consequences. For those in areas where the competition of truly emancipated Indians would have constituted an economic threat (as in the northern plains states, the Pacific Northwest, or the desert areas of New Mexico and Arizona), the reservations provided places for finally putting to rest Indian claims on land and jobs. For missionaries and anthropologists they provided a locus for proselytizing and research. But for most Americans the reservations were seen as living museums where part of our rich heritage was to be preserved in perpetuity.

But few Americans were aware of the true conditions of life in these places of perpetual internment, nor did they fathom the extent to which even the idea of preservation of traditional ways was disallowed by paradoxical "assimilationist" policies that demanded the sloughing off of Indian ways and the adopting of new ones—with rarely so much as a lick or a promise of where one might enjoy life in the new American mode. The farcical character of the whole charade was made clearly evident as more and more Hollywood film makers and Eastern commentators romanticized the life of the Indian. No longer solely objects of derogation, the "red men" came to be viewed as a heroic people, living reminders of a glorious past (but whose?). In some circles it even became fashionable to boast of possessing "Indian blood."

On June 2, 1924, America's original residents were finally granted citizenship. Four years later the Institute for Government Research published a report on "The Problems of Indian Administration," pointing out the dismal failure of assimilationist policy and setting forth bold recommendations. At last somebody seemed to be caring.

When John Collier became Commissioner of Indian Affairs in 1933, a new program was instituted to permit the Indians to retain their traditions without the overwhelming imposition of "white" ways. The Reorganization Act of 1934 also permitted Indians to sell their land to tribal members, to establish tribal councils to manage local affairs, and to incorporate into self-governing units. Since then progress has been very uneven. Some Indians have made significant gains. Here and there fallow lands have been irrigated and erosion halted. In some places education has been improved, especially with the long overdue demise of the assimilationist boarding schools. Birth rates have dramatically increased and death rates have declined as health and welfare problems are being dealt with more effectively through such government agencies as the Public Health Service, which took over health services from the Bureau of Indian Affairs in 1955.[8] Yet that same Bureau of Indian Affairs (a branch of the Department of the Interior) still maintains administrative control over most of America's Indians, now numbering approximately 800,000, the large majority of whom live on reservations, two-thirds of them concentrated in the states of Oklahoma, Arizona, New Mexico, and the Dakotas. The bureau's overall policies have vacillated significantly over the years, often subject to the whims of local agents who were far removed from the center of the bureaucracy in Washington. This has proven to be a mixed blessing.

Over the years some young Indians thought it best to leave the reservations and the villages to settle in the cities. They were often the best trained and the most success-oriented and they took their skills and talents with them, leaving a vacuum behind. Yet, in spite of the fact that some were integrated into the general community and found employment in specialized trades (for example, the high-steel workers among the Mohawks), most of those who relinquished their status as wards of the government suffered the plight of other "colored" minorities. Discriminatory practices in many parts of the country severely limited their opportunities for advancement and achievement.

For those who remain on the reservations life continues to be harsh.[9] In spite of the improvements that have taken place in recent decades, Indians remain members of a depressed minority situated in the bottom tenth of the economic hierarchy. As recently as 1970 the Census of Population showed that the average Indian had but five years of schooling, that the family income was only $1,500 per year, and that his rate of unemployment was a miserable 45 percent.

Young Indian people did not wait to see the 1970 census figures. They knew what was happening and many decided to fight. Following, and in many ways attempting to emulate, black militants, representatives of different tribal groups have formed Red Power organizations as both cultural centers and bases for challenging the system that in their view does little of a positive nature and much that is destructive to Indian peoples.

In some areas the loose confederation of Indian militants has gained notoriety and limited success. Perhaps the most dramatic cases have been the invasion and occupation of the abandoned island of Alcatraz and its empty prison buildings in 1970, the takeover of the Bureau itself in Washington in 1972, and the two-month siege of Wounded Knee in 1973. Other attempts to dramatize their cause, to bring all Indians together, or to effect change have been less successful. One of the many reasons for this record is the important fact that Pan-Indianism is a new idea. Most native Americans do not see themselves as brothers to members of distant (or sometimes even proximate) tribes. They are Navaho or Seminole or Cherokee or Sioux, not "Indians." And they often have very different notions of what they want and where they want to go. Still, there is a growing belief that all are owed reparations—of land, money, and respect. Whether they will obtain these goals in sufficient amounts to break the cycle of poverty and frustration remains to be seen.

The Colonists

For many years a debate has persisted over who first "dis-covered" America. Some have claimed that it was the Viking leader Leif Ericson who first set foot on these shores in 1004 A.D. Probably most people favor the view that it was Chris-topher Columbus, the Genoese sea captain whose several voy-ages were financed by King Ferdinand and Queen Isabella of Spain. Some even argue that ancient Jews sailed across the Atlantic long before Ericson or Columbus; this claim is based on the shaky evidence of the discovery in Tennessee of several large rocks with Hebrew inscriptions.

This debate sometimes takes the form of ethnic one-upman-ship. (Rumor has it that one prominent Italian-American jurist sought to raise money to hire his own historian to discredit the "Norsophiles" who claimed to have discovered an old Viking chart of the eastern coast, the "Vinland Map.") In one respect, the debate is also quite academic, for whichever European first set foot in America he was not the original dis-coverer. There were people living on the North American Con-tinent for thousands of years, long before *any* European crossed the Atlantic Ocean. The irony is that the Indians do not even receive credit for getting here first.

The first nationals to lay claim to substantial portions of American soil were the Spanish conquistadores who penetrated the southwestern sector of what was to become part of the United States and who established settlements on the Florida peninsula. Unlike the British who were to follow, the Spaniards mingled extensively with the native populations and frequently cohabited with Indian women. They left an indelible impression upon southwestern and Floridian culture. Their descendants, the Hispanos of mixed Spanish and Indian ancestry, are still to be found in the Southwest, especially in New Mexico. Had the Spaniards remained in power, intergroup problems, atti-tudes toward minority populations, and patterns of discrimina-tion would undoubtedly have assumed characteristics different from those that now exist. But this was not their destiny.

After the defeat of the Spanish Armada in 1588, rival nations began to establish and develop territories in the Western Hemisphere. Under the auspices of the West India Company the Dutch established trading posts in both North and South America—on the coast of Brazil, in the Antilles, at the estuary of the Hudson River (New York nee New Amsterdam), and northward along its banks (Fort Albany). Holland's control over these territories was short-lived, but the Dutch legacy lingers on, especially in the folklore and history of New York State and in the names of many famous families—Roosevelt, Vander Heuvel, Rensselaer, Vliet. (Moreover the Dutch left the English with a label—"Yankees"—an anglicized version of "Jan Kees," a sort of bumpkin.) In 1654 Holland lost her foothold in Brazil and, only a decade later, New Netherlands and Delaware[10] became British possessions.

France, too, had colonial ambitions in America and sent explorers and missionaries to stake out new lands. Eastern Canada and the huge Louisiana Territory came under French domination. Bitter warfare brought an end to French rule over Canada; the Louisiana Purchase (1803) ended French control over the Mississippi Valley and the Northwest territories. Yet, French nationalism persists powerfully in the Canadian province of Quebec where the majority of citizens are Roman Catholic, speak the French language, and retain many French customs. In the United States the imprint of France is still to be seen in Louisiana architecture and in festivals such as the famed Mardi gras.

But it was England, as we know, that became the supreme colonial power in North America. The English colonists consisted of tradesmen and fortune seekers, civil administrators and political refugees, religious dissenters and petty criminals. For the first time a large group of common folk crossed the Atlantic to settle here. Unlike the explorers from Spain and France, they came in family groups, and even several entire communities moved from the British Isles to America.

The establishment of British America was a struggle from its inception. The death toll—from the hardships endured en route, from diseases that plagued the settlers after arrival, from marauding Indians who attacked their villages—was exceedingly high. And for those who survived these hazards there were other problems.

Religious prejudices were transplanted from the mother country to New England and the mid-Atlantic colonies. Colonists often were set against one another in their desire to maintain their particular brand of Christianity. Fighting the invisible ogres of blasphemy, heresy, and sin, colonists perpetrated persecutions as acts of faith, the victims often being members of minority sects—Quakers, Unitarians, Roman Catholics, and others.[11]

In addition to the former residents of England who constituted the largest proportion of settlers, there were the Presbyterians from North Ireland, the Scotch-Irish, and the German refugees from the ravages of the Thirty Years' War. Small groups of Frenchmen, Welshmen, Irish-Catholics, and Sephardic Jews (of Spanish and Portuguese descent) were also numbered among the early colonists. Together, these North Europeans laid the cornerstone of modern American society and formed the basis of the "native" white majority.

Despite the immigration of millions of southern and eastern Europeans and thousands of Asians, Africans, and Latin-Americans in the late years of the nineteenth century and the first quarter of the twentieth century, the native white Americans or "Yankees" still constitute the largest and most powerful element in the population of the United States.

Afro-Americans

The first people of African descent to come to America arrived in 1619. Brought originally to Virginia and later to other colonies they were, like many whites, indentured servants. Servitude was not uncommon in the middle colonies and these black-skinned newcomers did not occupy a unique status. Some gained their freedom after serving their masters for a specified period of time; others became free through conversion to Christianity. Most remained as "unfree" men and women, but even they were not considered to be slaves. In fact, neither Virginia nor any of the other colonies of British America had yet recognized the institution of chattel slavery.

By the 1660s the condition of blacks began to deteriorate. The expansion of agriculture and the growing demand for a large and cheap labor force brought slavery to American shores. Africans, wrenched from their native villages and sold into bondage by Spaniards and Englishmen, by Muslims and Christians, and, sometimes, by fellow blacks, were taken to coastal ports, there to be transported under the most brutal conditions imaginable to the islands of the Caribbean and to the port cities of the east coast of America. Many died of disease and hunger and melancholia, en route; many—some say the lucky ones—by throwing themselves overboard or by inviting execution by proving too intractable. Once in the New World, the survivors were sold at auction like beasts of burden.

By the middle of the eighteenth century the practice of slavery was legalized in every English colony in America. In some places the new laws were soon rescinded. In fact, with the emergence of the United States as an independent nation, the slavery issue became the subject of congressional and local debate. The northern states began fairly early to abolish the practice by law, beginning with Pennsylvania where the Assembly, under the prodding of Thomas Paine, passed the first act for the emancipation of Negro slaves on March 1, 1780. Others followed suit.

In the South, however, the system was maintained intact. The "peculiar institution" had become a mainstay of the economic structure, and what some have called a "slavocracy" characterized a large section dominated by dependence on plantation labor.[12] There had been a brief period in the second half of the eighteenth century when declining profits in tobacco (the principal cash crop) seemed to portend a change in the social arrangements, but the invention of the cotton gin in 1793 and the rapid development of the British textile industry not only forestalled the anticipated change but made the southern planters even more intransigent.

The conditions under which the slaves lived and worked varied considerably not only from one region to another (the upper South as compared with the Piedmont or the Mississippi Delta) but also depended upon the size and character of the plantations themselves. Moreover, even within slave communities there was a definite stratification. Some blacks worked in the houses of their masters, benefiting from special treatment, and found themselves trapped between the world toward which they often aspired and that which they knew just beyond the big yard. Others, the majority, were field hands who did the grueling work of planting the seeds and picking the cotton and chopping the stalks and clearing the fields and planting and picking and chopping again in a never-ending cycle of back-breaking toil. Women and children, as well as the men, sweated their lives away in the fields.

Moreover, life in slave quarters was tempered and molded by events beyond the control of those forced to live there. Family life, for example, frequently meant the special bonds that existed between mothers and young children. Social activities were narrowly circumscribed. Freedom in all phases of life was highly limited. Yet, as in any local community (even concentration camps), a way of life did emerge, which significantly included patterns of adaptation that permitted blacks to cope with the system of enforced slavery. Thus, their customs often involved ways of playing the closed system to one's (slight) advantage. Blacks learned to sabotage, to feign illness, and to clown. They also tried to shield their children from their inevitable fate (sometimes by actually taking their lives).[13] Rarely was the system attacked directly. It was simply too dangerous.

For several years a great debate has been waged by scholars of the period—old-liners and revisionists, whites and blacks—over the question of how the slaves actually fared and how they survived. Some argue, for example, that even with the now widely conceded recognition that there was some sort of "slave culture," blacks still internalized the low status in which they were held and came to see themselves as inferior to whites. Others have said they never fully succumbed. That debate continues.

What is undisputed is the fact that by the 1830s slavery was beginning to come under severe attack. Many southerners, in order to justify their continued subjugation of the Negro, invoked the doctrine of racial superiority. Earlier few had argued that the slaves were *biologically* inferior and a menace to white society, but they did so now. Moreover, they underscored the idea that, as "property," the slave had no rights that whites were bound to respect. Even the Supreme Court was to support this argument when it upheld the finding of a lower court in the famous Dred Scott decision of 1857. Dred Scott, a slave, having been taken into a territory that prohibited slavery, considered himself a free man under the rules of the Missouri Compromise. The Court claimed that the compromise was unconstitutional since "Congress has no right to enact a law which deprived persons of their property in the territories of the United States."

Even so, there was great agitation to rid the nation of the institution of slavery and a powerful movement for abolition emerged in the North led by such white spokesmen as John Brown and such free blacks as Frederick Douglass.

Ultimately the slavery issue was to be resolved in the midst of the bloody Civil War. While President Lincoln insisted in the beginning that the war had nothing to do with slavery as such (indeed, early in the war Union soldiers returned slaves to their masters under flags of truce), the matter became one of central concern. For, in terribly oversimplified terms, the South fought to defend its way of life, which depended significantly on the slave system; the North fought to keep the Union whole. In a short time the emancipation of slaves was regarded as necessary, first politically and then morally, to achieve the northern objective.

On January 1, 1863, by Executive Order the President issued the Emancipation Proclamation. All slaves in the United States (referring to the rebellious Confederacy as well as the rest of the Union) were declared free—though not yet equal. Equality was to come with the Thirteenth Amendment to the Constitution. By the summer of 1863 the Union Army sought black recruits to fight for their country, and it is estimated that close to 200,000 eventually donned uniforms, half of them to see action on the battlefield.

At the end of the war Black Codes were proposed. These were laws that would give Negroes legal rights to marry and bear witness in a court of law but not, for example, to own land or to work in particular trades. The codes were never put into effect. Other measures were.

During Reconstruction the Afro-Americans gained equal status in law and, in many places, they did so in fact. A civil rights bill was passed by Congress in 1866, but vetoed by Lincoln's successor, President Andrew Johnson who then was in power. In 1868, a million Negroes were enfranchised. But the surge toward equal rights in the decade after the war began to wane and Radical Reconstruction, maintained in large part by federal forces, proved to be but a temporary interlude between slavery and institutionalized segregation.

Although the Sumner Act of 1875 secured equal rights in public transportation, in hotels, and in theaters and other places of amusement, it was to be declared unconstitutional by an 8 to 1 decision of the Supreme Court in 1883. Soon "Redemption" was to be fully under way. The era of segregation officially began with the Hayes-Tilden Compromise of 1876. Hayes, an Ohio Republican, won the Presidency in an electoral college victory over the popularly elected New York Democrat. This event, and the compromise which brought it about, was to be a major turning point. Local autonomy was returned to the states of the South, the Freedmen's Bureaus, which had been set up to help blacks adjust to the new conditions, were closed, and federal troops were withdrawn. In their wake many "carpetbaggers" left, too. With "Redemption" came the chipping away of the newly won rights of blacks. By the 1890's "Jim Crow" statutes divided southern society into a two-caste system, with whites occupying positions of power and Negroes reduced to second-class citizenship. The segregation laws prohibited the mixing of the races and barred "colored" people from virtually all white institutions.[14]

While the states with the heaviest concentration of blacks ignored or circumvented the Fourteenth Amendment (pertaining to citizenship) and the Fifteenth (specifying that the right to vote could not be denied because of race—though other tactics could be employed, like "grandfather clauses"), most people in the North seemed no longer to be interested in rallying to the cause of freedom. Moreover, the system of segregation which had emerged after 1876 was legally sanctified in the famous *Plessy v. Ferguson* decision of the U.S. Supreme Court which, in 1896, proclaimed the principle of "separate but equal" to be the law of the land.

At the time of the Plessy case, nine out of ten black Americans lived in the South, 80 percent in rural areas. While segregation existed in many states outside the old Confederacy, it was there that they suffered the most. With the curtailing of European immigration after World War I, Negroes began their northward migration. Between 1910 and 1920 a half million blacks moved to northern cities where they settled in tenement districts forming black islands in a sea dominated by people more foreign and yet, in many ways, no less alien than they. And they stayed. The city became their new home and the ghetto their jail.

Ralph Ellison, the black novelist, has poignantly described the problems they faced:

In relation to their Southern background, the cultural history of Negroes in the North reads like the legend of some tragic people out of mythology, a people which aspired to escape from its own unhappy homeland to the apparent peace of a distant mountain; but which, in migrating, made some fatal error of judgment and fell into a great chasm of maze-like passages that promise ever to lead to the mountain but end ever against the wall.[15]

Although the opportunity to escape southern conditions led to the ever-growing trek northward, blacks experienced residential, social, and economic discrimination wherever they went. Moreover, with World War I veterans returning and with *all-American* sentiment running at an all-time high, the new migrants frequently found themselves isolated, alone, and under attack whenever they dared to cross the color line. It was during this era that race rioting became a new feature of urban life. Thirty-three major interracial disturbances occurred in the United States between 1915 and 1949—eighteen of these between 1915 and 1919. With the exception of the Detroit riot of 1943 and the urban "burnings" of the 1960s, none of the more recent riots have been as fierce as those of the earlier period. The bloodiest of these were in East St. Louis and in Chicago, both cities in the northern state of Illinois.

The competition between whites who sought to maintain their superordinate positions and blacks who were hungry for work, housing, and respect continued and, by and large, blacks made but slow progress. And even this progress—especially stimulated by the emergence of prideful new political and cultural movements in the 1920s (the era of the Harlem Renaissance)—was slowed, then stopped altogether, by the Great Depression of the following decade. And as might be expected, competition for ever scarcer jobs served to intensify the prejudices of competitors. By 1940 a two to one black-to-white unemployment relationship emerged—and it persists to this very day.

During Franklin Roosevelt's "New Deal" some changes began to bring the Negro citizen closer to full equality before the law. Various groups, within and outside the black community, tried and sometimes succeeded in gaining fairer treatment for America's largest racial minority. World War II accelerated the move.

Northward movement increased again and so now did the trek to the West where the defense industry served as the magnet. President Roosevelt's Executive Order 8802 sought to assure fair employment practices. By 1940 one in four black Americans lived in the North or West and with the nation on wartime footing many found employment in factories earning higher wages than they had ever known. And at least a million blacks entered the armed forces. But even during the war they found themselves in segregated units of the army and navy.

The military was not ordered integrated until 1948 (President Truman's Executive Order 9981), three years after the end of World War II. The order was not finally implemented until 1952 when, during the height of the Korean War, President Eisenhower made the change in traditional policy.

In the early days of the postwar period, blacks in the North and in the South did gain new status in law, though relatively few advantages in fact. They shared in the economic boom of the era but, while the absolute gains they made were sometimes considerable, the gap between the racial categories black and white remained as wide as ever. Many thought that the independence movements in Africa might lead to their final and irrevocable emancipation. The African situation did not have that effect, but it served to provide a new reference to people who knew little of their origins or their heritage. Most important of all was the Supreme Court decision handed down on May 17, 1954, which, by unanimity, struck down the constitutionality of the separate but equal doctrine and opened the door to widespread desegregation. As is well known, this decision proved difficult to enforce and prompted a variety of legal subterfuges that sought to reverse or at least to forestall a 1955 directive to move toward desegregation "with all deliberate speed."

The apparent failure of the people to honor the court's decision, coupled with the seemingly unfulfilled promises that black Americans had rejoiced in, accelerated a movement that had been growing from the turn of the century: the movement for civil rights. That movement and the changes that have taken place during the sixties and seventies are the subject of Chapter Seven. Several points concerning this period should be made here, however, before moving on to the histories of other American minority groups.

First, in the decade between 1954 and 1963 the principal thrust for desegregation and, in many cases, integration came from a coalition of black and white reformers, most of whom tried to persuade their fellow countrymen to honor the nation's highest ideals. Many became disillusioned; many lost faith in interracial organizations; many said that cooperation was a mask for white co-optation. Yet most of those who marched and picketed and boycotted and rode the "freedom buses" during these years saw integration as the primary goal. The National Association for the Advancement of Colored People (NAACP), Congress of Racial Equality (CORE), and other civil-rights organizations were at the forefront of this movement. So, too, was the newly emergent Southern Christian Leadership Conference led by Dr. Martin Luther King.

The integration phase, if one can call it that, reached its height with the grand march on Washington in August of 1963 when 250,000 black and white Americans joined hands to sing "We Shall Overcome" and Reverend M. L. King offered his famous speech "I Have a Dream." Within a year the dream seemed shattered.

What happened is a complicated story, better saved for a later chapter. But it is important to note that whatever progress had been made up to that centennial celebration of the Emancipation Proclamation and rededication ritual had been much less the product of good-will than of hard work and political pressure.

In succeeding years integration was largely to be replaced by a new, more strident, and far more black-oriented ideology—Black Power. New and young leaders began to tire of promises of things to come and they felt that the civil-rights movement was failing to reach those who needed help most, especially those in the northern ghettos. While acknowledging certain victories—the Civil Rights Acts of 1964, 1965, 1968, for example —many of these leaders felt that the victories were, in reality, rather Pyrrhic. They had been won at too great a cost and the net result, it was often argued, was that white guilt had been assuaged but few blacks had really been helped.

Whatever the reality, and in our view there was more than a kernel of truth in their portrayal, the new leaders foreswore integration and concentrated on the issue of "getting it together," that is, the coalescence of community among black people throughout the nation. In many ways the wildest dreams of Stokely Carmichael and H. Rap Brown and other new-breed leaders were to be realized.[16] At least some of them.

Within a few years black people began to walk taller and to feel far freer to express the rage boiling up inside. Within a few years Black Power had become a household slogan (and "black" had replaced "Negro" as the proper term for the people who cried for it). Within a few years universities and other particularly vulnerable institutions conceded that they had been guilty of racism or, at least, had failed to cast a wide enough net and began actively to recruit black students who, in turn, then demanded and often got special programs in Black Studies. But during those same years the average wage of the black unskilled laborer fell further behind his white counterpart, the average reading level of ghetto children fell further behind that of white children, and the average contribution of white supporters of black liberation movements (no small factor) fell dramatically.

One thing is clear. Black Americans are moving and are determined not to see the second Reconstruction go the way of the first.

European Immigrants

The first census to include the "nationalities" of Americans was that of 1820 when all those who had entered the United States along the eastern seaboard and the Gulf Coast were listed by country of origin. According to this census there were 9,638,000 Americans, 20 percent of whom were Negroes and the rest mainly persons of Anglo-Saxon stock. Between 1820 and 1960 over 40 million immigrants came to the United States, the overwhelming majority from Europe and Canada.

Between 1820 and the beginning of the Civil War over 3,500,000 European immigrants arrived in America. Some were from England, some from Scandinavia, but the two largest groups came from Ireland and Germany. Severe economic and social conditions led many Irish citizens to seek a new life in the United States. Between 1847 and 1854 about 1,200,000 men, women, and children left the "emerald isle" for this country, and by the end of the Civil War period the Irish constituted 7 percent of the white population.

As many writers have pointed out, the Irish were in the vanguard of a new period of immigration—those who, despite their origins in the rural counties of Eire, foreswore the soil (or were too poor to push on) and settled in the growing cities along the eastern seaboard. As the late President Kennedy described them,

In speech and dress they seemed foreign; they were poor and unskilled; and they were arriving in overwhelming numbers. The Irish are perhaps the only people in our history with the distinction of having a political party, the Know-Nothings, formed against them in 1849.[17]

Indeed, they suffered severe discrimination in the new land and most often found employment only in the lowest-paying and hardest-working jobs: as ditchdiggers, or dockers, or "terriers" working on the railroads and in the canal beds. In some respects (clearly, not in all), the urban experience for blacks in the twentieth century—in terms of the attitudes of others and in terms of occupations—has its parallel in the Irish experience in the middle of the previous century.

In time, as they became acculturated to American ways and as others became even more visible targets for the animus of America Firsters, the Irish began the slow climb. It took many in and out of politics, including ward politics, and many more into public service, especially in the police force of New York, which used to be *the* Irish city, and Boston, which became and, in many ways, remains the political stronghold of the Irish clans so sharply portrayed in the novels of Edwin O'Connor. (In this generation many political science departments have their Irish-American specialist on urban politics, a Murphy or a Flynn or a Daniel Patrick Moynihan.)

The Irish also were to dominate the hierarchy of the

Catholic Church in America. Even today the percentage of Irish-American compared with Italian- or German-American bishops and archbishops (to say nothing of parish priests) far exceeds their proportion of the population. (It should be noted that, while for the Irish, parish and precinct are frequently one and the same, priests have frequently spoken out on non-ecclesiastical subjects, and the range of opinion grows wider with each passing year. One thinks, for example, of the spectrum from conservatives Cardinal McIntire and Cardinal Spellman to those radical pacifists and outspoken critics of Vietnam policy, Father Dan Berrigan and his brother, Father Philip Berrigan.)

Many German Catholics came to America, too. But they rarely linked politics and parochialism so neatly as did the Irish. They were more German than Catholic and, like thousands of their Protestant countrymen who came to America before the Civil War, often moved out from the port cities of the East, dispersed themselves widely across the land and entered a myriad of occupations. Many became homesteaders in the Middle West and others settled in such cities as Baltimore, Buffalo, St. Louis, Minneapolis, and, especially, Milwaukee. (In these cities German-Americans began various businesses, including such to-be-famous breweries as Anheuser-Busch, the makers of Budweiser, and Schlitz, "the beer that made Milwaukee . . . .")

Germans—Protestants as well as Catholics—came in the beginning of the nineteenth century, in the middle (especially as political refugees after the failures of reform in 1848), and throughout the rest of the century. In time, they were to become the largest immigrant group to come to America. Yet, oddly enough, one rarely thinks of Germans as "immigrants" or "an ethnic group." And never as the largest group of all. Why not?

For one thing, they did not arrive in a single wave that lasted but a decade or two like so many others. For another, they shared many of the values and cultural traits of the Scandinavians among whom they often settled, including the work ethic of the old Anglo-Americans as well. While they retained some of their cultural baggage, they "gave" a good deal of it away (like the Sunday picnic, the kindergarten, New Year's parties, and the frankfurter or "hot dog"). Moreover, they were themselves a rather heterogeneous group, which made stereotyping far more difficult. The Milwaukee brewers were a far cry from the Pennsylvania "Dutch" (the word is a corruption of *Deutsch*).

During the early part of the twentieth century some German-Americans did undergo a difficult period when their original "fatherland" became their new country's enemy. During World War I many Germans suffered from discrimination by fellow Americans; to avoid identification and ostracism, some anglicized their names: Stein to Stone, Schmidt to Smith, Battenberg to Mountbatten, and Feldmann to Mansfield.

A similar attitude did not emerge during World War II, and few German-Americans were singled out, officially or unofficially, as dangers to American security. Unlike their Japanese-American counterparts, they were never evacuated from any centers of population or placed in concentration camps.

On the other hand, some groups of German-Americans had been sympathetic to the aims of Nazism in the 1930s (including anti-Semitic policies), but most of the "Bünde" folded with the onset of American involvement. And of course the overwhelming majority of Americans of German origin supported and defended the United States and applauded its victory in Europe under the leadership of their *landsmann*, Dwight David Eisenhower.

Long before, in the realization that immigration was going to continue to grow, the Castle Garden immigration depot was opened in New York in 1855. The depot was put to the test in the years following the Civil War (a war in which many immigrants fought side by side with citizens). After the war immigration began to flow more freely; the flow became a stream, and the stream, a torrent. By the middle of the 1880s hundreds of ships were sailing toward the eastern seaboard carrying human cargo. Between 1880 and 1914 about 7,500,000 eastern and central Europeans—Hungarians, Bohemians,

Table 1   Total Numbers of Immigrants to the United States by
          Area of Origin: 1820–1971

Area of Origin	Totals	Percentage
Europe	35,630,398	78.2
America (North and South)	7,641,268*	16.8
Asia	1,782,711	3.9
Australia and New Zealand	101,762	.2
Africa	82,317	.2
Pacific Islands	23,207	.1
All Other	271,453	.6
All Countries	45,533,116	100.0

* Includes 3,991,417 from Canada.
Source: U.S. Immigration and Naturalization Service, *Annual Report: 1972*, Washington, D.C., 1972, Table 137, p. 92.

Slovaks, Czechs, and Russians (almost one-half of whom were Jewish)—immigrated to the United States. During approximately the same period 4 million Italians, mainly from *Il Mezzogiorno* (the south) and from Sicily, came to this country.

Primarily peasants and laborers, these immigrants from south, central, and eastern Europe represented economically some of the more impoverished peoples of the Continent. Many had come to work in the expanding industries of this country, intending to return to their homelands. Some "birds of passage" went back and forth (as do southern Italians, Spaniards, and Greeks who work in Germany and Scandinavia today). Some, like the Jews, had no homelands to which to return. It was these sojourners about whom Emma Lazarus wrote:

Give me your tired, your poor,
Your huddled masses yearning to breathe free,
The wretched refuse of your teeming shore,
Send these, the homeless, tempest-tost, to me:
I lift my lamp beside the golden door.[18]

The new arrivals to Ellis Island (which replaced Castle Garden as the portal of entry in 1892) were not the adventurers, explorers, traders, or conquerors of an earlier era. Yet they were also pioneers. For "the experience of the immigrants recapitulated the early American pioneer hardships, in many ways on harder terms, since the difficulties they encountered were those of a jungle society rather than a jungle wilderness."[19] These newcomers have been aptly called "the uprooted."[20]

Because of their limited resources few of these immigrants ventured far beyond the ports of debarkation or the inland cities along the main railroad lines. They found employment as laborers and miners, workers in heavy industry and in the needle trades. Jobs were obtained through old-country connections, employment agencies, or through newly found friends and neighbors. The tasks they performed were arduous, the hours long, the conditions frequently intolerable, and the paychecks often inadequate to provide for growing families. For the first generation there was little time for recreation. What little leisure they had was spent within the confines of neighborhoods where attempts were made to keep Old World traditions alive.

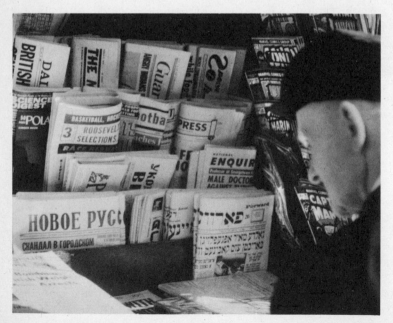

Members of each immigrant group tended to gather together, and ethnic islands became a natural feature of the urban topography. Somewhat like the local communities of medieval Jews, these modern ghettos emerged in the older sections of the cities. But, as individuals improved their economic and social positions, they moved "uptown," leaving their older neighborhoods to those who followed. In the metropolitan centers of the North the pattern was often repeated: The areas of original settlement successively became the ghetto communities of the older settlers, then the Irish and Germans, East Europeans, Jews, Italians, and most recently blacks from the South and Puerto Ricans.

Many children of European immigrants found themselves torn between the customs of their parents and the world into which they sought admission. For them the past was to be forgotten, the future lay ahead. Theirs was the generation of acculturation, and they were often caught between two conflicting cultures. They were learning the norms of American life and, in doing so, frequently evoked the antagonism, even the wrath, of those who had already "arrived." Fear of the stranger had greeted their parents; now hostility toward those eager to compete added fuel to the smoldering embers of anti-foreign prejudice. Restrictive practices became commonplace, and increasing numbers of jobs, schools, fraternities, restaurants, and clubs became forbidden territory. The signposts were clear: "Americans Only," "Irish Need Not Apply," "No Jews Allowed." In 1894 the Immigration Restriction League began. It was to be the strongest force against unrestricted acceptance of immigrants for the next quarter of a century.

Following World War I mounting isolationism and anti-foreign feelings reached their peak. In 1921 and again in 1924 restrictive legislation was passed, sharply curtailing the immigration of "undesirable" national groups and setting forth rigid quotas favoring north Europeans and all but excluding others. In 1921 the Johnson Act, signed by President Harding, provided that the annual number of aliens permitted to enter the United States from any nation was not to exceed 3 percent of the total number of foreign-born members of that particular nationality residing in this country in 1910. The Immigration Law of 1924 limited immigration even more severely. The

Table 2 Principal Sources of Immigration to the United States: 1820–1971 (*These figures include immigration to Alaska and Hawaii*)

Country of Last Permanent Residence	Totals for last 151 Years*	Peak Years
Germany	6,925,736	1882
Italy	5,199,304	1907
Great Britain	4,804,520	1907
Ireland	4,715,041	1851
Canada	3,991,417	1888
U.S.S.R.	3,347,118	1924
Mexico	1,642,916	1882
Sweden	1,267,574	1913
Norway	853,783	1924
France	733,009	1882
Greece	588,160	1924
West Indies	544,688	1851
Poland	487,778	1907
China	450,900	1921
Turkey	376,842	1913
Denmark	361,095	1882
Japan	370,033	1907
Netherlands	352,594	1882
Switzerland	343,421	1883
Portugal	369,665	1921
Cuba	309,225	1961
Spain	229,235	1921
Belgium	198,738	1924
Czechoslovakia	133,285	1921

* Source: U.S. Immigration and Naturalization Service, *Annual Report: 1972*, Washington, D.C., 1972, Table 137, p. 92.

formula provided for the admission of 150,000 persons each year, with national quotas fixed at 2 percent of the total of foreign-born members of any given nationality group residing in the United States in 1890. These enactments served to close the "golden door."[21] (The McCarran Act of 1952 sealed it even tighter. It was not opened until legislation—initiated just before John F. Kennedy was assassinated and signed by his successor, Lyndon Johnson—changed the system from being quota-based to a much more open and equitable one.)

Jews

Included among the millions of potential immigrants effectively barred from entry into the United States were hundreds of thousands of European Jews, the vast majority of whose coreligionists had come to America after 1880. Jews were not, however, newcomers to this country. As early as 1654 twenty-three Jewish refugees from Brazil settled in New Amsterdam. By the time of the Revolution almost three thousand Jews— mainly of Spanish and Portuguese descent (called Sephardim)— were living in the seaboard colonies.

The first Jewish settlers, generally traders and merchants, found little opposition to their presence in the cities and towns where they worked and lived. There were scattered instances of discrimination in the days of Dutch control; some Jews suffered religious persecutions in the English colonies, where they were sometimes forbidden to hold public office or to bear arms. But these barriers were frequently offset by the fact that many Protestants looked with favor upon the "Israelites" in their midst—the descendants of the ancient Hebrews whose testaments had so markedly influenced Christian thought. By 1700 freedom of worship was widely recognized and in 1740, when the Jews of British America were granted full citizenship, they achieved a degree of freedom probably unmatched anywhere in the world.

The Sephardim were joined by Ashkenazic Jews (from eastern and central Europe) who began coming to America during the late Colonial period. Shortly after the turn of the nineteenth century, economic conditions and political unrest

DAVID N. MIELKE

prompted the migration of German Jews. In 1836 the first communal migration of Jews—large families and even whole communities—moved to America. Throughout the nineteenth century the number of Jews emigrating from Germany rose steadily. It is estimated that the American Jewish population was 15,000 in 1840, 50,000 in 1850, 150,000 in 1860, and 250,000 in 1880.

Many of the German Jews left the seaboard cities and moved to smaller communities to the south and west. In many instances they went as peddlers and stayed to build the retail emporia that are now to be found scattered in towns and cities across the nation. (It is frequently noted that the Jewish-owned store is as commonplace in a southern town as the Confederate monument that stands in the square.) Not surprisingly, the Jews often had to live down traditional stories and legends about "those Jewish peddlers"; so, too, had the Yankee peddlers of an earlier period. Yet blatant discrimination was rarely to be found. Like their more cosmopolitan countrymen from the upper strata of German-Jewish society, these Jews had little difficulty in establishing themselves economically, in forming religious congregations, and in adapting themselves to local patterns. It was not until the wave of east European immigration began rolling toward the United States that anti-Jewish discrimination gained a significant foothold in this country.

In 1880 250,000 Jews were living in the United States; by 1924 the number exceeded 3 million. Beginning in the 1880s Jews from Poland, Russia, Romania, and other east European lands migrated to America. Included were large numbers who fled from pogroms and other insufferable conditions in their lands of original domicile—which few would call homelands. Economically impoverished and traditional in their religious beliefs, the largest percentage of these immigrants remained in the larger cities where they could find work (especially in the expanding garment industry) and where they could continue their religious practices. Like other ethnically distinct groups, east European Jews began to develop their own communities.

The conspicuousness of their dress, uniqueness of their

customs, strangeness of their everyday language (Yiddish), and their Orthodox faith, all combined to reinforce traditional images of Jews as a clannish and mysterious people. Along with other recent immigrant groups they became the targets of anti-foreign sentiments.

In spite of their old-country ways the Jewish immigrants possessed several cultural traits that enhanced their adjustment and rapid mobility in American society. Years of relegation to marginal occupational roles, traditions that placed high value on education and the learned professions, and emphasis on familial responsibility, all served to aid many Jews in their struggle to find acceptance and prosperity in competitive America.

Yet the very fact that a substantial number of Jews began to surpass others in the rapidity of their ascent increased animosity and fanned the embers of anti-Semitism (an old phenomenon distinct from general anti-foreign attitudes). Because some Jews were extremely successful financially, they were referred to as "unscrupulous money changers" and "crass capitalists" (especially by the Populists and their sympathizers). Because other Jews were deeply engaged in radical politics and labor organizations, others tried to paint all Jews "red." And some, like the members of the Ku Klux Klan and even as notable and powerful a figure as Henry Ford, ignoring the ridiculous contradictions in their allegations, called the Jews *both* "parvenu" and "pinko"—and "Christ-killers," too. Moreover, the search for scapegoats during the Great Depression often found the Jews, including such advisers to President Roosevelt as Bernard Baruch, as targets for the bitter frustrations felt by many Americans. (As mentioned previously, the rise of Nazism evoked some sympathy here as well, and several new "hate" organizations sprang up to defame the Jews.)

It was during this era (the late 1930s) that about two hundred thousand European Jews—mostly from Germany and Austria—managed to migrate to the United States. Many more refugees from Nazi-dominated countries would have come had it not been for America's restrictive immigration laws. Reactions against the horrors practiced by the Nazi regime greatly served to reduce anti-Jewish sentiments. Since World War II virulent anti-Semitism has shown a marked decline, although restricted neighborhoods and social discrimination still exist in many of our cities and suburbs. Nevertheless the epidemic of swastika daubing in 1960, the temple bombings in 1962, the rise of George Lincoln Rockwell's American Nazi Party and other neo-Nazi organizations, the emergence of certain reactionary patriotic movements of the radical right in the early 1960s, and the occurrence of "black anti-Semitism" and Third World anti-Zionism on the part of the radical left in the late 1960s indicate the continued existence of anti-Semitic feelings in certain segments of the population. And it may be a portent. As the author suggested in late 1969:

American Jews, delighted at Israeli victory in the Six-Day War, have evinced much less enthusiasm for their own country's protracted conflict in Southeast Asia and its stalemated war against poverty at home. Other groups in American life share the sense of frustration. In the search for scapegoats that may soon ensue, Jews may find themselves most vulnerable to attack from right, left, and below. By seeking reform and compromise on most issues instead of radical change they may come increasingly to appear too white for the black militants, too red for the white conservatives, and too yellow for their own children.

Jews are not unaware of such possibilities. They know that latent anti-Semitism can be revived in America as it has been in the past. But they do not seem worried. They feel they can ride out the coming storms. Like their forebears who came to settle on the Lower East Side, the majority of Jews still believe in America and in the American people.[22]

While the situation has changed—and not for the better—since these words were written, they still seem to be an accurate portrayal of the position of most Jews in the United States at the present time.

Asian Americans

The Lower East Side of New York, where the Russian-Jewish immigrants first congregated, was sometimes referred to as an

"Oriental enclave," for to some people the Jews were Orientals. Few Asians would see them as such, though as we shall see the American Jews did prove to have many traits in common with Chinese-Americans and some with Japanese-Americans as well. And the latter "true" Orientals had certain things in common with one another, not the least being similar looks that set them apart from other immigrants and, with other factors, made them special targets for racist attacks, especially in the late part of the nineteenth century when their principal immigration began.

Actually, the first Chinese came to America during Gold Rush days, in the late 1840s. Over the years their immigration increased sharply and by 1882 there were about 320,000 Chinese people living in America, mostly on the West Coast. Most of them had come from a single province in Southeast China where economic conditions forced many men to leave home as contract laborers or "coolies" to work in this country as miners or railroad workers during the early days of westward expansion. Many intended to return to China to attain new status based on the wages of their toil. As a result of this hope and because of strong filial ties, few made much effort to adapt to western institutions. And some did return, but most stayed in the United States. Many suffered from vicious attacks. There were outright murders in Los Angeles in 1871 and a massacre of twenty-nine persons took place in Rock Spring, Wyoming, in 1885.[23]

When the railroads were finished and the mines were shut down, many Chinese moved back to the West Coast cities, where they turned to occupations that had nothing especially Oriental about them—running hand laundries, cigar shops, curio shops, and restaurants—and few remained in outdoor labor. Moreover, since "merchants" had higher status in the eyes of immigration officials than "workers," many called themselves merchants.

Immigration officials were an important factor in the lives of the Chinese. California, the state with the largest Chinese population, had long looked with disfavor upon these (and,

it turned out, other) Orientals. They repeatedly passed discriminatory legislation—deemed essential in the face of the
"yellow peril"—to curtail the activities of the Chinese residents.
In 1882 the Chinese became the first group singled out by the
federal government for separate treatment, when the Chinese
Exclusion Act was passed. (It was renewed in 1892, and in 1902
all Chinese immigration was made illegal. The ban was not lifted
until 1943 when China was our military ally and then only a
crack: 105 persons were to be admitted each year. The Act of
1965 has changed things considerably.)

The restriction against immigration did not reduce anti-
Chinese sentiments. "Chinatowns," inhabited mainly by single
men, were considered by many Americans to be centers of
licentiousness, narcotic addiction, corruption, and mystery.
Traditional ties and loyalties, clan connections and "company"
allegiances, gave these areas local "community control" years
before that phrase was to become a part of everyday rhetoric.
Ever-present prejudice and blatant discrimination increased
the pressure for ingroup solidarity in Chinese neighborhoods as
well. On their "turf" and in their own way, economic and welfare and educational institutions were established as were
places of recreation and amusement. (Even today, as is well
known, Chinese-Americans find solace in their own communities and want to maintain their own dualistic culture patterns.
Resistance to widespread school bussing in San Francisco by
many Chinatown residents is but a single case in point.)

Chinese-Americans suffer much less prejudice and discrimination than in earlier years; still Chinatowns remain—especially
in San Francisco, Los Angeles, and New York—and so do
many problems. But most of these have to do with internal
conflicts in the communities, as between citizens and recent
immigrants from Hong Kong, or between shop owners and those
who work in the ubiquitous sweatshops, or between the old
guard and the "red" guard, sometimes composed of the children
of middle-class Chinese-Americans. Also, as might be expected,
the shift of American foreign policy toward Peking after almost
a quarter of a century of support for Nationalist China and

the Chiang regime has confused and angered many Chinese-Americans who felt a sense of kinship with Taiwan. It has also delighted many others who see China the country, not the political entity, as their homeland.

The Japanese were a half step behind the Chinese at each phase of their early settlement—and in their early travails—in America. The first Japanese settlers came in 1869, twenty-one years after the first Chinese; and the large migration took place a decade after the major Chinese immigration and *after* the Chinese Exclusion Act had been invoked. The latter point is important, for it shows that while the two groups were frequently lumped together, significant distinctions were also made between them.

Save for the few members of the Wakamatsu Colony of pioneers who came here in the late 1860s under very special circumstances, no Japanese migrated to this country again until 1885; until then almost no one could leave Japan. With a shift in the policy of the new Mejii regime, however, many departed their native land to find work in Hawaii and in the United States itself. When they arrived here some sought work in the cities, but it was hard to obtain and so they turned to mining and logging and, particularly, farm labor. The latter proved to be advantageous to employers and newcomers alike —for a large number of immigrants had worked the soil before and took pride in what they could do with it. But they proved too good for some Californians to tolerate.

As they saved and began to buy land for their own farms or, as in the case of quite a few members of the second generation, left their jobs as laborers or domestics and sought to enter competitive vocations, prejudices began to mount and they also came to feel the brunt of racism used as "a mask for privilege," to use Carey McWilliams' phrase. The Japanese and Korean Exclusion League was formed to protest against "unfair competition."

Immigration was greatly reduced in 1907 as a result of President Theodore Roosevelt's "Gentlemen's Agreement with the Japanese Government" to stop the issuance of passports to potential farm workers. (Others, including some merchants and many students, continued to come.) But this was not enough to satisfy the Californians. They sought and got their own Alien Land Law in 1913; it prevented the Japanese ("aliens ineligible for citizenship") from purchasing their own farms. Owing to World War I and the need for produce, the threat of denial— and of removal—was stayed. In fact, immigration restrictions themselves were lifted and about seventy-five thousand Japanese entered the country, to become mostly farm laborers. One student of the period writes that "farm income reached a peak in 1920 when the Japanese in California produced land crops valued at 67 million dollars."[24] He also points out that

. . . after the war, the release of war workers from city factories, the return of soldiers, and the "increasing danger" from a rising nationalistic Japan reignited agitation against the Japanese. Although they had developed much of the marginal land of California, they were accused of having secured the richest and most desirable farm land.[25]

And as one might now expect, the land law was soon amended and ultimately served to curtail sharply Japanese agricultural activities—though it did not stop them entirely.

The Japanese reaction to discrimination was quite different from that of many other ethnic groups, including the Chinese. For the most part they eschewed a "ghetto" existence but they did tend to help one another. This became especially important in the cities to which many farm workers and former owners had to move. While feeling pressure from the *Issei* (first generation) they found solace among their kinfolk—and their "ken folk" (people from the same district, or *ken*). Yet the *Nisei* (the second generation) were more inclined to be attracted to the world beyond the "Little Tokyos" of Seattle, San Francisco, and Los Angeles.

Following the attack on Pearl Harbor almost the entire Japanese-American population—citizens and aliens alike—were removed by military decree from the cities of the West Coast and placed in "security" camps in the desert, the Rocky Mountains, and as far away as Arkansas. (Japanese-Americans living in other parts of the country were placed under surveillance, but were not interned.) This unprecedented action of the government was prompted by fear of disloyalty from the Japanese-American minority, the seeds of suspicion often having been sown by those for whom the Japanese had long been an economic threat. Eventually the order was rescinded, and a year after the evacuation, the Japanese began to resettle. Many established new homes in the Midwest, some in the mountain states and in the East, and others finally returned to the West. It is estimated that the Japanese-Americans suffered a financial loss of over $350 million through the forced evacuation. Although Congress appropriated some money for restitution to these displaced persons, few were able to recoup their losses, many could not offer sufficient proof of their claims, and no government, of course, could compensate them for the disruption of their lives.[26]

More often than not, the Japanese had to begin again in different occupations from those they had engaged in prior to the war. Without sufficient funds only a small number could return to their prewar activities. Nonetheless, in the main the status of Japanese-Americans has improved considerably since 1945. Being more widely dispersed throughout the country, they now occupy a minority-group position somewhat analogous to that of American Jews.[27]

In addition to the half million Chinese and almost as many Japanese who crossed the Pacific to the United States, many thousands of Filipinos also made this journey. Their emigration came about as a result of the special circumstances whereby the Philippines became a territory of the United States in 1898 at the end of the Spanish-American War. Most of those who came were laborers or domestics and some have remained in such positions over the years. The United States Navy, for example, still uses Filipinos as mess stewards on shore and shipboard. Some resent this automatic treatment. Others are pleased to have their "niche" even in the context of a sort of uniformed domestic service. In recent years, an increasing number of well-educated Filipinos, including many doctors, have come to continue their studies or to find work in the United States.

Spanish-surnamed Americans

Because of their particular history many of the Filipinos are classified not only with other Asian-Americans but with those now listed under the rubric "Spanish-surnamed." However, relative to other people with Spanish names, the Filipinos comprise a tiny minority. While receiving their names from the same source—if at a considerably earlier time—the "Spanish-surnamed" are in fact, a multigroup minority that includes descendants of very early settlers living in areas taken over from Mexico after the Treaty of Guadalupe Hidalgo at the end of the

Mexican-American War, recent immigrants from Mexico and other Latin-American countries, and Puerto Ricans, who have been citizens since 1917.

Oldest are the Hispanos of mixed racial parentage—Spanish and Indian—whose history dates back to the days of the Spanish conquest. The Southwest has been their traditional home for over four centuries. They became American citizens by default when New Mexico, California, and other southwestern territories were ceded to the United States after the Mexican-American War in 1848. Prior to their annexation, the social patterns of Mexican society prevailed in these territories, and the lifeways of many Hispanos still mirror those of their countrymen south of the Rio Grande.

Shortly after the turn of the twentieth century, increasing numbers of Mexican laborers crossed the border to work in the United States. Restrictions on overseas immigration during World War I gave impetus to the migration from Mexico; almost a million Mexicans entered the country between 1910 and 1930. Most of these found employment in southwestern states —Texas, Arizona, and California; some became migratory workers moving northward and eastward with the seasons. Over half of these newcomers took up residence in the United States and, while few sought to obtain citizenship, their offspring became Americans by birth.

Characteristically, the second generation sought access to what was denied their parents, and some gained entry to "Anglo" society. The majority, however, found the paths to American-style success blocked by barriers of prejudice and discrimination and especially by a particular form of racism that implied that Mexicans were ideally suited for "stoop labor" and therefore should be restricted to what they "did best." This widespread attitude served to keep many influential people in the Southwest from making the necessary changes in the educational system and in social welfare to assist the Mexican workers in moving off the fields and up the ladder of social mobility. The slum *barrios* in El Paso and San Antonio, in Trinidad, Colorado, in Tucson, Arizona, and in Los Angeles and San

Diego are living reminders of these facts of social life for our Mexican-American citizens; so, too, are the labor camps and rural settlements that pockmark the fertile valleys of California. In these places (and similar ones throughout the Southwest) two types of migrants from Mexico are to be found: the "wetbacks," who cross the border illegally in search of employment; and the "braceros," legal entrants with permits to work as contract laborers. (The *bracero* program has been sharply curtailed. At its height in 1960 427,000 entered. Few were admitted under the special provisions of the Mexican Laborer Acts after 1965 and none by 1970. All Mexicans must now enter legally, under the revised Immigration and Nationality Act.)

In the recent past these two groups served to heighten anti-Mexican prejudice of both white citizens (or "Anglo" as they are referred to in that part of the country) and those of Mexican descent. Willing to work for lower wages or contracted in large groups for agricultural and industrial employment, they constituted an economic threat of several sorts. In addition to depressing the value of local labor, they were often seen as a part of the Mexican-American community and everyone named Ramirez or Gonzales or Diego got tainted with the same stigma.

Of late, instead of resenting this grouping of contract laborers and others with themselves, Mexican-Americans have joined with them to fight for union representation and collective bargaining in the vineyards, lettuce fields, and orange groves where they toil. And not only is there a growing sense of cohesiveness beginning to assert itself among the disparate members of *La Raza* but a demand for both political power and recognition of cultural pride is being voiced by an increasing segment of this minority of 5 million people.

"Chicano" used to be a term of derogation (a corruption of "Mexicano") but, for many so labeled, it has now become a term of pride and solidarity. As one well-known Mexican-American has said, "Call us whatever you like, *we* know what we are and are proud of it."[28]

Increasingly the voices of Mexican-Americans — Cesar

Chavez in California, Corky Gonzales in Colorado, Ries Tijerina in New Mexico, and a variety of new leaders in Texas—have been raised and many, Anglos and Mexican-Americans, are listening closely. And they are seeing changes that will alter both the public stereotypes ("Frito bandito") and the substance of life for Mexican-Americans. Like other peoples so often categorized as "colored" minorities, they are seeking a legitimate and equal place in a pluralistic America. They are determined to be recognized for something far more important than the ubiquitous taco stands that dot the byways of the Southwest.

Often grouped with Mexican-Americans are the Puerto Ricans. Although they too are of mixed racial origins and are Spanish-speaking, they are a distinct—and distinctive—people.

Puerto Rico, an island in the Caribbean, has been an American possession since the Spanish-American War. By their own choice Puerto Ricans became United States citizens in 1917. (Until recently, few other Americans knew this, nor much else about these fellow citizens. In fact, until the mid-1950s many mapmakers misspelled the name of their home island, calling it "Porto Rico.")

Migration from the island to the mainland began early in this century; it has fluctuated with economic conditions in the states. Since World War II, Puerto Rican migration has risen sharply, in large part because of increasing job opportunities, the appeal of the popular culture of large cities, and dramatically improved transportation facilities, which have brought Puerto Rico closer to the mainland.

As in earlier days, New York is the gateway for new arrivals, and as in the past, many who first arrive in New York remain there. Puerto Ricans—like their predecessors from southern and eastern Europe and southern blacks whose migration to New York has paralleled their own—have found employment in the garment industry and as service workers in this great commercial and tourist center. While Puerto Ricans are to be found in all parts of the country—including Alaska and Hawaii—over three-fourths of their total number live in

New York City. In 1970 slightly more than a million Puerto Ricans were living in the United States, 750,000 of these in New York City (including 211,000 born there).

Like other newcomers to the city, many Puerto Ricans have found themselves relegated to the worst and most overpriced neighborhoods. Their children attend overcrowded schools; they often hold the lowest-status jobs; they frequently suffer "winter temperatures and more chilling social contacts."[29] Despite the fact that in many ways they have come better prepared for life in the United States than other ethnic minorities, they are still having difficulty climbing the ladder.[30]

The Puerto Rican migrants are a literate group; in addition to Spanish, 40 to 50 percent know English when they arrive. They are far more likely to have come from urban areas and have a much higher proportion of skilled and semiskilled workers than the native population. Furthermore, in contradiction to the assertion that "primarily Puerto Rico's unemployed come to New York," it has been found that the migrants were more regularly employed at home than the rest of the population and received a slightly higher income than the Puerto Rican average. They come not to seek work, but to seek *better* work. Lastly, they have maintained a sense of interdependence that has helped to solidify the Puerto Rican community.

The last characteristic has not always been based upon the desire to maintain a separate identity. It has come about in part as a defensive reaction against the conflicts that exist between Puerto Rican attitudes toward "race" and those which they confront upon migration. Puerto Ricans are the first large minority group to migrate to the urban centers of the United States who bring with them a tradition of widespread social intermingling and racial exogamy. While it is true that lighter-skinned Puerto Ricans generally have higher status on their home island than in this country, there are a great many exceptions. It is said that while "on the mainland, the color of a person determines what class he will belong to; in Puerto Rico, a class a person belongs to determines his color. . . ." This differential image of color may account largely for the tenacity with which many Puerto Ricans cling to their separate identity as Spanish-Americans.

Some Puerto Ricans, reacting to discrimination against them, have tried a new ploy, to call themselves Cubans. Until the Castro Revolution there were some Cubans in the United States, many of them laborers and growers. Afterward the ranks swelled rapidly (over 350,000 were admitted between 1961 and 1970), and the group that came included many middle-class people who were (or thought they would be) dispossessed. In addition, with the failure of the Bay of Pigs invasion in 1961, many Cuban refugees of various social classes were welcomed into this country and in many places given special and favorable treatment. While by and large they have done well, they are still resented and envied by other recent immigrants, the traditional competitors for unskilled and semiskilled jobs, such as blacks, especially in places like southern Florida, where half of all Cuban refugees live.

Finally, it should be noted that there are other Spanish-surnamed people to be found throughout the United States. Some are regular immigrants and some are refugees from Franco's regime in Spain; others are from such Caribbean islands as the Dominican Republic; and many others are from South America, including in recent years a number of students and physicians.

Conclusion

Many of those who migrated to America left their countries of origin seeking freedom and a new life in the New World. Some came to make their fortunes; some to escape religious persecution, political tyranny, or economic deprivation; and some were unwillingly brought in the chains of bondage. For most, immigration was the beginning of a new and exciting adventure, but for others the journey to America was a bitter and harrowing experience.

In this brief sketch of America's principal immigrant groups we have only touched upon the reception of newcomers by those already in the United States. In Chapter Three we turn to a discussion of various proposals for coping with "strangers" in the land, an interpretation of these, an examination of the patterns of ethnic separation that emerged, and a consideration of a statistical breakdown of America's racial, religious, and ethnic composition in 1972.

NOTES

1. There are many general texts that describe the history of and reaction to America's minorities. Among the most useful are Oscar Handlin, *The Uprooted* (Boston: Little, Brown, 1951); Marcus Lee Hansen, *The Atlantic Migration: 1607–1860* (New York: Harper Torchbook, 1961); Marcus Lee Hansen, *The Immigrant in American History* (Cambridge: Harvard University Press, 1940); John Higham, *Strangers in the Land: Patterns of American Nativism, 1860–1925* (New Brunswick: Rutgers University Press, 1955). See also Charles F. Marden and Gladys Meyer, *Minorities in American Society*, 3rd ed. (New York: American Book Company, 1968); and Richard A. Schermerhorn, *These Our People: Minorities in American Culture* (Boston: Heath, 1949).

2. John Collier, "The United States Indian," in J. B. Gittler (ed.), *Understanding Minority Groups* (New York: Wiley, 1956), pp. 34-36. See also Frank Lorimer, "Observations on the Trends of Indian Populations in the United States," in Oliver La Farge (ed.), *The Changing Indian* (Norman: University of Oklahoma Press, 1942). Lorimer cites estimates of the number of aborigines in the Western Hemisphere at the time of the first white settlement as between 8 and 13 million.

3. See, for example, Ruth Benedict, *Patterns of Culture* (Boston: Houghton Mifflin, 1934); Paul Radin, *The Story of the American Indian* (New York: Liveright, 1944); and Peter Farb, *Man's Rise to Civilization* (New York: Dutton, 1968).

4. John Collier, *Indians of the Americas* (New York: Mentor Books, 1947), pp. 116-117.

5. Marden and Meyer, *op. cit.*, pp. 361-362.

6. Pierre van den Berghe, *Race and Racism* (New York: Wiley, 1967), p. 86.

7. Alden Stevens, "Whither the American Indian?" in Milton L.

Barron (ed.), *American Minorities* (New York: Knopf, 1958), p. 148.

8. Marden and Meyer, *op. cit.*, pp. 362-371. See also William and Sophie Brophy, *The Indian: America's Unfinished Business* (Norman: University of Oklahoma Press, 1966).

9. See Murray Wax, *Indian-Americans: Unity and Diversity* (Englewood Cliffs, N.J.: Prentice-Hall, 1971).

10. Delaware had been a Swedish possession. It was surrendered to the Dutch in 1655.

11. See Arnold and Caroline Rose, *America Divided* (New York: Knopf, 1953), pp. 28-31.

12. See Kenneth M. Stampp, *The Peculiar Institution* (New York: Vintage Books, 1956).

13. There is considerable controversy over these issues. See Stanley Elkins, *Slavery* (University of Chicago, 1959); and Ann J. Lane, *The Debate over Slavery: Stanley Elkins and His Critics* (Urbana: University of Illinois Press, 1971). See also Peter I. Rose (ed.), *Slavery and Its Aftermath* (Vol. I of *Americans from Africa*) (New York: Atherton Press, 1970), especially pp. 103-194.

14. See C. Vann Woodward, *The Strange Career of Jim Crow* (New York: Oxford University Press, 1957), p. 8.

15. Ralph Ellison, *Invisible Man* (New York: Random House, 1962).

16. See Peter I. Rose (ed.), *Old Memories, New Moods* (Vol. II of *Americans from Africa*) (New York: Atherton Press, 1970), especially pp. 237-320.

17. John F. Kennedy, *A Nation of Immigrants*, rev. ed. (New York: Harper & Row, 1964), p. 18.

18. Emma Lazarus, "The New Colossus," *Poems* (Boston: Houghton Mifflin, 1889), pp. 202-203.

19. Max Lerner, *America as a Civilization* (New York: Simon and Schuster, 1958), p. 88.

20. Handlin, *op. cit.*

21. See, for example, William S. Bernard, *American Immigration Policy—A Reappraisal* (New York: Harper & Row, 1950), pp. 23-24. Also see Benjamin M. Ziegler (ed.), *Immigration: An American Dilemma* (Boston: D. C. Heath, 1953).

22. Peter I. Rose, "The Ghetto and Beyond," in Peter I. Rose (ed.), *The Ghetto and Beyond* (New York: Random House, 1969), p. 17.

23. See, for example, Rose Hum Lee, *The Chinese in the United States of America* (New York: Oxford University Press, 1960), Francis L. K. Hsu, *Challenge of the American Dream: The Chinese in the U.S.* (Belmont, Calif.: Wadsworth, 1971); and Stan-

ford M. Lyman, *Chinese-Americans* (New York: Random House, 1973).

24. Harry H. L. Kitano, *Japanese-Americans* (Englewood Cliffs, N.J.: Prentice-Hall, 1969), p. 17.
25. *Ibid.* See also William Petersen, *Japanese-Americans: Oppression and Success* (New York: Random House, 1971).
26. Leonard Bloom and Ruth Riemer, *Removal and Return* (Berkeley: University of California Press, 1949), pp. 202-204.
27. Stanford M. Lyman, "Japanese-American Generation Gap," *Society*, 10 (January-February 1973), 55-63.
28. See John H. Burma (ed.), *Mexican-Americans in the United States* (New York: Schenkman, 1970); and Ellwyn Stoddard, *Mexican-Americans* (New York: Random House, 1973).
29. Clarence Senior, *Strangers—Then Neighbors* (New York: Freedom Books, 1961), p. 22. See also Elena Padilla, *Up from Puerto Rico* (New York: Columbia University Press, 1958); Christopher Rand, *The Puerto-Ricans* (New York: Oxford University Press, 1958); and Patricia Sexton, *Spanish Harlem* (New York: Harper, 1965).
30. See report by Edward C. Burks, "Affluence Eludes Blacks, Puerto-Ricans," *The New York Times*, August 17, 1972, p. 33.

ᒘᕼᕆᕫᕫ

ONE AMERICAN
OR MANY?

Coming Full Circle

Sometime in the spring of 1970 the "American saga" seemed
to come full circle. An attempt was made by a dozen Indians
to establish a beachhead on Ellis Island, the station to which
thousands upon thousands of European immigrants had first
touched American shores. The motorboat failed and the plot to
seize the island on the East Coast as others had seized the
island of Alcatraz in San Francisco Bay was foiled.

When some person suggested that the Indians were stupid
for attempting an invasion and occupation of the island without
proper equipment, one retorted, "We're stupid? It was your
ancestors who landed on these shores, thought they were somewhere else and called us Indians. Indians live on the other side
of the world!"

That bit of repartee is more profound than it seems on the
surface. It bespeaks, in a few words, the frustration of many
American minorities who know that they are seen as lazy,
ignorant, sneaky, sullen, argumentative, or aggressive while
the members of the dominant group fancy themselves as para-
gons of virtue, as the normal human specimens, modal types.
In the United States this majority is preeminently white, Protestant and of European background. Its standards are those set,
by and large, by its legacy; and so, in a way, are its prejudices.

Ko Lum Bo

But suppose, as George Stewart once suggested, that the English and other north Europeans had not settled our eastern shores first. Suppose that the approach had been from the west and that Asians, rather than Europeans, had landed and established political control and, for all intents and purposes, political and cultural hegemony over the new territories. Stewart put it this way:

> . . . during one of the vigorous and expansive periods of the Chinese Empire, one of their navigators (who might have been named Ko Lum Bo) conceived the idea of sailing eastward from China and thus arriving at Ireland, which was known to be the farthest outpost of Europe. The Chinese wished to reach Ireland, it may be believed, because they had heard tales that those barbarous islanders made a certain drink called Wis Ki.
>
> Ko Lum Bo made his voyage, and discovered a country that he supposed to be part of Ireland, although he was disappointed in not finding any Wis Ki being manufactured by the natives.
>
> During the course of the next two centuries the Chinese colonized this country, eventually discovering it to be not Ireland, but a wholly new continent. Nevertheless they continued to call the natives Irish, or sometimes Red Irish.
>
> The Chinese colonists introduced their own well-established ways of life. They continued to speak Chinese, and to practice their own religion. Being accustomed to eat rice, they still ate it, as far as possible. Vast areas of the country were terraced and irrigated as rice paddies. The colonists continued to use their comfortable flowing garments, and pagodas dotted the landscape. In short, the civilization was Asiatic and not European.[1]

Dropping this delightful and pointed social science fiction, we remind ourselves that it was the English, Scotch-Irish, and north Europeans who did come, brought with them much of their own cultural baggage, which, from the start, they thought superior to that of the natives. Manners of speaking and dressing, of organizing communities, even of worship were transplanted from the old country. Of course, the New World (and, especially, the hinterlands of North America) was of a scale that was hard to comprehend. As the new society developed, adjustments were constantly necessary. Innovations were commonplace. Even so, many aspects of the core culture were retained. And so, like the Chinese who never did come (at least not in the manner imagined), the English and others who did developed a new or, better stated, modified version of their old societies. And all who were here (meaning the variegated Indian peoples) or were to come (including thousands of slaves and millions of immigrants) were to be affected by the laws and lifeways of the Anglo-American Establishment, which, in time, broke from the motherland but remained—like the "hippie" of recent years with all his new trappings—an unmistakable product of its early socialization.

Immigrants and the American Dream

As noted in the preceding chapter, for four centuries America served as a magnet—first for the rich and venturesome and later for the tired and poor and "tempest-tost." The majority of immigrants—English, Irish, German, Scandinavian, Italian, Jewish, and Slav—came, of their own free will, ready and willing to share in the wealth and bounty of America. Many were disillusioned; many suffered from discrimination by those who had so recently been newcomers themselves; many found it difficult to reconcile their Old World and its ways with the new. And yet, in time, one group after another began the slow climb and, for many, the "American dream" (of opportunity) proved more than a catch phrase.

In spite of the divisions and conflicts among the varied groups that are so much a part of American history and American folklore, for those who were white, almost all things were considered possible. As Raymond Aron, the French sociologist, has accurately observed:

> As far as I am concerned, the greatest achievement of American society is to have drawn millions of people from the lower classes of Europe and made them into good American citizens. That is an

extraordinary performance, an unprecedented marvel of acculturation.

But you didn't do it without paying a heavy price. Poverty in America is aggravated by ethnic heterogeneity, by the unfinished acculturation of certain fragments of the American population. You have a permanently unintegrated fringe, consisting chiefly of blacks and Puerto-Ricans. You did very well in assimilating national minorities, but not nearly as well with racial minorities.[2]

There are various explanations of these facts of American life. One that is the simplest is quite persuasive. Those who proposed programs for the best way of integrating disparate peoples into a single nation did so generally without regard to color and yet rarely were "colored people" ever seriously considered on a par with white immigrants. They dealt with marginal men, not invisible ones—at least not until recently, as we shall see.

Theories of Integration

The nature of adjustment of increasing numbers of immigrants to life in America has been of concern to both scholars and politicians since the early days of the colonial period. In the deliberations and debates over the problem of integrating ethnically heterogeneous peoples into a unified, English-speaking national group, various courses of action with explicit goals in mind have been promulgated. The three principal theories of adjustment—offered by the Founding Fathers, by the newcomers themselves, or by their spokesmen—have been popularly referred to as "Anglo conformity" (a term coined by George Stewart and Mildred Cole), "the melting pot," and "cultural pluralism."[3] Sociologists, ever wont to give more precise designations to social processes, came to call these *assimilation, amalgamation,* and *accommodation,* respectively.

Assimilation

During the eighteenth century the majority of those who had come to America—white, Protestant, Anglo-Saxon—saw themselves standing on the threshold of a new world. The United States itself was conceived in the spirit of liberty and dedicated to the belief "that all men are created equal . . . endowed by their Creator with certain inalienable Rights." However, the authors of these phrases shared the belief of many others that American social norms and values of the future lay within the framework of traditionally British social, religious, and cultural institutions; and, while America was envisaged as an asylum for Europe's refugees, some of the leading figures of the day had strong reservations about what the effects of unrestricted immigration might be. In a letter to John Adams, George Washington wrote:

My opinion, with respect to immigration, is that except of useful mechanics and some particular descriptions of men or professions, there is no need of encouragement, while the policy or advantage of its taking place in a body (I mean the settling of them in a body) may be much questioned; for, by so doing, they retain the language, habits and principles (good or bad) which they bring with them.[4]

Most of those who were of the opinion that an open-door policy should prevail emphatically maintained that the immigrant should take off his foreign mantle and quickly adapt himself to *American* ways. John Adams made this position quite clear when he wrote:

They come to a life of independence, but to a life of labor— and, if they cannot accommodate themselves to the character, moral, political and physical, of this country with all its compensating balances of good and evil, the Atlantic is always open to them to return to the land of their nativity and their fathers. . . . They must cast off the European skin, never to resume it.[5]

If the Founding Fathers had their ideas about the best course of national integration, so, too, did many of the newcomers.[6] The immigrants often envisioned America as a vast land, ready, willing, and able to provide economic and social opportunities in an atmosphere free from harassment and interference. By the mid-nineteenth century many came to this country with clear intentions of maintaining their separate cultural identities. The Germans, for example, who settled in Wisconsin, Missouri, and Texas, succeeded in establishing several settlements where the German language was the vernacular and where German nationalism persisted. In time the Germans scattered more widely across the land where they adapted themselves to many "native" institutions. Some, however, retained a nostalgic longing for the fatherland.

The Scandinavians were more successful. Their settlements in the farmlands of the northern Middle West became strongholds of church-centered Norwegian and Swedish traditions. Isolation from the dominant drift of American social patterns permitted their widespread and long-lived retention of indigenous lifeways, which continue, in some measure, to this day.

As indicated in the preceding chapter, the Irish—and most of the other immigrants who came later—tended to concentrate in urban areas where it was more difficult to maintain a separate existence. Yet, the presence of these new immigrants in the same communities as "native" Americans brought about a reevaluation of sentiments about assimilation. The newcomers—whose backgrounds differed even more radically than those of the Germans or Scandinavians from those of the early settlers—were often viewed as constituting a substantial threat to the established majority. "Could these aliens ever become real Americans?"

Labor unrest and agitation attributed largely to the foreign elements in the population, the specter of Catholicism in Protestant America, and the identification of immigrants as denizens of the urban slums revived and reinforced xenophobic attitudes. As a result of these developments, movements arose to keep the United States American. In 1882 the first restrictive legislation was passed to limit the flow of immigrants (in this case, Chinese laborers) to the United States. In the years that followed, resentment grew as increasing numbers of European nationals established their own ethnic communities where Old World ties were perpetuated. No longer could the dominant group avoid coming to grips with the problem of immigrants who arrived at the rate of a million a year and whose political strength alone was very great. A new kind of assimilationist policy emerged to enforce more directly the adoption of American ways. This was the "Americanization movement," which, through propaganda and education, sought to break down the immigrants' ties to the past.

Not all the advocates of this plan were anti-foreign; indeed, many felt that this was the only way to develop a united nation, a unified people. But most protagonists of Americanization would have agreed, essentially, with the position of one American who not so long ago stated:

> I am sure foreign people make a mistake in keeping customs of their own land alive and featured in this country. If this country meets their expectations they should forget the folklore of Europe, St. Patrick's Day Parades, German Days, and get behind American things. If they can't do this they should be returned to the land they love. This country is supposed to be the world's melting pot. If they won't melt, they should not belong.[7]

Amalgamation

While the assimilation—or "Anglo conformity"—idea was the most prevalent one through much of our history, there were other attitudes toward the new Americans. Many people of the dominant North European heritage hoped to develop a society where the "best" traditions of Europe would be blended into a dynamic unity. This conception of amalgamation was established in the years immediately following the American Revolution and is illustrated in the visiting Frenchman Crèvecoeur's description of the American:

> He is either a European or the descendant of a European; hence, that strange mixture of blood, which you will find in no other country. . . . He is an American, who, leaving behind him all his ancient prejudices and manners, receives new ones from the new mode of life he has embraced, the new government he obeys, and the new rank he holds. . . . Here individuals of all nations are melted into a new race of men, whose labours and posterity will

one day cause great changes in the world. Americans are the western pilgrims, who are carrying along with them the great mass of arts, sciences, vigor, and industry, which began long since in the east. They will finish the circle.[8]

Men like Crèvecoeur, Ralph Waldo Emerson, and, later, Frederick Jackson Turner argued that the problems of diverse peoples would best be resolved through the gradual fusion of cultural traits into a new and unique system.

At the height of the period of new immigration, long after the great influx of groups from northern Europe had ended, others revived the theme of amalgamation. Thus, the English writer Israel Zangwill expanded the notion to include persons from every corner of the globe. In a play, "The Melting Pot," he portrayed America as a crucible:

There she lies, the great melting pot—listen! Can't you hear the roaring and the bubbling? There gapes her mouth—the harbour where a thousand mammoth feeders come from the ends of the world to pour in their human freight. Ah, what a stirring and a seething—Celt and Latin, Slav and Teuton, Greek and Syrian,— black and yellow— . . . Jew and Gentile. . . .[9]

The politician William Jennings Bryan echoed the sentiments of Zangwill: "Great has been the Greek, the Latin, the Slav, the Celt, the Teuton, and the Saxon; but greater than any of these is the American, who combines the virtues of them all."[10]

The problem of immigrant adjustment was often presented as an either/or proposition. Some argued that newcomers must become apostates from their old and established ways—"get behind American things"—and reconcile themselves to the new and strange way of life of the host society. Others urged that people should merge themselves in a "natural" process of cultural fusion. The former view presumed that, by forcibly assimilating immigrants to a single, already established pattern, they would, in time, benefit from a way of life superior to that which they brought to America. Many newcomers, however, were understandably reluctant to quit their familiar ways, and the one-way process of Americanization never in fact took place. So, too, the melting pot philosophy, while more democratic in intent, was an unrealistic ideal. People simply did not mix together in the great crucible to form a new American, a blend of the cultural ingredients of Europe, Africa, and Asia. Recognition of these facts encouraged the emergence of the idea of cultural pluralism.

Accommodation

The history of our disparate ethnic, religious, and racial groups, as we have indicated, shows that newly arriving immigrants sought out their compatriots who earlier had come to America. They formed national and ethnic colonies in the farmlands and the cities—for example, Scandinavians in the northern Midwest; Irish in Boston, New York, and Philadelphia; Poles in Buffalo, Hamtramck, Michigan, and western Massachusetts; Little Italies and Little Jerusalems in the major urban centers. The United States became a checkerboard of minority groups and, as Milton Gordon suggests, "Cultural pluralism was a fact in American society before it became a theory—a theory with explicit relevance for the nation as a whole. . . ."[11]

This theory developed into an image of the United States as strengthened by *diversity.* Rather than absorption or fusion, advocates of pluralism saw America as "a multiplicity in a unity, an orchestration of mankind."[12] Jane Addams, John Dewey, and Randolph Bourne were among those who spoke out against the policy of "Americanization" and the destruction of indigenous cultural values of immigrants. But no one more eloquently presented the case for cultural pluralism than the philosopher Horace Kallen:

As in an orchestra, every type of instrument has its special timbre and tonality, found in its substances and form; as every type has its appropriate theme and melody in the whole symphony, so in society each ethnic group is the natural instrument, its spirit and culture are its theme and melody, and the harmony and dissonances and discords of them all make the symphony of civilization, with this difference: a musical symphony is written before it is played; in the symphony of civilization the playing is the writing, so that there is nothing so fixed and inevitable about its progressions as in music, so that within the limits set by nature they may vary at will, and the range and variety of the harmonies may become wider and richer and more beautiful.[13]

Cultural pluralism was thus based on the assumption that there is strength in variety, that the nation as a whole benefits from the contributions of different groups. Cultural pluralism involves giving *and* taking and, most importantly, the sharing of and mutual respect for ideas, customs, and values. In such terms America can be seen as a mosaic of ethnic groups, a "nation of nations," each retaining its unique qualities while contributing to the overall pattern.

All spokesmen for cultural pluralism emphasized the fact that ethnic groups ("nationalities," as they were called) should have the right to remain separated, and Kallen, in an oft-quoted sentence, suggested that individuals who were *born* into such groups were inextricably bound to them. He said that "men may change their clothes, their politics, their wives, their religions, their philosophies, to a greater or lesser extent, [but] they cannot change their grandfathers."[14]

The fact is that America remains in many ways what it has always been, a *structurally pluralistic country,* a nation of ethnic blocs whose members are joined by the labels they have inherited, by the tribal ties of kinship, social organization, and economic interests; and by the prides and prejudices of others. (Other factors—religion, class, region—are important too and, as we shall see, need to be "factored in" along with ethnic ties.)

Those minority individuals who tend to be found enjoying a truly high degree of social integration are likely to be members of the academic community, or artists, writers, journalists, hippies, freaks, and, perhaps, criminals. But these are the exceptional cases, those "in which persons from different ethnic backgrounds interact in primary group relations with considerable frequency and with relative comfort and ease."[15] For most Americans close social relations occur within what Gordon calls the *ethclass*, defined as "that sub: ociety created by the interaction of the vertical stratification of ethnicity with the horizontal stratification of social class."[16] In simple terms this means, for example, that, by and large, upper-class "WASPs" associate with those who share their ethnicity and their social-class position; while middle-class Jews, middle-class Italian-Americans, working-class Polish-Americans, or poor white southerners interact, in the main, with their own kind as well.

Numerous empirical studies of American social structure (including those by Stanley Lieberson, Nathan Glazer, Benjamin Ringer, Andrew Greeley, and Norbert Wiley) point to this fact of structural pluralism. In fact it is doubtful that there can be any clear understanding of social stratification in the United States without a concomitant examination of the ethnic factor.

White Immigrants and Nonwhite Minorities

There is a problem left unanswered in the many discussions of assimilation in American life, including cultural pluralism. Usually all racial, religious, and nationality groups are included in both the explanations of what has happened and in blue-prints for the future. Proponents tend to deny or overlook fundamental differences among the voluntary immigrants, the various Indian nations whose lands were overrun, and, especially, the blacks whose migration was enforced and who comprise over a tenth of the present population.[17]

Many writers, sociologists, and others have long argued—and perhaps wanted to believe—that blacks would take their place, all other factors being equal, in the manner of the earlier immigrants. While it is patently naïve to refer to people whose ancestors came when only Indians and Pilgrims populated the land as "newcomers," it is true that their urban experience is relatively recent and that the northward trek, made by so many black men and women in the past eighty years, does represent an important internal migration. And there are certain parallels. But even in such terms the analogy does not hold completely.

During the past century, hope and a belief in the American dream and definite opportunities were important incentives. Overcoming various obstacles, many Irish-, Italian-, Polish-, and Jewish-Americans did manage to make it, and they found successful accommodation in the new environment. But what is also true is that opportunities for Europe's immigrants—even the desperately poor—were far greater than those afforded nonwhite people and, especially, blacks. As economist John Kenneth Galbraith is reported to have quipped: "If you have to be poor, at least have the good sense to be born at a time when *everybody* is poor."[18]

There was yet another problem. Not only did black people enter the urban economy at the wrong time according to the Galbraith dictum but also, unlike most other American minority groups, they did not have the same choices to inspire them nor did they have the same positive self-imagery which they could fall back upon (as the Irish and the Jews and the Chinese and even the Puerto Ricans had done in their own time). They were different.

This last point opens a Pandora's box, one with both practical and theoretical implications. The argument that blacks will resolve their dilemma in the manner of other cases of "immigrant adjustment" assumes that their dilemma is the same. It is not and, in many ways, it never was.

Sociologist Robert Blauner, one of the leading opponents of the Negro-as-immigrant school, recently wrote that

. . . the entrance of the European into the American order involved a degree of choice and self-direction that was for the most part denied people of color. Voluntary immigration made it more likely that individual Europeans and entire ethnic groups would identify with America and see the host culture as a positive opportunity rather than an alien and dominating value system. It is my assessment that this element of choice, though it can be overestimated and romanticized, must have been crucial in influencing the different careers and perspectives of immigrants [the] colonized in America, because choice is a necessary condition for commitment to any group, from social club to national society.

Sociologists interpreting race relations in the United States have rarely faced the full implications of these differences. The *immigrant model* became the main focus of analysis, and the experiences of all groups were viewed through its lens. It suited the cultural mythology to see everyone in America as an original immigrant, a later immigrant, a quasi-immigrant or a potential immigrant. Though the black situation long posed problems for this framework, recent developments have made it possible for scholars and ordinary citizens alike to force Afro-American realities into this comfortable schema. Migration from rural South to urban North became an analog of European immigration, blacks became the latest newcomers to the cities, facing parallel problems of assimilation. In the no-nonsense language of Irving Kristol, "The Negro Today Is Like the Immigrant of Yesterday."[19]

Unique Americans

The black experience in America is unique—it has no real parallel. And black Americans are unique. Paradoxically, blacks may well be at once the most estranged and the least foreign of all the citizens: most estranged because of their special history, which began in subjugation, continued in separation, and persists to this day under various forms of segregation; least foreign because, ironically, having been cut off from their native roots, they had few guides but those of the master and his agents. This is not to say that no "Africanisms" survived. Of course they did. Still, most black Americans, for good or ill, were imbued with many of the same goals and aspirations of those of the dominant group. Many of their cultural traits were similar too.

What they said and what they ate, what they believed and, in some ways, the way they worshiped, were heavily southern Americana. And so with their names. And in these names one finds the true paradox of being both a part of and apart from society. Names are labels by which others know you. Black people's names are those of whites, usually white masters. It is little wonder that one of the symbolic gestures in the new search to assert both self-hood and people-hood by young blacks is to cast off their "slave names" and to adopt African ones—or simply to call oneself "X."

By and large this assertion did not come about until quite recently. For years black people—named Smith and Jones and Brown and Washington—quested often the American Dream and sought to take their place with whites. For many, the venture proved quixotic. Some succeeded, however, and became black equivalents of the white *nouveaux riches,* with all the material trappings to indicate having arrived. Others eschewed such life styles and sought other benefits in the dominant society, especially through higher education and work in the professions. They often found that barriers remained, and rejection often heightened smoldering bitterness and exacerbated doubts about the rightness of seeking to integrate in the first place.

They sometimes proved more akin to the Arabs in French Algeria than the Italians or Jews or Irish-Americans with whom they were so often compared. As Raymond Aron points out:

> The French never established an integrated society in Algeria. Ironically, the young Algerians who came closest to being French, by education and training, were usually the most hostile. But this is understandable, because they were the most sensitive to their rejection by the French ruling class.[20]

Persistent relegation to inferior status and the internalization of values regarded as most typically American (such as the idea of individual achievement through hard work) have led, especially in recent years, to a different sort of response on the part of blacks compared with members of most other American ethnic groups. Some began to argue that the more they learned about the wider society and its members' unwillingness to honor its own lofty ideals, the less they should encourage their "brothers" and "sisters" to accept its basic tenets. Since whites appeared eager to maintain their position of preeminence, many blacks began saying that integration was, in fact, highly dysfunctional for blacks—just as it was in Algiers.

These observations are not to suggest that all social scientists who see blacks as the latest immigrants are white supremacists. But they may be quite naïve in assuming that admitting black children to white schools, opening neighborhoods, and saying, in effect, "You're as good as I am," will solve the problem. Assimilation may have been the goal at one time but it is being severely challenged (see Chapter Seven).

Many observers have failed to accept the uniqueness of the black experience and have offered what in an earlier reference to immigrants was called an either/or response. In the present context the argument goes like this: If black people are not to be segregated, they must be integrated. Integration, in these terms, turns out to be little more than a liberalized and modernized version of "Anglo conformity" (or, today, Euro-American conformity). Indeed and, perhaps, ironically, the pluralism that many wanted for others (and sometimes for themselves) was rarely even considered as a model for blacks, the people who by all counts would benefit most by accepting their uniqueness.

Until recently many liberal integrationists—in the universities, in the government, and even in the civil-rights movement itself—saw but one side of the problem. They recognized but failed to understand the counter culture that grew out of reactions to barriers erected by whites during and after slavery. And so they said, "Throw off your unacceptable ways and become like me." James Farmer, the founder of the Congress of Racial Equality, once put this point of view in very clear perspective. Writing on integration, he said:

. . . we [Blacks] learned that America simply couldn't be color-blind. It would have to become color-blind and it would only become color-blind when we gave up our color. The white man, who presumably has no color, would have to give up only his prejudices. We would have to give up our identities. Thus, we would usher in the Great Day with an act of complete self-denial and self-abasement. We would achieve equality by conceding racism's charge: that our skins were afflicted; that our history is one long humiliation; that we are empty of distinctive traditions and any legitimate source of pride. . . .[21]

Farmer would probably agree that segregation and integration (as social policies) are at once logical opposites and two sides of the *same* coin.

This interpretation, until recently, was very difficult for many integrationist-minded people (including some of those who have analyzed the assimilation processes discussed earlier) to accept. They, like the segregationists, tended to think about black/white relations in dichotomous terms.

An illustration of this viewpoint is what Robert Blauner has called "a dogma of liberal social science." The stance began with Gunnar Myrdal's monumental volume, *An American Dilemma*, in which he asserted that the Negro is "an exaggerated American" and that his principal values are "pathological elaborations" of those commonly shared. Historian Kenneth Stampp referred to those who were "white men with black skins" and Nathan Glazer and Daniel P. Moynihan, in their study of New York City, asserted that "the Negro is only an American and nothing else. He has no values and culture to guard and protect."[22]

These ideas were put forth by others, too, relying in no small measure on the work of the late E. Franklin Frazier, one of America's best-known black sociologists. For example, here is what Frazier wrote in his 1957 revision of *The Negro in the United States*:

Although the Negro is distinguished from other minorities by his physical characteristics, unlike other racial or cultural minorities the Negro is not distinguished by culture from the dominant group. Having completely lost his ancestral culture, he speaks the same language, practices the same religion, and accepts the same values and political ideals as the dominant group. Consequently, when one speaks of Negro culture in the United States, one can only refer to the folk culture of the rural Southern Negro or the traditional forms of behavior and values which have grown out of the Negro's social and mental isolation. . . .[23]

Frazier went on to say that "Since the institutions, the social stratification, and the culture of the Negro minority are essentially the same as those of the larger community, it is not

PARDON ME, SIR. WHY ARE YOU FOLLOWING ME?

I'M YOUR SIT IN.

YOU MUST HAVE THE WRONG PARTY. **I'M** NOT A LUNCH COUNTER.

I'M A **SOCIAL** SIT IN, NOT A PROPERTY SIT IN. WE INTE-GRATE **PEOPLE**.

DON'T GET ME WRONG. I UNDERSTAND WHAT YOU'RE TRYING TO DO. BUT I **CAN'T** TAKE YOU TO WORK WITH ME.

HAVE YOU EVER TAKEN A COLORED PERSON TO WORK WITH YOU?

BELIEVE ME, I WOULD IF I FOUND ONE QUALIFIED. I'M ON **YOUR** SIDE. **YOU** DON'T WANT **ME!**

WONDERFUL. WE CAN DISCUSS IT AT WORK.

LOOK, I **DO** MY BIT! EVERY DAY I **DELIBERATELY** SIT NEXT TO ONE OF YOU ON THE BUS! DON'T I GET **SOME** TIME OFF FOR LIBERALISM?

HAVE YOU EVER TAKEN A COLORED PERSON HOME WITH YOU?

HOLD ON! I NEVER MIX MY HOME LIFE WITH MY POLITICS! HOW LONG DO YOU EXPECT TO STAY WITH ME?

WHITHER YOU GOEST, BABY, I GOEST.

CIVIL RIGHTS USED TO BE SO MUCH MORE TOLERABLE BEFORE NEGROES GOT INTO IT.

strange that the Negro minority belongs among assimilationist rather than the pluralist, secessionist or militant minorities."[24]

Frazier, in our view, may well have been both correct and highly misleading. He assumed, along with many commentators on the Black Experience (both black and white), that to have a culture, a unique culture, one must possess a distinctive language, a unique religion, and a national homeland. As Blauner suggests, this view may be appropriate for what anthropologists would call a holistic culture, complete with the institutions of an integrated social system. To be sure, black Americans did not possess this kind of culture. But they developed their own life styles and sensitivities, often combinations of lower-class and quasi-ethnic characteristics, characteristics not brought from abroad but developed through encounters with racist America.

Black writers such as Richard Wright, LeRoi Jones, and Ralph Ellison—in quite different ways, to be sure—have portrayed the extent to which blacks have had to respond to the "either/or" interpretation. In his brilliant novel *Invisible Man*, Ellison wrote:

I am an invisible man. No, I am not a spook like those who haunted Edgar Allan Poe; nor am I one of your Hollywood ectoplasms. I am a man of substance, of flesh and bone, fiber and liquids, and I might even be said to possess a mind. I am invisible, understand, simply because people refuse to see me. Like the bodiless heads you see sometimes in circus sideshows, it is as though I have been surrounded by mirrors of hard distorting glass. When they approach me they see only my surroundings, themselves, or figments of their imagination—indeed, everything and anything except me. Nor is my invisibility exactly a matter of biochemical accident to my epidermis. That invisibility to which I refer occurs because of a peculiar disposition of the eyes of those with whom I come into contact. A matter of construction of their inner eyes, those eyes with which they look through their physical eyes upon reality.[25]

In contrast to most whites, most blacks find themselves in a perpetual state of cultural schizophrenia. They long had, and continue to have a sense of what W. E. B. Du Bois called "twoness." "One ever feels his twoness," he wrote, "an American, a Negro; two souls, two thoughts, two unreconciled strivings; two warring ideals in one dark body . . ."[26]

Vernon Dixon argues that "the application of the 'either/or' conceptual approach to race relations produces racial harmony [only] when the blacks and whites embody total sameness."[27] And this is an impossibility. Therefore, he proposes a new and different approach, called by the rather cumbersome term "diunitalism," in which one simultaneously recognizes the similarities *and* differences between blacks and whites. Above all the analyst (and, presumably, the policymaker) must learn to understand the ambiguity that marks the social position and often helps shape the personalities of black Americans, whose blackness is both part and parcel of their relations to white society.

Pluralism and Discrimination

In an ironic sense, demands by blacks arguing that they too belong to an ethnic group have strengthened the general ideology of pluralism. What is sauce for the goose is sauce for the gander and, responding to black pressures, many "old ethnics" have become ethnophilic ganders (see Chapter Eight). In principle at least, the doctrine of pluralism is once again coming to pervade present-day conventional morality concerning intergroup relations in the United States. The nation-of-nations motif is extolled by public officials, educators, and religious leaders. School children are told that every group member has the right voluntarily—not by will of the majority—to retain (or give up) his or her separate identity, that people should be judged as individuals, not as members of racial, ethnic, or religious groups.

In practice, of course, the persistent social cleavages between such groups in American society are reflected in patterns of prejudice and discrimination that deny the very rights implied in the idea of pluralism. These patterns are most noticeable in the areas of civil rights, housing, education, employment, religion, and, especially, social interaction. But this does not mean that cultural pluralism is merely a sham, the verbal espousal of which allows many Americans to proclaim tolerance while practicing intolerance. Careful examination of majority-minority relationships reveals a far more complex situation than this contradiction between principle and practice suggests.

Moreover, the notion of pluralism itself has obscured the complex nature of the adjustment of diverse groups to American life, for it lumps together socially and sociologically distinctive processes.[28]

Acculturation

Acculturation pertains to the result of contact between groups possessing differing cultures, to the frequent changes in their behavior patterns and attitudes. In the United States the dominant group has sometimes adopted the traits of minorities. Well-known examples include such linguistic adaptations as "moccasin," "faux pas," "kibbitz," and "gesundheit," and such ethnic dishes as pizza, "Danish" pastry (which, incidentally, is known in Denmark as *wiener brot*), and "sacramental" wine. Sometimes the majority have accepted more active social forms: Latin-American dances, "soul" music, the games of mah-jongg and chess, the sports of judo, lacrosse, soccer, and jai alai.

Generally, as noted previously, the cultural patterns of the dominant groups have been taken over by minority groups. Many members of racial and ethnic minorities have adapted themselves to the folkways of the dominant culture. They have accepted, as their own, patterns of living, dress, and speech—much in the way that Washington, Jefferson, and John Adams had hoped would be the case. Constantly exposed to the dominating modes of life of the majority group, most minority-group members accommodate themselves to expected behavior patterns.

This "behavioral assimilation," as Gordon calls it, is largely evident in public activities. Taking over dominant-group behavior patterns does not necessarily lead to a substantial amount of social interaction on a close, personal basis between members of the established majority and minority-group members. Instead, behavioral assimilation is limited either to such general norms as a common respect for law and order, acceptance of modes of employer-employee relationships, conformity to styles and fashion touted by the mass media, and widespread acceptance of the symbols of success as nurtured by advertisers, or to rather formal settings such as work situations, public education, professional meetings, and the like.

Behavioral Assimilation and Social Separation

The more personal the nature of a potential situation for social interaction, the greater are the barriers to primary and intimate intergroup participation. The case of the Jewish members of a middle-sized community in New York State, studied by the late John Dean, is illustrative. In this town there is little discrimination in the economic sector of life, and Jews are conspicuous in commercial enterprises and in the professions. But political participation is relatively limited, and those Jews who are in public office tend to be appointed rather than elected. Participation in community services is very high among the Jews, but they are prevented from assuming leadership roles "where these entail membership in groups governed by the norm of social exclusiveness."

Such social exclusiveness and restrictive practices were found most prevalent in organizational life. On the basis of these findings, Dean hypothesized that "the larger the proportion of Jews in the community, the more Jews are excluded from socially elite organizations and residential areas."[29] Comparable research on the relations of other minority groups with the larger community suggests that, by substituting the names of other ethnic groups for "Jews," this hypothesis states a valid generalization about dominant-minority relations in many parts of the United States.

Despite the outward manifestations of acceptance and a high degree of behavioral assimilation, various minorities have been—and are—excluded from social cliques, informal groups, and even such communal activities as religious services and leisure-time pursuits. In the study cited above, Dean reported that field staffs who investigated Jewish-Gentile relations in a number of American cities found that there is virtually no intimate, social mixing—that is, interaction among close friends, including visits to each other's homes—between Jews and Christians. More recently Andrew Greeley has noted a similar phenomenon occurring between Protestants and Catholics living in a middle-class Chicago suburb.[30]

It is evident that the structural definitions of social situations—as formal or informal, secondary or primary—are relevant cues to the levels at which behavioral assimilation breaks down and social separation is required and maintained. It should be noted, once again, that the actual levels of acceptance or tolerance vary markedly; that the behavior of those in "dominant groups" is far from uniform; and that within all minorities differential modes of reaction to rejection and discrimination prevail.

Not all members of minority groups wish to have close relationships with others who differ from them culturally. The desire to maintain social distance is most clearly evident among members of certain religious groups—such as Mennonites and Hasidic Jews—who, in order to retain their systems of belief intact without threat of exposure to or enticement from the members of other faiths, avoid almost all intergroup activities. Similarly, certain cultural traditions may be thought to be threatened by the overpowering influence of a cordial host society. Solomon Poll's description of the Hasidim of Williamsburg, Brooklyn, provides an illustration of social separation:

Resistance to Americanization is such that although there is no physical wall to isolate them, a strong "sociological wall" separates this group from activities that might encroach on its cultural stability. All the institutions, including the economic activities of the group, are such that they are conducive to a Hasidic "way of life."[31]

Yet, such intensive resistance to general Americanization and to opportunities to develop and maintain relationships on the basis of personal considerations rather than ethnic status is not the prevailing mode. In fact, most members of minority groups welcome opportunities for acceptance as individuals rather than as members of minorities—and this still includes many blacks despite the growing pride in self and community referred to previously. Many would be satisfied not to have their minority-group membership used as a basis for acceptance or rejection. And, in some areas of life, such is actually the case.

Not all minority-group members are discriminated against "equally." Studies of social distance have shown that certain realms of social life are more open than others and that, even within these spheres, minority groups and their members are ranked according to various criteria of acceptability. In certain occupations that stress performance standards, Jews, blacks, and other American minority-group members have found acceptance without becoming apostates—minority status being considered irrelevant. As suggested earlier, notable cases include parts of the academic world, the arts, entertainment, sports, the "demi-world," and the underworld.

Nevertheless, in the everyday world—removed from the academy, the ball park, the arena, or the theater, where people are patrons or spectators or engage in a certain amount of risk-taking—many members of minority groups are unable to be exempted, unable to bridge the status gap. They turn instead to traditional occupations, select friends from within their own groups, withdraw into the minority community, and resign themselves to a life wherein their status as members of minority groups becomes of utmost importance to them, whether they wish it or not. And where the gap between the dominant and minority group is great, social inbreeding within the minority community heightens group cohesion and simultaneously reinforces the image of clannishness.

There are variations, but the general and pervasive pattern is one of behavioral assimilation and social exclusiveness. Although they are increasing, instances of acceptance by the majority of minority-group members on an equal-status level remain infrequent. And such acceptance is an essential requirement if the ideal of cultural pluralism is to be achieved.

America's People Today

The United States remains a nation of separate racial, religious, and ethnic groupings. Information regarding the racial and religious composition and national origin of the population is readily available in the periodic reports of the U.S. Bureau of the Census and other sources. This kind of information, however, should be understood in the context of the methods used for data-gathering; the meanings of "race," "creed," and "ethnicity," each present different problems for both enumerators and analysts. "Race," for example, has been assessed on the basis of information that "cannot be hidden from the enumerator, about which [he] can make assumptions without serious error, and about which people will be willing to furnish information."[32] Until 1960 this meant that the census-taker was the ultimate judge of the racial designation of a given respondent and, as a result, statistics often reflect the biases of enumerators rather than the racial identity of respondents. (Since 1960 self-classification has been the method of defining both race and ethnic affiliation, probably resulting in greater accuracy than in earlier censuses.)

Racial Groups in the United States

The extent to which the social definition of "race" (referred to in Chapter One) has long affected the ultimate percentages given for the population is indicated in the description of the category "Negroes." As noted earlier, for many decades the U.S. Bureau of the Census claimed that "in addition to persons of Negro descent and of mixed Negro and white descent . . . [it] includes persons of mixed American-Indian and Negro descent, unless the Indian ancestry very definitely predominates or unless the individual is regarded as an Indian in the community."[33]

To the present day, while "white" and "Negro" (however loosely the terms may be defined) are set aside as separate and distinct groupings, others are categorized by a combination of color and place of ancestral origin. Included among the "other races" are American Indians, Japanese, Chinese, and Filipinos; under the heading "all other" are grouped Aleuts, Asian Indians, Eskimos, Hawaiians, Koreans, Indonesians, Polynesians, and "other races not shown separately."[34]

According to these criteria, the 1970 Census indicates that 87.4 percent of the American population is white, 11.2 percent is Negro, and 1.4 percent, other. Census Bureau studies show that, compared with the last decennial enumeration, there has been only a slight change in the proportional representation of racial groups in the United States. Moreover, in spite of increasing northward migration, five of every ten Negroes in

the country still reside in the South. Change has been more dramatic in the increase of blacks (or Negroes) in the overall percentage of city residents. Comparing 1960 with 1970, a rise from 53 percent to 58 percent is noted for the "central city."[35] An increase in the percentage of whites moving *from* these same inner-city areas to the suburbs has also been noted, thereby increasing the ratio of blacks rather markedly, especially in certain centers. In addition to Washington, a city with 71 percent Negroes in 1970, Newark, Gary, and Atlanta already have black majorities.[36]

In contrast to the situation of Negroes, members of other nonwhite groups are most heavily concentrated west of the Mississippi; seven of every ten members of this category live in the West, eight of ten in the coastal area. The only states with a substantial proportion of non-Negro nonwhites are Alaska (20 percent—mainly Aleuts, Eskimos, and Indians) and Hawaii (67 percent—mainly Japanese and Chinese).

Table 3 presents a breakdown of all racial groups enumerated in the 1970 Census.

Religious Groups in the United States

In American society the freedom to worship in one's own way is a fundamental guarantee of the Bill of Rights. There is a proliferation of religious organizations, ranging in structure from the highly bureaucratized Roman Catholic Church to the transitory and loosely organized storefront Protestant churches. Some religious groups are basically fundamentalist; others are more liberal in their interpretations of sacred writings and theology.

Despite this diversity in organization and religious perspective (and despite the proclivity of Americans to search for new avenues for expressing religious feelings—as in the current appeal of Hare Krishna and Zen, which do not follow orthodox western religious traditions) Americans remain a church-going people. The United States, as Will Herberg once suggested, is a nation ever caught in a paradox of "pervasive secularism and

Table 3   Racial Groups in the United States 1970

Race	Number in Hundreds of Thousands	Percentage of Total
White	177,747	87.4
Negro	22,580	11.2
Other races		1.4
Indian	793	
Japanese	591	
Chinese	435	
Filipino	343	
All other	721	
Totals	203,210	100.0

Source: U.S. Bureau of the Census, 1970 *Census of Population*

mounting religiosity."[37] While the commitment of many Americans to the basic tenets of their faiths becomes increasingly vague, both membership and the number of new religious edifices continue to increase. This trend may be related to the expectation that, in this country, every individual is expected to have a religious "brand name" by which to be identified—Protestant, Catholic, or Jew. Herberg and others have observed that religious identification according to these major faiths has replaced, in considerable measure, group identification on the basis of nationality background—so most Americans are affiliated with one of the three.[38]

In 1971, for example, a study made by the National Council of Churches of Christ in the United States of America indicated that there were over 320,000 churches and synagogues in this country with approximately 130 million members.[39] (In a study conducted in 1957 it was learned that only 3 million people denied some kind of religious identification. Moreover, Gallup and other pollsters have repeatedly shown that Americans mistrust "atheists." Many studies show that, all other things being equal, an atheist would be the last person most people would vote for on a list that included Protestants, Catholics, Jews, blacks, women, and atheists.)

Over two-thirds of those who are fourteen years of age

or over belong to one of the Protestant denominations, the largest group being Baptists, the next Methodists, then Lutherans, and then Presbyterians (including those called Congregationalists). Also included here are those who belong to the "black churches" such as the African Methodist Episcopalian, those who sometimes claim they are not truly Protestants, like Quakers and Unitarians, and those who are members of the latest revival movement, the "Jesus freaks." Roman Catholics comprise 25 percent of those fourteen years of age or over and 3 percent are Jewish.

Ethnic Groups in the United States

The distinctions between the major religious denominations in America are fairly well defined and membership statistics are not difficult to obtain. Racial breakdowns, while open to many criticisms regarding their validity and reliability, are likewise available, but accurate data on ethnic-group membership and identification are far more elusive. As noted in Chapter One, ethnic divisions include various kinds of groupings: those with common national backgrounds, those whose racial designation places them in a special category with which they identify themselves and are so identified by others, and those whose group identity may transcend both racial and national boundaries. The complexity of the problem of ethnic classification is illustrated by such facts as the following: Jews are both a religious and cultural minority; the descendants of Irish, Italian, and Polish immigrants are predominantly Roman Catholic, but they also are members of distinctive national ethnic groups; Puerto Ricans, mainly Catholic, sometimes considered to be Negroes, bring distinctive cultural and linguistic patterns from Puerto Rico to the mainland; black Americans, at least to some degree, are culturally as well as racially identifiable, especially when compared with others, like West Indians, who may share their looks but not necessarily their outlooks.

Overlapping of this kind prevents the clear-cut enumeration

of ethnic-group membership. Moreover, there are few reliable statistics on the national origins of the native-born. Estimates are most frequently based on projections of statistics on immigration to the United States—as indicated in Table 2, Chapter Two. Although census enumerators continue to request information about country of birth from both the respondent and his parents, such data do not provide a valid basis for ascertaining the true size or constituency of nationality groupings in America today. Most people now living in this country were born here, as were most of their parents, and projections of immigration statistics alone do not, and cannot, indicate the degree to which individuals have retained their identity with the land or cultural traditions of their forebears.

The problem of estimating the size of ethnic groups is further complicated by the increasing incidence of intermarriage between individuals of different nationality backgrounds. (Members of religious groups, however, have remained relatively endogamous, as, even more strongly, have members of racial groups.) Several recent studies indicate that class affiliation and residential propinquity are, in large measure, the determinants of marital choice for those of differing national but similar religious and racial backgrounds.[40] The rising rate of intermarriage among Irish, Poles, and Italians indicates a greater crossing of ethnic borders than ever before; Roman Catholics are becoming less bound by historic patterns of "intranational" marriage.

This trend in exogamous marriage does not mean that enclaves of national-ethnic groups no longer exist. There are still communities where traditional schisms, between English and Irish, between French- and English-Canadians, between Chinese and Japanese, remain little changed. Moreover, even in those places where "international" marriage is fairly commonplace, many third- and fourth-generation Americans continue to retain a strong sense of identification with the country from which grandparents or great-grandparents migrated. A recent survey of Northampton, Massachusetts, for example, found that residents often make a *single* selection when asked to indicate with which of the larger known ethnic groups in the community they most strongly identify themselves.[41]

Thus, while in some instances the traditional barriers between certain ethnic divisions are becoming increasingly blurred, national-ethnic groupings, as well as those based upon racial or religious factors, persist in the United States.

The Continuation of Intergroup Tensions

There persist, too, although with marked changes in recent years, patterns of social discrimination and prejudice rooted in the lifeways of this nation's "dominant" and "minority" groups. Almost all of America's immigrants and many of their descendants at one time or another have been the targets of discrimination, and many have been its perpetrators—group prejudice is not confined to the majority. One might expect that this historical experience, especially within the context of an open (or semi-open) society with a strong democratic ethos, would work toward the elimination of group barriers and inter-group tensions—and in the long run this may be the case. But, as we know, group antipathy and friction continue. Why do these patterns persist?

This question cannot be easily answered. One clue is offered, however, by the fact that each new group, in seeking its place among those already in the United States, sought to integrate but was often thwarted by others engaged in the same struggle for acceptance. Max Lerner writes:

From the beginning there were stereotypes imposed upon the more marginal immigrants. As was perhaps natural, the members of each new wave of immigration were assigned the lowliest tasks, the longest hours of work, the poorest and dirtiest living quarters. The basic pattern was, however, for the immigrants of each new influx to be in time absorbed by the rest, yielding the role of strangeness in turn to the still later comers. Most of them moved up the hierarchical ladder while those who followed grasped eagerly to the lowly places that had been relinquished.[42]

This pattern of group mobility, which shows a rough correlation between time of arrival and social status (notable exceptions are low-status American Indians, on the one hand, and relatively high-status Jews, on the other), may help to account for the fact that "there has never been any real alliance of minority groups to withstand the prejudice and discrimination from the majority."[43] The rationale for this bold statement will be developed in the succeeding chapters on the nature of prejudice and discrimination and the reactions of minority groups to their status.

NOTES

1. George Stewart, *American Ways of Life* (Garden City, N.Y.: Doubleday, 1954), pp. 11-12.
2. As quoted in Milton Vorst, "Talk with 'a Reasonable Man,'" *New York Times Magazine,* April 19, 1970, p. 96.
3. See, for example, Milton M. Gordon, "Assimilation in America: Theory and Reality," *Daedalus*, 90 (Spring, 1961), 263-285.
4. *The Writings of George Washington* (W. C. Ford, Collector and Editor) (New York: Putnam, 1889), Vol. XII, p. 489. This quotation is discussed in greater detail by Milton M. Gordon, *op. cit.*, pp. 266-267.
5. This letter was published in *Nile's Weekly Register*, 18 (1820), 157-158. See discussion in Marcus L. Hansen, *The Atlantic Migration, 1607–1860* (Cambridge: Harvard University Press, 1940), pp. 96-97.
6. See Nathan Glazer, "Ethnic Groups in America: From National Culture to Ideology," in M. Berger, T. Abel, and C. H. Page (eds.), *Freedom and Control in Modern Society* (Princeton, N.J.: Van Nostrand, 1954), p. 163.
7. This is the comment of a lifelong Yankee resident of a small town in upstate New York. See Peter I. Rose, "Small-Town Jews and Their Neighbours in the United States," *Jewish Journal of Sociology* (England), 3 (December 1961), 187.
8. Michel Guillaume Jean de Crèvecoeur, *Letters from an American Farmer* (New York: Albert and Charles Boni, 1925), pp. 54-55; originally published in London, 1782.
9. Israel Zangwill, *The Melting Pot* (New York: The Jewish Publication Society of America, 1909), pp. 198-199.

10. As quoted in Robert E. Park and Ernest W. Burgess, *Introduction to the Science of Sociology* (University of Chicago Press, 1924), p. 734.

11. Gordon, *op. cit.*, pp. 274-275.

12. Horace M. Kallen, "Democracy versus the Melting-Pot," *The Nation*, 100, February 18, 1915, pp. 190-194, and February 25, 1915, pp. 217-220; see also Horace M. Kallen, *Cultural Puralism and the American Idea* (Phila.: University of Pennsylvania Press, 1956).

13. Kallen, "Democracy versus the Melting-Pot," February 25, 1915, *op. cit.*, p. 220.

14. *Ibid.*

15. Gordon, *op. cit.*, pp. 279-285. See also Gordon, "Social Structure and Group Relations, *Freedom and Control* . . . ," *op. cit.*, pp. 141-157.

16. Milton M. Gordon, *Assimilation in American Life* (New York: Oxford University Press, 1964), pp. 51 ff.

17. See L. Paul Metzger, "American Sociology and Black Assimilation: Conflicting Perspectives," *American Journal of Sociology*, 76 (1971), 627-647. See also Stanford M. Lyman, *The Black American in Sociological Thought* (New York: Capricorn Books, 1972).

18. As quoted in Charles Silberman, *Crisis in Black and White* (New York: Random House, 1964), p. 41. See also James Weldon Johnson, *Black Manhattan* (New York: Knopf, 1930); Claude McKay, *Harlem: Negro Metropolis* (New York: Dutton, 1940); and Oscar Handlin, *The Newcomers* (Cambridge: Harvard University Press, 1959).

19. Robert Blauner, *Racial Oppression in America* (New York: Harper & Row, 1972), pp. 56-57. Irving Kristol's article (referred to by Blauner) and several others dealing with the question of "The Negro as Immigrant" appear in Peter I. Rose (ed.), *Nation of Nations* (New York: Random House, 1972), pp. 197-275, *passim*.

20. As quoted in Milton Vorst, *op. cit.*, pp. 96-97.

21. James Farmer, *Freedom—When?* (New York: Random House, 1965), p. 87.

22. Nathan Glazer and Daniel Patrick Moynihan, *Beyond the Melting Pot* (Cambridge: MIT Press, 1963), p. 53.

23. E. Franklin Frazier, *The Negro in the United States* (New York: Macmillan, 1957), p. 680.

24. *Ibid.*

25. Ralph Ellison, *Invisible Man* (New York: Random House, 1947), p. 3.

26. W. E. B. Du Bois, *The Souls of Black Folk*, 1903. (As published in New York: Fawcett Publications, Premier Americana Editions, 1961, pp. 15-16.)

27. See Vernon J. Dixon, "Two Approaches to Black-White Relations," in Vernon J. Dixon and Badi Foster (eds.), *Beyond Black or White* (Boston: Little, Brown, 1971), pp. 22-66 ff.

28. Gordon, *op. cit.*, pp. 279-285. See also Gordon, "Social Structure in Group Relations," *Freedom and Control . . ., op. cit.*, pp. 141-157.

29. John P. Dean, "Patterns of Socialization and Association Between Jews and Non-Jews," *Jewish Social Studies*, 17 (July 1955), 249-251. Dean's hypothesis was substantiated in the author's study of isolated Jews. The majority of small-town Jews interviewed indicated that they enjoyed a degree of intimate interfaith socializing unparalleled in the urban community; see Rose, *op. cit.*, p. 182.

30. Andrew Greeley, *Why Can't They Be Like Us?* (New York: Dutton, 1971).

31. Solomon Poll, *The Hasidic Community of Williamsburg* (New York: Free Press, 1962), p. 3.

32. Donald Bogue, *The Population of the United States* (New York: Free Press, 1959), p. 122.

33. U.S. Bureau of the Census, *1960 Census of Population Supplementary Reports*, PC (S1)-10, Washington, D.C., p. 2.

34. *Ibid.*

35. U.S. Bureau of the Census, *U.S. Census of Population: 1970 General Population Characteristics* PC (1)-B1, *United States Summary*.

36. Statistical Abstract, 1972, pp. 21-23.

37. Will Herberg, *Protestant–Catholic–Jew* (New York: Doubleday, 1955), p. 14.

38. *Ibid.*, Chaps. 2 and 3; see also Ruby Jo Kennedy, "Single or Triple Melting Pot? Intermarriage Trends in New Haven: 1870–1940," *American Journal of Sociology*, 58 (January 1952), 56-59.

39. *Yearbook of American Churches* (New York: National Council of Churches of Christ in the United States of America, 1970), p. 225.

40. See, for example, A. B. Hollingshead, "Cultural Factors in the Selection of Marriage Mates," *American Sociological Review*, 15 (October 1950), 619-627; and Kennedy, *op. cit.*

41. Peter I. Rose, "The Public and the Threat of War," *Social Problems*, 11 (Summer, 1963), 65-66. For an excellent analysis of the persistence of ethnic identity, see Nathan Glazer and Daniel Patrick Moynihan, *op. cit.*

42. Max Lerner, *America as a Civilization* (New York: Simon and Schuster, 1957), p. 503.
43. Arnold and Caroline Rose, *America Divided* (New York: Knopf, 1953), p. 65.

FOUR

PREJUDICE

On Being Culture-Bound

Members of all societies usually view and judge others from their own culture-bound and group-centered frames of reference. They tend to like what is familiar to them and devalue the strange, the foreign. Kipling described such ethnocentrism in the closing stanzas of his poem "We and They":

All good people agree,
  And all good people say,
All nice people like Us, are We
  And everyone else is They:

But if you cross over the sea,
  Instead of over the way,
You may end by (think of it!) looking on We
  As only a sort of They![1]

According to William Graham Sumner, ethnocentrism "leads a people to exaggerate and intensify everything in their own folkways which is peculiar and which differentiates them from others."[2] It is often difficult for Americans to understand how people in other lands can worship their ancestors, practice infanticide, or engage in polygamy. Many find it hard to comprehend the fact that great numbers of Hindus have lived on the brink of starvation while cattle roamed Indian streets. Why, it is asked, do some Moslem women cover their faces, some Balinese women go bare-breasted, and the Siriono Indians of Bolivia wear no clothes at all? Why do so many nations emerging from colonial status favor socialism over our political system? These patterns of behavior and attitude, strange and generally unacceptable according to American standards, are apt to be explained away as examples of a lower level of cultural development, as exotic legacies from a more primitive past, as evidence of how different some folks are from "rational" Americans.

In "Foreign Children," another poem well known to many Americans who grew up between 1885 and 1935, the Scottish author Robert Louis Stevenson expressed these biases quite explicitly.

Little Indian, Sioux or Crow,
Little frosty Eskimo,
Little Turk or Japanee,
O! don't you wish that you were me?

You have seen the scarlet trees
And the lions over seas;
You have eaten ostrich eggs,
And turned the turtles off their legs.

Such a life is very fine,
But it's not so nice as mine:
You must often, as you trod,
Have wearied, not to be abroad.

You have curious things to eat,
I am fed on proper meat;
You must dwell beyond the foam
But I am safe to live at home.

Little Indian, Sioux or Crow,
Little frosty Eskimo,
Little Turk or Japanee,
O! don't you wish that you were me?[3]

It is sometimes surprising for Americans to learn that everything they do is not thought worthy of emulation. There are many people throughout the world who cannot see any point in women's suffrage, some who are aghast at the permissiveness of our quest for marital partners, and others who regard rules against premarital intercourse as unnatural. And there are those who think it odd, if not downright ignorant, to worship *merely* a single God; others who cannot understand why anyone should pay obeisance to any God at all.

Students of intergroup relations are well aware that not only those "over the sea" are viewed (and view others) ethnocentrically. These distinctions between "they" and "we" exist *within* societies as well. In modern industrial societies most individuals belong to a wide array of social groups that differentiate them from others—familial, religious, occupational, recreational, and so on. Individuals are frequently caught in a web of conflicting allegiances. This situation is often surmounted by a hierarchical ranking of groups as referents for behavior. In most societies, including our own, the family is the primary reference group. In the United States, ethnic or racial identity and religious affiliation are also relevant referents. Members of other ethnic, racial, and religious groups are often judged and graded on the basis of how closely they conform to the standards of the group passing judgment.

Thus, several studies have shown that in American society many, probably most, whites holding Christian beliefs, who constitute both the statistical majority and the dominant group, rank minorities along a continuum of social acceptability. They rate members of minority groups in descending order in terms of how closely the latter approximate their image of "real Americans." The ranking often comes out like this: Protestants from Europe, Irish Catholics, Iberians, Italians, Jews, Spanish-Americans, American-born Chinese and Japanese, blacks, and foreign-born Orientals.[4] While most Americans probably find those of English or Canadian ancestry acceptable citizens, neighbors, social equals, and kinsmen by marriage, relatively few grant all these prerogatives to those relegated to lower-status positions.[5]

There is an interesting correlate to this finding. Investigators have found that minority-group members themselves tend to accept the dominant group's ranking system—with one exception: Each tends to put his own group at the top of the scale.[6]

Ranking is one characteristic of ethnocentric thinking; generalizing is another. The more another group differs from one's own, the more one is likely to generalize about its social characteristics and to hold oversimplified attitudes toward its members. When asked to describe our close friends, we are able to cite their idiosyncratic traits: We may distinguish among subtle differences of physiognomy, demeanor, intelligence, and interests. It becomes increasingly difficult to make the same careful evaluation of casual neighbors; it is almost impossible when we think of people we do not know at firsthand. Understandably, the general tendency is to assign strangers to available group categories that *seem* to be appropriate. Such labeling is evident in generalized images of "lazy" Indians, "furtive" Japanese, "passionate" Latins, and "penny-pinching" Scots.

Ranking others according to one's own standards and categorizing them into generalized stereotypes together serve to widen the gap between "they" and "we." Freud has written that "in the undisguised antipathies and aversions which people feel toward strangers with whom they have to do we may recognize the expression of self-love—of narcissism."[7] In sociological terms, a function of ethnocentric thinking is the enhancement of group cohesion. There is a close relationship between a high degree of ethnocentrism on the part of one group and an increase of antipathy toward others. This relationship tends to hold for ethnocentrism of *both* dominant and minority groups.[8]

Many writers refer to such antipathetic attitudes as bases for "group prejudice." For example:

It is this very group consciousness, or ethnocentrism, which lays the foundations of group prejudice. If there were no strong feelings for one's own group, there would not be strong consciousness of other groups. An awareness of one's own group as an in-group and of the others as out-groups is fundamental in group relationships.[9]

Defining Group Prejudice

Group prejudice may be defined as "a system of negative beliefs, feelings, and action-orientations regarding a group of people."[10] This definition characteristically emphasizes the negative side of prejudice. Literally, of course, "prejudice" refers to positive as well as negative attitudes. Yet, because of the detrimental psychic and social consequences that often result from hostile attitudes, sociologists usually concern themselves with "negative prejudice."

The definition of group prejudice stated above incorporates the three major dimensions of all attitude systems: the *cognitive* (beliefs), the *affective* (feelings), and the *conative* (predispositions to act in particular ways, or policy orientations).[11]

The cognitive component pertains to the "intellectual" side of prejudice, for it involves knowledge, however faulty. This is expressed in stereotypical conceptions and misconceptions of various social groups, for example: whites who believe that blacks are shiftless, ignorant, and oversexed; Gentiles who imagine that Jews are avaricious, brash, clannish, and too intelligent for their own good; Englishmen who think of the Irish as argumentative, heavy drinkers; Irishmen who imagine Englishmen to be stuffy bores. By analogy, cognition refers to "cranial" reactions, that is, pictures in the mind's eye. While the ethnocentric individual frequently generalizes about groups he knows little or nothing about, the prejudiced person generalizes about groups he *thinks* he knows well.

The affective dimension refers to the way one *feels* about the group he perceives. The emotions evoked are "visceral" in that they are often manifest in feelings of revulsion, fear, hate, or indignation, as illustrated by the following expressions:

"It makes me sick just thinking about my kids going to school with those Puerto-Ricans."

"Every time I see a black man on the street at night I get scared stiff."

"Don't you just hate the way Jews exploit everybody? I simply can't stand them."

"I know it's wrong but I really shiver at the thought of rooming with an African student next year."

Often emotions aroused in the prejudiced person are based upon the stereotypes he holds of certain people. If one thinks that Greeks are underhanded or sharp businessmen, this tends to elicit apprehension in dealing with them. Similarly, if one believes that Mexicans typically carry knives, one may well feel frightened when confronted by a member of this group.

Group prejudices involve both thoughts and feelings about people. "However false as to fact, prejudice has a certain logic, a logic not of reason but of the emotions. . . . Prejudice is more than false belief; it is a structure of false belief *with a purpose,* however unconscious."[12] This is why prejudice as an attitude represents a predisposition to act in a particular way toward a social group. It is a state of readiness for action but not in itself overt behavior or discrimination.

Prejudice and Discrimination

Social discrimination may be defined as the differential treatment of individuals considered to belong to particular groups or social categories.[13] Although frequently they are opposite sides of the same coin, prejudice and discrimination, as both analytical and concrete concepts, should not be confused. The difference between prejudice as an attitude and discrimination as overt behavior was summed up by an English judge in his comments to nine youths convicted of race rioting in the Notting Hill section of London:

Everyone irrespective of the color of his skin, is entitled to walk through our streets in peace with their heads held erect and free from fear. . . . These courts will uphold [these rights] . . . *think what you like.* . . . But once you translate your dark thoughts into savage acts, the law will punish you, and protect your victim.[14]

American civil-rights workers have also recognized the significance of the distinction. The late Dr. Martin Luther King in his first address to the Atlanta, Georgia, "Jaycees" put it bluntly: "The law may not make a man love me, but it can restrain him from lynching me, and I think that's pretty important."[15]

The prejudiced person may not actually behave outwardly the way he thinks or says he will act. Attitudes do not always lead to hostile or aggressive actions. Furthermore, many individuals discriminate against others without harboring negative feelings toward the groups to which they belong. Dean and Rosen have found that "conformity with the practices of segregation and discrimination is often quite unrelated to the intensity of prejudice in the individuals who conform."[16] Social contact itself and the conventions characteristic of the particular circumstances in which contact takes place often help to determine how an individual will act at a given time. Sometimes people may even behave toward others in direct opposition to their own predispositions. The situation itself frequently provides the cues for "appropriate" behavior. For example, many liberals conform to practices of segregation when vacationing in the South; and southerners, who hold moderate views about the desegregation issue, often remain silent on the matter in their home communities.

By comparing the presence or absence of prejudicial attitudes on the part of individuals with their willingness or reluctance to engage in discriminatory activity, Robert K. Merton described the relationship between prejudice and discrimination. The paradigm that he devised includes four types of persons and their characteristic response patterns.[17]

The Unprejudiced Nondiscriminator

This "all-weather liberal," as Merton calls him, sincerely believes in the American creed of freedom and equality for all, and practices it to the fullest extent. He is the vigorous champion of the underdog, takes the Golden Rule literally, and cherishes American egalitarian values. It would appear that a liberal individual such as this would be most able to influence others in the realm of intergroup hostility and discrimination. Yet, as Merton indicates, his effectiveness is limited by certain "fallacies."

First there is the "fallacy of group soliloquies." Liberals tend to expend their energies in seeking out one another and talking chiefly to others who share their point of view. The feeling of agreement that logically ensues by interacting mainly with those who agree leads to the second fallacy, that of "unanimity." Through discussions with likeminded individuals the liberal may feel that many more people agree with his attitudes regarding ethnic relations than do in fact. Finally, there is the "fallacy of privatized solutions," depicted by Merton as follows:

> The ethnic liberal, precisely because he is at one with the American creed, may rest content with his own individual behavior and thus see no need to do anything about the problem at large. Since his own spiritual house is in order, he is not motivated by guilt or shame to work on a collective problem.[18]

The problem of the unprejudiced nondiscriminator is not one of ambivalence between attitude and action—as in the case of the two types described below—but rather it is a lack of awareness of the enormity of the problem and of a clear-cut approach to those who are not so liberally inclined.

The Unprejudiced Discriminator

The many homeowners throughout the urban North who deny having any personal feelings against black people and yet steadfastly try to keep them out of their neighborhoods for fear of altering the character of those neighborhoods illustrate the case of the unprejudiced discriminator who is, at best, a "fair-weather liberal." More pragmatic than all-weather liberals, they discriminate when such behavior is called for, seems to be appropriate, or is in their own self-interest. Expediency is the motto, and the creed is to "live and let live; a man's got to get along."[19] Merton suggests that the "fair-weather liberal" is frequently the victim of guilt because of the discrepancy between conduct and personal beliefs and is thus especially amenable to the persuasion of the liberal.

The Prejudiced Nondiscriminator

This third type might be called the "timid bigot." Like so many of the gentle people of prejudice, he is not an activist. He feels definite hostility toward many groups and he subscribes to the conventional stereotypes of minority-group members. Yet, like the "fair-weather liberal," he too reacts to the exigencies of the situation. If the situation—as defined by law or custom—precludes open discrimination, he conforms: he serves black customers, sits next to them on buses or trains, sends his children to school with black children. "What can I do," he says, "fight the system, fight city hall?"

Although both the "fair-weather liberal" and the "fair-weather illiberal" share the theme of expedience, Merton states:

> Superficial similarity in behavior of the two in the same situation should not be permitted to cloak a basic difference in the meaning of this outwardly similar behavior, a difference which is as important for social policy as it is for social science. Whereas the timid bigot is under strain when he conforms to the creed, the timid liberal is under strain when he deviates. . . . He does not accept the moral legitimacy of the creed; he conforms because he must, and will cease to conform when the pressure is removed.[20]

The Prejudiced Discriminator

This is the person who embodies the commonly held assumption that prejudice and discrimination are mutually dependent. This "active bigot" neither believes in the American creed nor acts in accordance with its precepts. Like the all-weather liberal he conforms to a set of standards; but in this case "his ideals proclaim the right, even the duty, of discrimination."[21] He does not hesitate to express his basic attitude—"all whites are superior to colored people"—or to convert it into overt behavior. He is willing to defy law, if necesary, to protect his beliefs and vested interests.

Each of these categories is, of course, an *ideal type.* It is seldom, in reality, that one finds a single individual who is all saint or all sinner. Moreover, while it is true that many people prejudiced against one minority, say Italians, often tend to dislike others, such as Jews and blacks,[22] prejudice toward one minority does not necessarily mean prejudice toward all. Anti-black southerners are not, ipso facto, anti-Semites.[23]

Nor do dominant groups have a monopoly on prejudice. Many minority-group members subscribe to images of other minorities that coincide with those held by members of the dominant group: The anti-Semitism manifested by some blacks, for example, or anti-black sentiments expressed by some Jews, both of which came to light during the famous school crisis in New York City in 1968–1969.[24] Furthermore, for many racial, religious, and ethnic minorities the dominant group represents "the enemy camp." Thus there are anti-white Negroes and anti-Gentile Jews who go so far as to seek to avoid all social relations with their "adversaries."[25]

Theories of Prejudice

There are many explanations for the causes of prejudice and the grounds for discrimination.[26] Prior to the twentieth century, theories of prejudice focused primarily on physical traits and group differences. Some writers attempted to prove that certain groups are innately superior to others; others speculated that there is an instinctive aversion of people to the unfamiliar that accounts for antipathy toward aliens and strangers.

Early Classifications of Races

In spite of the influence of Voltaire, Rousseau, and others who argued that there is a universal oneness in human nature, the eighteenth and nineteenth centuries saw the birth of a doctrinaire theory of group prejudice. Taxonomical classifications of human "races" paved the way for elaborate schemes that "proved" that some varieties of mankind were superior to others and that, inevitably, sought to justify the maltreatment of nonwhite people by Europeans.[27]

For example, the eighteenth century scientist, Carl von Linne (also known as Linnaeus) divided Homo sapiens into four racial groupings, each of which was purported to instill a distinctive "mentality" in its members. The African (*Afer niger*) was said to be slow and negligent, cunning and capricious. The American Indian (*Americanus rufus*) was described as tenacious, free, and easily contented. The Asiatic (*Asiaticus luridus*) was viewed as a haughty, stern, and opinionated fellow. The European (*Europaeus albus*) was envisaged as possessing the traits of liveliness and creativity and was considered to be superior to the other racial types. While Linnaeus based his typology on color—black, red, yellow, white—and region, others (such as J. F. Blumenbach, Anders Retzius, Samuel G. Morton, and Josiah C. Nott) divided human beings into categories according to other physical attributes, and each series of measurements led to a different kind of classification of "races."

These classifications, devised by Europeans or white Americans, for the most part seemed to come to the same conclusion: "Nonwhites are innately inferior." The equation of somatic differences with culture traits gave birth to the theory of racial superiority or racism. Throughout the Western world it was asserted that colored people were degenerate, simple-minded, untamed, uncivilized. Racism was used by several writers to justify the slave system in the United States and to sanction exploitation by American, British, and other colonialists, many of whom viewed conquest and subjugation as the "white man's burden." Darwin's theory of evolution and the possibility of "separate creation" gave added legitimacy to the doctrine. The superordinate status of whites was taken to be evidence that the fittest survive and that the aggressive, not the meek, inherit the earth.

Since its inception, the dogma of racism has persisted in various forms. Nietzsche, Gobineau, H. S. Chamberlain, and Adolf Hitler, among others, argued that certain "racial" groups possess the traits of leadership, greatness, and nobility, while others are born to follow, to serve, or to be exterminated as useless parasites.

"Natural" Differences

Early in the twentieth century several social scientists—for example, the sociologists Charles H. Cooley and W. I. Thomas —rejected the doctrine of racial superiority and the supposition that racial origins determine culture patterns. Yet, in recognizing that groups do in fact differ in their racial and ethnic composition, some scholars held to the view that man instinctively dislikes the strange and different. They saw xenophobia as an inborn trait passed from one generation to the next. This was an element in the social thought of the early American sociologist F. H. Giddings, who argued that men identified with the members of their own social groups and excluded outsiders, owing to a "consciousness of kind." It was natural, he claimed, for people to like what they know and to fear the unknown. For a time even Robert E. Park, the scholar who was to become one of the major guiding forces behind the empirical study of inter-group relations, subscribed to the view. In 1924 Park wrote that "it is evident that there is in race prejudice as distinguished from class and caste prejudice, an *instinctive* factor based on the fear of the unfamiliar and uncomprehended."[28]

Intelligence Testing

Those who assume biological superiority (and inferiority) and innate or natural group aversion imply that something inherent in ethnic bodies largely determines the thoughts, abilities, and group-focused loves and hates of their members. To most modern social scientists such a view is unacceptable. To be sure, individuals have certain potentialities that are, in large measure, biologically inherited. Idiosyncratic differences are very great: Some people are strong and others weak, some are intelligent and some are feeble-minded. But the strong and the intelligent are to be found in all racial and cultural groups. The manner in which a given individual is able to optimize whatever innate potentialities he may possess is dependent, in part at least, upon the opportunities afforded to him in the social milieu into which he is born and in which he is raised. And, it is the studied conclusion of the members of the American Anthropological Association that "all races possess the ability needed to participate fully in the democratic way of life and in modern technological civilization."[29]

With the development of systematic methods of investigation and a scientific orientation toward social life itself, the ideas that certain groups are born to lead and others to follow, that xenophobia is rooted in the genes, were found to be theoretically and empirically untenable. However, this conclusion did not mean that research on the relationship between racial background and behavior ceased. On the contrary, it took new forms—often variations on old themes that sought, by use of such culturally biased instruments as intelligence tests, to demonstrate white/black differences. Perhaps the best example of this line of thinking is to be found in Audrey Sheuey's volume *The Testing of Negro Intelligence* (1958)[30] and in the more recent controversial debates over the work of Arthur Jensen.[31]

Sheuey, after an extensive review of the literature in which I.Q. test scores of white and black subjects were compared, concluded that the data clearly belie the claim that there are no native differences. The biggest problem was the leap she made between the consistency of the findings that blacks scored proportionately lower and the argument that this was attributable to innate intellectual inferiority rather than cultural bias.

In perhaps the most pointed gibe at Sheuey's work (and the work of others who make similar claims) Adrian Dove, a social worker from the Watts section of Los Angeles, clearly illustrated that the vast majority of white people would flunk his "Dove Counterbalance Intelligence Test," while most blacks, Dove claimed, would do quite well. The test consisted of thirty multiple-choice questions, including the following:

Which word is out of place here? (a) splib, (b) blood, (c) gray, (d) spook, (e) black.

A "handkerchief head" is a(n) (a) cool cat, (b) porter, (c) "Uncle Tom," (d) hoddi, (e) preacher.

Cheap "chit'lin's" . . . will taste rubbery unless they are cooked long enough. How soon can you quit cooking them to eat and enjoy them? (a) 15 minutes, (b) 2 hours, (c) 24 hours, (d) 1 week (on a low flame), (e) 1 hour.

Hattie Mae Johnson is on the county. She has four children and her husband is now in jail for nonsupport, as he was unemployed and was not able to give her any money. Her welfare check is now $286 per month. Last night she went out with the biggest player in town. If she got pregnant, then 9 months from now, how much more will her welfare check be? (a) $80, (b) $2 less, (c) $35, (d) $150, (e) $100.

"Hully Gully" came from (a) "East Oakland," (b) Fillmore, (c) Watts, (d) Harlem, (e) Motor City.[32]

Sometime after the debates over Sheuey's book had simmered down, psychologist Arthur Jensen gained widespread attention for an article published in the *Harvard Educational Review* in the Winter of 1969 in which, on the basis of his research, he claimed the following: (1) Compensatory education programs designed to improve intellectual performance of those euphemistically called "culturally disadvantaged" have failed to raise I.Q. scores. (2) Children with low I.Q.s tend to be handicapped genetically as well as culturally (or environmentally). (3) The genetic proclivity for certain types of performances is an important factor not merely in determining potential differences in intelligence ratings from the same group but also differences between groups. (4) One should recognize and compensate for the fact that rote learning seems easier for some than abstract learning.[33]

Aware that he might raise, once again, the specter of "scientific racism," Jensen nevertheless felt that a number of important questions about the relationship between nature and nurture needed consideration especially by people who were concerned with the attainment of improved education for all children.

Reactions, especially to the shakiness of some of Jensen's assertions, as expected, were harsh—in some cases quite extreme. "Jensenism" became a word that was linked to "imperialism" and "fascism" and "genocide" by militant critics. Even those who attended the annual business meetings of the American Anthropological Association found themselves asked to vote on the censure of the *Harvard Educational Review* for publishing Jensen—and they proceeded to do so without protest. (The protest came later, and it was not only from reactionary quarters.[34])

As Christopher Jencks, an authority on educational research, noted in a lengthy review of Jensen and his critics:

Were there a dispassionate observer, who could look at these arguments without political or personal bias, I think he would conclude that neither Jensen nor his critics have offered a persuasive explanation of IQ differences between blacks and whites. He would probably also conclude that neither geneticists nor social scientists know enough about the determinants of IQ scores to design a study which would fully resolve our present confusion. Nonetheless, Jensen's decision to reopen this ancient controversy without first gathering more evidence strikes me as a serious political blunder.[35]

However valid Jencks' conclusion may be, the topic has been reopened and the debates have forced us to examine a number of important assumptions, not the least being those related to the persistent blurring of the study of race per se (and of race differences) and the study of prejudice and discrimination and their effects. The significance of the distinction becomes clearly apparent when one moves away from the emotionally charged realm of "intelligence" and "performance" to that of health and illness.

It has long been asserted by some that racial purity is a virtue and that, by sticking to one's own race, many problems can be avoided. Perhaps, as some blacks now argue (and as many whites have long contended) there is a psychological truth embedded in the assumption but not necessarily a physiological one. Recent medical research has shown several important negative results of endogamy (marriage to a member of one's own group, especially an ethnic or racial one) in the so-called race-based diseases, such as sickle-cell anemia, thalasemia, and Tay-Sachs disease, which are prevalent among blacks, Mediterranean peoples, and Ashkenazic Jews, respectively.

The suggestion here is that, as the famous geneticist Theodore Dobzhansky has noted, "Faced with a revival of 'scientific' racism, one is tempted to treat the matter with the silent scorn it so richly deserves . . . [Yet] it may perhaps be useful to add a warning against exaggerations which some writers bent on combatting racism are unwittingly making."[36] Or, as the author of this text once suggested, making official statements such as the unanimous declaration of the American Anthropological Association cited above, denies to the discreditors the notion that those categorized as members of a given racial group (such as the far from "pure" American Negroes) are innately inferior, but in another sense it begs several questions that remain scientifically legitimate.[37] The study of race and the ideology of racism must be dealt with as separate phenomena.

Social Structure and Individual Personality

Concern about racism is clearly at the center of most current discussions of prejudice in American society. But various students of the subject tend to concentrate their attention on one or another aspect of the overall problem. Some students focus on the social system and its various parts (organizations, classes, and institutions), its rules or norms, and its purported values. Society itself is often the principal unit of analysis. Others eschew so grand a scope of study, preferring to concentrate on individual behavior and personality. George A. Kourvetaris has called these polar approaches "macroscopic" and "microscopic."[38] [The author would prefer to label them "hypermetropic" and "myopic" for it is not so much the tube through which one looks as the ability of the eye (in this case, the mind's eye) to deal with what is observed. Those in the former category are farsighted, those in the latter category are often so nearsighted that they fail to take into account the significant surroundings that, inevitably, help to understand what one sees up close.] Still, whatever terms are used it is important to recognize the tendency of many to see only a part of the whole.

Economic and Psychological Interpretations

Followers of Marx and a good many other social scientists view prejudice as primarily the result of the strained relationship between the exploited and the exploiter. Carey McWilliams, for example, argues that anti-Semitism has traditionally been "a mask for privilege" and is based on the efforts of those in economically advantageous positions to exclude rising groups.[39] Oliver Cox and others have hypothesized that the whole system of race relations and segregated patterns, especially in the United States, is directly related to the maintenance of a cheap labor supply.[40] In not very different terms many contemporary analysts of American racial patterns argue that they are a form of domestic colonialism based on a continuing policy of exploitation of poor people, especially those who belong to such "Third World groups," as blacks, Puerto Ricans, Mexican-Americans, Asian-Americans, and Indians.[41]

The colonial model, at least when applied to the situation of Third World Americans, according to William J. Wilson, involves four fundamental components: (1) The racial-group's entry into the dominant society is forced and involuntary. (2) The members of the dominant group administer the affairs of the suppressed or colonized group. (3) The culture and social organization of the suppressed group are destroyed. (4) Racism exists, that is, "a principle of social domination by which a group seen as inferior or different in terms of alleged biological characteristics is exploited, controlled and oppressed socially and psychically by a superordinate group."[42]

While all social scientists do not agree that economic interests play the most important role in bringing about and maintaining prejudice and discrimination, many have found that intergroup conflict continues in large part because of the gains—both material and psychological—that are realized by assuming an attitude of superiority and enforcing social distance between one's own group and others. Early studies of "social distance" suggested that the principal basis for differential ranking of ethnic groups is the desire to maintain or enhance one's social position by associating with groups considered to be of high status and by disassociating from those low in the prestige hierarchy.[43] More recent investigations have found anti-Semitism and anti-Negro sentiments to be most common among people dissatisfied with their own economic position or among those whose status has declined.[44]

In 1945 Bruno Bettelheim and Morris Janowitz documented the relationship between downward mobility and increased antipathy toward Jews and Negroes.[45] In Social Change and Prejudice, a volume published years after the initial study, they summarized the findings of various national-sample surveys conducted to reexamine the relationship.[46]

In their original investigation Bettelheim and Janowitz suggested that from among the 150 young veterans they interviewed in Chicago, those enjoying moderate upward mobility were more tolerant than those who had experienced no change in status, those who were rising very rapidly, or, especially, those experiencing downward mobility. In explaining these differences the authors said that "one can argue that, given American values which legitimate social mobility . . . the moderately upwardly mobile person is likely to have relatively effective personal controls." This theme of effective controls was crucial to the revised theoretical orientation of the investigators. In their more recent work they place heavy stress on new developments in ego psychology in which the person is viewed as part of, not apart from, his wider social milieu. In these terms prejudice is no longer seen as a reflection of an inherently weak ego straining against unacceptable inner strivings (as many psychologists have long contended); rather the emphasis is on the protective shield prejudice affords to those whose identity is threatened, as in the case of those experiencing sudden changes of status.

In societies such as our own, where prejudice is a "normal" rather than an "abnormal" fact of social life, Bettelheim and Janowitz assert that it must be understood in functional terms. In popular parlance, prejudice helps to pump up the egos of those who feel deprived or threatened; it reduces anxiety about one's own status; it adds in the assertion of superiority. "Unless other means of ego support are found for the person seeking identity and fearing its loss, prejudice can be expected to exist in one form or other."

The notion that prejudice may prove advantageous to certain individuals is something that bigoted demagogues *and* militant minority leaders have long known. This idea also has long been explored by social scientists. Thus in the 1930s in his classic study of race relations, *Caste and Class in a South-*

ern *Town*, John Dollard examined the functions of prejudice. Dollard was particularly impressed with the level of "social inertia," the reluctance to change traditional patterns mainly because of the gains accruing to those middle-class whites who maintained the institutions of segregation.[47] Among the advantages he saw were those in the spheres of economics, sexual activities, and ego gratification linked to what Dollard called "prestige."

The psychological advantages of prejudice can be demonstrated more clearly in Freudian than in Marxian terms. Some writers have explained prejudice as a means of deflecting aggressions created by personal frustrations.[48] The thesis develops as follows: One goes through life seeking gratification for felt needs and, while many such needs have their origin in the organic structure of the individual, there are others which are culturally determined. These are learned early in life and are canalized and directed toward certain goals. When goal-directed behavior is blocked, hostile impulses are frequently created in the individual who, unable to determine the real source of his frustration but in an attempt to overcome it, manifests "free-floating aggression."[49] Such undirected aggression finds a "legitimate" point on which to focus which becomes a substitute for the actual frustrating agent. Usually the target is weak and unable to strike back. This process is well known: The boss berates his employee, who takes it out on his wife, who in turn berates the children. And so it goes.

Free-floating aggression is often directed toward a minority group or outgroup whose status in society puts it in a vulnerable position. One observer has made the point in graphic—though extreme—terms:

> The rich take to opium and hashish. Those who cannot afford them become anti-Semites. Anti-Semitism is the morphine of the small people. . . . Since they cannot attain the ecstasy of love they seek the ecstasy of hate. The Jew is just convenient. . . . If there were no Jews the anti-Semites would have to invent them.[50]

When aggression is displaced in this manner the target is a scapegoat. In sociological parlance, scapegoating is the expression used to describe the psychological mechanism of displacing aggression. It refers to placing one's own "iniquities" or "sins" upon others. The scapegoat is therefore a whipping boy for the frustration-invoked hostility of the individuals or groups who use it. And, as Albert Camus has suggested, anyone and anything can become a scapegoat:

We are all exceptional cases. We all want to appeal against something. Each of us insists at all costs that he is innocent, even if he has to accuse the whole human race and heaven itself.[51]

The reader who examines these economic and psychological explanations of the basis of prejudice may ask what predisposes certain individuals to attempt to exploit others or to seek scapegoats upon whom they can transfer their own inadequacies. One attempt to answer this question was made by a group of behavioral scientists who hypothesized "that the political, economic, and social convictions of an individual often form a broad and coherent pattern as if bound together by a 'mentality' or 'spirit' and that this pattern is an expression of deep-lying trends in his personality."[52] This statement is taken from the well-known study of *The Authoritarian Personality*, which, more than twenty years ago, presented a new approach to the investigation of prejudice. The major concern of this large-scale research, conducted in the United States during and after World War II, was to understand the "potentially fascistic individual, one whose structure is such as to render him particularly susceptible to anti-democratic propaganda."[53]

Both quantitative and qualitative research techniques were employed in this investigation. Questionnaires administered to groups of college students (and later to noncollege groups) provided background information about the respondents. Stereotype-laden questions were used as bases for the development of scales of anti-Semitism, ethnocentrism, politico-economic conservatism, and fascism. Two types of interviews were administered to the extreme scorers on these scales: one, nondirective, aimed at getting at basic ideology; the other, clinical-genetic, designed to elicit case history material.

Analysis of data thus obtained suggested that antipathy toward minorities and ethnocentric thinking—called "social discrimination" by the authors—are generalized ideological systems pertaining to groups and group relations. Highly prejudiced individuals were found to possess the following personality characteristics: glorification of power; the tendency to view people as good or bad, and things as black or white; deep concern with status and toughness; repression of sexual feelings; conception of the world as a jungle; cynicism about human nature; the proclivity to blame others rather than themselves for misdeeds and trouble. Outgroup hostility was especially prominent among the defense mechanisms of these "authoritarians." Concerning these extreme scorers, the authors wrote:

> . . . the basically hierarchical, authoritarian, exploitative parent-child relationship is apt to carry over into a power-oriented, exploitively dependent attitude toward one's sex partner and one's God and may well culminate in a political philosophy and social outlook which has no room for anything but a desperate clinging to what appears to be strong and disdainful rejection of whatever is relegated to the bottom.[54]

This study, in other words, concluded that many, perhaps most, highly prejudiced persons are mentally disturbed.[55] This conclusion no doubt holds for many individuals of "rigid personality," including at least some of the leaders of extremist hate movements and, perhaps, quite a few of their followers.[56] But these all-weather bigots are hardly representative of the vast number of Americans who manifest racial and ethnic prejudice and discriminate against minority groups. In fact, follow-up studies of hypotheses presented in *The Authoritarian Personality,* using similar or identical research instruments (especially the "F scale"), report that prejudice and discrimination characterize the attitudes and behavior of many "normal" people.[57] Moreover, careful testing of the hypotheses of this pioneering work suggests that bigotry is by no means confined to politically conservative or reactionary individuals, and that authoritarian personalities are to be found among both the right and the left segments of the nation's citizenry.[58] Given the fact that these patterns are widespread, adequate sociological explanation of prejudice and discrimination cannot be confined to psychological deviation alone. Prejudice and discrimination constitute a major social problem precisely because most of their practitioners *conform to established beliefs and values.*

Socialization and Social Conformity

Rather than conceiving of group prejudice as an inborn tendency or a characteristic in one's basic personality, most sociologists today view it as a social habit. This thesis derives from the general proposition that cultural traits are learned. In the process of learning the ways of their groups—the process of socialization—individuals acquire both self-perceptions and images of others. If the teaching is effective, the individual internalizes (in substantial measure, but never fully) the sentiments and customs of his social milieu—including the "appropriate" prejudices. As sociologists MacIver and Page have written:

The individual is not born with prejudices any more than he is born with sociological understanding. The way he thinks as a member of a group, especially about other groups, is at bottom the result of social indoctrination, in both its direct and its indirect forms, indoctrination that inculcates beliefs and attitudes, which easily take firm hold in his life through the process of habituation.[59]

A former southerner put it this way:

I grew up just 19 miles from Appomattox. The teaching I received both in school and from my parents was hard-core South, with no chance of insight into the thinking and ways of other peoples. I was taught to look down upon Negroes, tolerate Jews (because we had to do business with them) and ignore Catholics.

We celebrated Jefferson Davis's birthday, but ignored Lincoln's;

the name Robert E. Lee was spoken with reverence and Appomattox was a shrine. The Golden Rule only applied to others who were either Methodist or Baptist, white and without a foreign-sounding name. . . .[60]

The internalization of social prejudices does not require direct contact between the learner and the members of groups held in low esteem. If the agents of socialization—parents or peers or community leaders—are themselves prejudiced people, they are apt to be effective teachers of group antipathies whether the objects of their attitudes are immediate neighbors or distant outgroups.

The lessons learned in this "natural" process of acculturation constitute a serious problem for those educators and other persons who attempt to make more realizable the values of the American ethos. They are competing with the home, playground, and, sometimes, the mass media, which for many people represent the normal and desirable way of life, a way of life that all too often is inconsistent with and disruptive of ideals of freedom, social equality, and unhampered opportunity. This situation is aggravated by the fact that group antipathy has been found to exist not only among upper-status individuals but, more significantly perhaps, among members of the rank and file. Both feel that they have material or psychological stakes in institutionalized patterns of prejudice—and act accordingly.

Institutionalized Racism

Many contemporary writers and most militant minority-group leaders consider institutionalized racism to be the principal source of prejudice against nonwhite peoples. Their explanations find expression in many forms—from academic rhetoric to the argot of the street—but the theme remains more or less the same. The core argument is that a faulty belief in their own superiority is deeply ingrained in the minds of white people and in their social mores. They have internalized the same views as those promulgated by the protoanthropologists and perpetuated by those who, for several centuries, claimed to be lifting and carrying "the white man's burden." The late Whitney M. Young put it succinctly when he wrote that "racism . . . is the assumption of superiority and the arrogance that goes with it."[61]

As noted earlier, many southerners found scientific racism a justification for the exploitation of Africans during the first half of the nineteenth century, a time when the institution of slavery was being severely challenged. Increasing evidence suggests that others shared their views but, instead of putting down the blacks, they put them out, out of their minds. Joel Kovel, for example, in his psychohistory *White Racism* contends that in this country racism is still manifest in efforts to control (or what he calls the pattern of "dominative racism") or to avoid ("aversive racism").

He explains that:

In general, the dominative type has been marked by heat and the aversive type by coldness. The former is clearly associated with the American South, where, of course, domination of blacks became the cornerstone of society; and the latter with the North, where blacks have so consistently come and found themselves out of place. The dominative racist, when threatened by the black, resorts to direct violence; the aversive racist, in the same situation, turns away and walls himself off.[62]

To pursue the point one step further, it is interesting to note that, like de Tocqueville long before him, Kovel asserts that aversive racists have been more intense in their reaction than their dominative countrymen. De Tocqueville made the point: "The prejudice of race appears to be stronger in the states that have abolished slavery than in those where it still exists; and nowhere is it so intolerant as in those states where servitude has never been known . . ."[63] In recent years, the degree of compliance with school desegregation orders reflects, at least in some measure, levels of prejudice; and, in keeping with the observations of de Tocqueville and Kovel, southern districts, in many of which attitudes appear to be changing rapidly, are desegregating less slowly than many communities in the North.

In the North, people who long overlooked what was happening in their midst, while condemning southerners for their racial prejudice, are revealing that they are by no means immune to racism themselves.

Racism refers to a special kind of prejudice, a prejudice directed against those who are thought to possess biologically or socially inherited characteristics that set them apart. We should not forget that not so long ago many otherwise unrelated people were grouped into racial categories and victimized by such infamous rules as the Nuremberg Laws, which led to the placement of Jews, half-Jews, and quarter-Jews into a single hated category, one of the first steps toward Hitler's "final solution." Those barbarous laws were the most extreme recent example of what has come to be called "institutional racism."

In the sociological literature, however, institutional racism is not a clear-cut concept and some scholars have sought to clarify it or, at least, to distinguish between racial prejudice and cultural prejudice. Thus Richard A. Schermerhorn suggests a continuum ranging from the "maximal racist" to the "minimal racist."[64] The author generally favors this distinction, but is haunted by a memory that makes it almost too academic. Engaged in a public debate with an English columnist about race relations in Great Britain, I described the plight of what were then known as the "coloured immigrants" and was told that I had failed to distinguish between racial and cultural prejudice. To claim that the immigrants were unfit because of the color of their skin was patent nonsense, said my adversary. It was simply that they weren't English! My rejoinder was that it mattered little if one was on the short end of the stick.[65] The idea of a "minimal racist" may be, on reflection, an unfortunate label.

Having criticized an English opponent for misusing an important sociological distinction, I hasten to praise British scholars for making another. Some social scientists in Britain distinguish between *racialism* (the ideology of racial supremacy) and *racism* (a social policy). The latter, of course, is based on the former, and it is that to which most Americans refer when they speak of institutionalized racism.

Institutionalized racism then pertains to ingrained prejudices as reflected in customs and laws concerning what is expected, what is required, what is forbidden—and with whom. As shall be noted in the next chapter, various segments of society have systematically denied equal opportunity to certain specific groups in such a way that, in one sense, many are involved in discriminatory patterns. In many cases such involvement is inadvertent and many persons are innocent victims, themselves being entrapped in a web of social relationships (the reluctant discriminators previously mentioned are a case in point). Many others do, in fact, harbor prejudices, having learned them as a part of a general socialization experience in a "prejudiced society."

Conclusion

Group prejudice, as we have seen, has been attributed to basic economic interests, to authoritarian personality structure, to reactions to frustration, to social conformity, to poor education. There are, of course, other interpretations; for example: the emphasis upon the symbolic significance of the presence of a particular minority in a certain area;[66] the idea that contact with certain minorities under certain circumstances increases rather than decreases prejudice;[67] and what Allport has called "earned reputation"—the notion that individuals react to ethnic traits that are in fact menacing and threatening and therefore evoke realistic hostility.[68]

Each of these interpretations possesses more than a kernel of truth, and each may help to explain prejudice of a particular sort. Group prejudice is not a unidimensional phenomenon. Although we have not exhausted the various explanations for its occurrence, one thing appears certain: Prejudice is learned, not inherited.

NOTES

1. Rudyard Kipling, "We and They," in *Debits and Credits* (London: Macmillan, 1926), pp. 327-328. By permission of Mrs. George Bambridge, the Macmillan Co. of London & Basingstoke, the Macmillan Co. of Canada, and Doubleday & Co., Inc.

2. William Graham Sumner, *Folkways* (Boston: Ginn, 1906), p. 13.

3. Robert Louis Stevenson, "Foreign Children," in *The Works of Robert Louis Stevenson* (New York: Walter Black, Inc., 1926) (originally published in 1883).

4. For a further discussion of this phenomenon, see W. Lloyd Warner and Leo Srole, *The Social Systems of American Ethnic Groups* (New Haven: Yale University Press, 1945), pp. 283-296.

5. See, for example, these early discussions and studies of "social distance": Robert E. Park, "The Concept of Social Distance," *Journal of Applied Sociology*, 8 (1924), 339-344; and E. S. Bogardus, *Immigration and Race Attitudes* (Boston: Heath, 1928). See also E. L. Hartley, *Problems in Prejudice* (New York: Kings Crown Press, 1946).

6. Hartley, *ibid.* See also R. Zeligs and G. Hendrickson, "Racial Attitudes of 200 Sixth-Grade Children," *Sociology and Social Research* (September-October 1933), 26-36.

7. Sigmund Freud, *Group Psychology and the Analysis of the Ego* (New York: Boni and Liverright, 1950), p. 55.

8. Catton and Hong have found that "after social dominance has been taken into account, the appearance of ethnocentrism in minorities is a further factor in the development of majority hostility." William R. Catton, Jr., and Sung Chick Hong, "The Relation of Apparent Minority Ethnocentrism to Majority Antipathy," *American Sociological Review*, 27 (April 1962), 190.

9. Joseph B. Gittler, "Man and His Prejudices," *The Scientific Monthly*, 69 (July 1949), 43-47. See also Herbert Blumer, "Race Prejudice as a Sense of Group Position," *Pacific Sociological Review*, 1 (Spring, 1958), 3-7.

10. Daniel Wilner *et al.,* "Residential Proximity and Intergroup Relations in Public Housing Projects," *Journal of Social Issues*, 8 (No. 1, 1952), 45. For several discussions of the definition of prejudice, see Gordon W. Allport, *The Nature of Prejudice* (Cambridge: Addison-Wesley, 1954), pp. 3-16; Brewton Berry, *Race and Ethnic Relations* (Boston: Houghton Mifflin, 1958), pp. 369-371; John Harding *et al.,* "Prejudice and Ethnic Relations," in Gardner Lindzey (ed.), *Handbook of Social Psychology* (Cambridge: Addison-Wesley, 1954), Vol. II, pp. 1021-1061; George Simpson and J. Milton Yinger, *Racial and Cultural Minorities,*

rev. ed. (New York: Harper & Row, 1958), pp. 14-19; and Robin M. Williams, Jr., *The Reduction of Intergroup Tensions* (New York: The Social Science Research Council, Bulletin #57, 1947), pp. 36-43.

11. See Bernard M. Kramer, "Dimensions of Prejudice," *Journal of Psychology*, 27 (April 1949), 389-451.

12. Arnold M. Rose, "Anti-Semitism's Root in City Hatred," *Commentary*, 6 (October 1949), p. 374.

13. This is essentially the same definition used by Robin M. Williams, Jr., *op. cit.*, p. 39.

14. As reported in *Time*, September 29, 1958, p. 58. Italics supplied.

15. As reported in *The New York Times*, October 21, 1966, p. 28.

16. John P. Dean and Alex Rosen, *A Manual of Intergroup Relations* (University of Chicago Press, 1955), p. 58.

17. Robert K. Merton, "Discrimination and the American Creed," in R. M. MacIver (ed.), *Discrimination and National Welfare* (New York: Harper & Row, 1949), pp. 99-126. The passages to follow are largely summary statements of Merton's thesis. Only direct quotations will be noted.

18. *Ibid.*, p. 105.

19. See, for example, Robert O. Blood, "Discrimination Without Prejudice," *Social Problems*, 3 (October 1955), 114-117.

20. Merton, *op. cit.*, p. 108.

21. *Ibid.*, p. 109.

22. See Allport, *op. cit.*, p. 68.

23. See, for example, E. Terry Prothro and John A. Jenson, "Interrelations of Religious and Ethnic Attitudes in Selected Southern Relations," *The Journal of Social Psychology*, 32 (August 1950), 45-49.

24. See, for example, Herbert J. Gans, "Negro-Jewish Conflict in New York," *Midstream* (March 1969).

25. See, for example, Gerhard W. Ditz, "Outgroup and Ingroup Prejudice Among Members of Minority Groups," *Alpha Kappa Deltan* (Spring, 1959), 26-31; and Catton and Hong, *op. cit.*, pp. 178-191.

26. For a more detailed discussion of various explanations of the causes of prejudice, see Allport, *op. cit.*, pp. 206-216; Arnold M. Rose, "The Causes of Prejudice," in Francis E. Merrill (ed.), *Social Problems* (New York: Knopf, 1950), pp. 402-424; Arnold M. Rose, "The Roots of Prejudice," in *The Race Question in Modern Science* (a UNESCO publication) (New York: Whiteside, Inc., and William Morrow and Company, 1956), pp. 215-243; and Robin M. Williams, Jr., *op. cit.*, pp. 36-77.

27. See Oscar Handlin, "The Linnaean Web," in *Race and Nationality in American Life* (Garden City, N.Y.: Doubleday, 1957), pp. 57-73; and Cyril Bibby, *Race, Prejudice and Education* (New York: Praeger, 1960), pp. 40-62.

28. Robert E. Park and Ernest W. Burgess, *Introduction to the Science of Sociology* (University of Chicago Press, 1924), p. 578. Italics supplied. Park later modified his position. For example, in "The Nature of Race Relations," in Edgar T. Thompson (ed.), *Race Relations and the Race Problem* (Durham, N.C.: Duke University Press, 1939), pp. 3-45, he wrote: "Race consciousness, therefore, is to be regarded as a phenomenon, *like* class or caste consciousness, that enforces social distances." Italics supplied.

29. This is the closing sentence of a resolution passed by the Fellows of the American Anthropological Association, November 17, 1961. A similar resolution was adopted at the annual meeting of the Society for the Study of Social Problems in 1961.

30. Audrey Sheuey, *The Testing of Negro Intelligence* (Lynchburg, Va.: Randolph-Macon Women's College, 1958). Cf. Melvin M. Tumin (ed.), *Race and Intelligence* (New York's Anti-Defamation League, 1963).

31. Arthur R. Jensen, "How Much Can We Boost I.Q. and Scholastic Achievement?", *Harvard Educational Review*, 39 (Winter, 1969), 1–123.

32. As reported in *The New Republic*, December 16, 1967, p. 7. N.B. The answer is (c) in each case. The full text of the "test" appeared in *The Denver Post*, July 8, 1968, p. 6.

33. Jensen, *op. cit.* See also Christopher Jencks, "Intelligence and Race," *The New Republic*, September 13, 1969 pp. 25-29.

34. The sharpest barb came from anthropologist Jerry Hyman who facetiously suggested that the Association had not gone far enough. He suggested "That it is incumbent on all members dedicated to Truth to seek out and destroy any remaining copies of publications that include the views of Herrnstein, Shockley and Jensen so that our libraries and institutions of learning not be used to disseminate such unscientific and potentially damaging material. That special attention be paid to the destruction of *The Atlantic Monthly, Harvard Educational Review* and *New York Times* in that their complicity in this deception has been more energetic and more constant than other publications. That the method of destruction shall be left to the conscience of the individual fellow or voting member but that fire is a particularly symbolic and therefore appropriate mechanism." (Quoted

from *Newsletter of the American Anthropological Association*, 13 (February 1972), 2-3.

35. Jencks, *op. cit.*, p. 29. See also H. J. Eysink, *The I.Q. Argument* (New York: Library Press, 1971).

36. Theodore Dobzhansky, "Comment," *Current Anthropology*, 2 (October 1961), 31.

37. Peter I. Rose, *The Subject Is Race* (New York: Oxford University Press, 1968), p. 41.

38. George A. Kourvetaris, "Prejudice and Discrimination in American Social Structure," in P. Allan Dionisopoulos (ed.), *Racism in America* (Dekalb: Northern Illinois University Press, 1971), pp. 32-41.

39. Carey McWilliams, *A Mask for Privilege: Anti-Semitism in America* (Boston: Little, Brown, 1948).

40. Oliver C. Cox, *Caste, Class and Race: A Study in Social Dynamics* (Garden City, N.Y.: Doubleday, 1948).

41. See, for example, Jack Forbes *et al.*, *The Third World Within* (Belmont, Calif.: Wadsworth, 1972); and Joan W. Moore, "Colonialism: The Case of the Mexican-Americans," *Social Problems*, 17 (Spring, 1970), 463-472.

42. William J. Wilson, "Race Relations Models and Explanations of Ghetto Behavior," in Peter I. Rose (ed.), *Nation of Nations* (New York: Random House, 1972), p. 262. The definition of "racism" is from Robert Blauner, "Internal Colonialism and Ghetto Revolt," *Social Problems*, 16 (Spring, 1969), 396.

43. See, for example, studies by E. S. Bogardus, including: "Social Distance and Its Origins," *Journal of Applied Sociology*, 9 (1925), 216-226; "Analyzing Changes in Public Opinion," *Journal of Applied Sociology*, 9 (1925), 372-381; "Social Distance: A Measuring Stick," *Survey*, 56 (May 1926), 169-170; and "Race Friendliness and Social Distance," *Journal of Applied Sociology*, 11 (1927), 272-287.

44. See, for example, A. A. Campbell, "Factors Associated with Attitudes Toward Jews," in T. M. Newcomb and E. L. Hartley (eds.), *Readings in Social Psychology* (New York: Holt, Rinehart and Winston, 1947), pp. 518-527.

45. Bruno Bettelheim and Morris Janowitz, *The Dynamics of Prejudice* (New York: Harper & Row, 1950).

46. Bruno Bettelheim and Morris Janowitz, *Social Change and Prejudice* (New York: Free Press, 1965).

47. John Dollard, *Caste and Class in a Southern Town* (New Haven: Yale University Press, 1937), esp. Chaps. 6 to 8.

48. See John Dollard *et al.*, *Frustration and Aggression* (New

Haven: Yale University Press, 1939). "When Marxists have described the dynamic human interrelationships involved in the class struggle . . . they have introduced unwittingly a psychological system involving the assumption that aggression is a response to frustration." *Ibid.*, p. 23.

49. See, for example, Clyde M. Kluckhohn, "Group Tensions: Analysis of a Case History," in L. Bryson, L. Finkelstein, and R. M. MacIver (eds.), *Approaches to National Unity* (New York: Harper & Row, 1945), p. 224.

50. Quoted by Allport, *op. cit.*, p. 343.

51. Albert Camus, *The Fall* (Justin O'Brien, tr.) (New York: Vintage Books, 1963), p. 81.

52. T. W. Adorno *et al.*, *The Authoritarian Personality* (New York: Harper & Row, 1950), p. 1.

53. *Ibid.*

54. *Ibid.*, p. 971.

55. See Bettelheim and Janowitz, *op. cit.*; and Selma Hirsch, *The Fears Men Live By* (New York: Harper & Row, 1955).

56. See, for example, Leo Lowenthal and Norbert Guterman, *Prophets of Deceit* (New York: Harper & Row, 1949).

57. See, for example, Richard Christie, "Authoritarianism Reexamined," in Richard Christie and Marie Jahoda (eds.), *Studies in Scope and Method of "The Authoritarian Personality"* (New York: Free Press, 1954), pp. 123-196. See also Muzafer and Carolyn Sherif, *Groups in Harmony and Tension* (New York: Harper & Row, 1953).

58. See Edward A. Shils, "Authoritarianism: 'Right' and 'Left,' " in Christie and Jahoda, *op. cit.*, pp. 24-49.

59. Robert M. MacIver and Charles H. Page, *Society: An Introductory Analysis* (New York: Holt, Rinehart & Winston, 1949), p. 407.

60. Letter to the Editor of *The New York Times*, May 16, 1963. The letter was signed by Tom Wilcher.

61. See Whitney M. Young, Jr., *Beyond Racism: Building an Open Society* (New York: McGraw-Hill, 1969).

62. Joel Kovel, *White Racism: A Psychohistory* (New York: Pantheon, 1970), pp. 31-32.

63. Alexis de Tocqueville, *Democracy in America* (New York: Vintage Books, 1945), Vol. I, p. 373.

64. R. A. Schermerhorn, *Comparative Ethnic Relations* (New York: Random House, 1970), pp. 73-74.

65. The exchange took place at the World Affairs Conference at the University of Colorado in Boulder, April 14–18, 1969. See also Peter I. Rose, "Outsiders in Britain," *Transaction*, March 1967.

66. See, for example, Lewis Browne, *How Odd of Jews* (New York:

Macmillan, 1943); and Arnold M. Rose, "Anti-Semitism's Roots in City Hatred," *op. cit.*

67. See Allport, *op. cit.*, Chap. 16.
68. *Ibid.*, p. 217.

DISCRIMINATION

Patterns of Discrimination

In Chapter Three we described intergroup relations in the United States as marked by a general acceptance of dominant cultural norms by most citizens, concurrent with persisting patterns of social separation based upon real or spurious group differences. Throughout the study a central theme has been the fact that certain elements in the population assume positions of social superiority and frequently attempt to maintain social distance by setting up psychological and physical barriers, that is, discriminating, against certain racial, religious, and ethnic minorities. As Robin Williams succinctly put it, "Discrimination may be said to exist to the degree that individuals of a given group who are otherwise fully qualified are not treated in conformity with the universal, institutionalized codes."[1]

The denial of the franchise, separate and unequal education, unfair hiring practices, restrictive neighborhoods, exclusive social clubs, and anti-miscegenation laws are examples of the various ways in which minority groups may be—and often are—treated. Perhaps most of those who maintain the practices of discrimination do so not out of deep-seated hatred, but through a reluctance to change what, to them, are economically, psychologically, and socially acceptable arrangements. Thus, it is not surprising to find that many Americans are "fair-weather liberals," who do what is expected more often than they do what is "right."

Not so long ago many middle- and upper-class whites in the South regularly employed black servants whose jobs involved intimate contact with the family, such as cooks, maids, even wet-nurses for the children. Yet these very same people were reluctant to allow blacks to drink from the same water fountain, swim in the same pool, go to school with white youngsters. Northern whites, more self-righteous perhaps but equally inconsistent, were less concerned with "ritual pollution" but kept (and many continue to keep) blacks from their neighborhoods, their clubs, even their churches. Indeed, the height of northern hypocrisy is most clearly manifest each Sunday morning when they faithfully proclaim the brotherhood of man—in segregated churches.

These inconsistent behavior patterns demonstrate the segmental quality of discrimination and the fact that large numbers of people subscribe to those forms of behavior that are acceptable according to the social and cultural definitions of the situations in which they find themselves. Relatively few are willing to cut the cake of custom, especially when they feel (or are made to feel) that their vested interests are threatened. In this way the fair-weather liberal often chooses to be a reluctant discriminator.

In addition to an understanding of its institutional settings, it is important to recognize the varying degrees of discrimination and the specific ways in which individuals are denied their civil and social rights. *Defamation, avoidance, threat, coercion, segregation, colonization, relocation,* and *elimination* describe points along a continuum of discriminatory practices. Of these practices, the present chapter deals with three distinctive modes, which we call *derogation, denial,* and various forms of *aggression.*[2] This listing is not exhaustive, for the varieties of discrimination, as the continuum above suggests, are numerous. Yet these three patterns—ranging from the use of epithets to the practice of group annihilation—should serve to indicate both the varying degrees of intensity and the social forms discrimination may take.

Derogation

Ethnophaulisms are derogatory terms used by the members of one ethnic group to describe the members of another. These are the core of the language of prejudice and, when openly expressed, become a form of discrimination known as *antilocution*. The old saying that "sticks and stones may break my bones but names will never hurt me" is misleading, for articulated antagonisms may serve to reinforce the images we hold of others and may have serious psychic consequences for those on the receiving end. The repeated reference to the adult black male as "boy" or the married black woman as "miss," to cite examples graphically portrayed by Richard Wright, is like a stain that leaves an indelible imprint on the recipient's personality.[3]

Unintentional references to color, verbal slips, and testimonials are frequently construed by minority-group members as derogatory. Included here are such old-fashioned expressions as "free, white, and twenty-one," "he treated me white," and "your face may be black, but your heart is as white as mine." Color-laden phrases are closely related to those expressions that slip out, often with no intent to harm or disparage. Examples are numerous: "nigger toes" (referring to Brazil nuts), "jew him down," "he's scotch all right," "I've been gypped," and the well-known jingle "Eenie, meeny, miney, moe/Catch a nigger by the toe." Sometimes, in an attempt to indicate friendliness, the white person may say to the Negro, "You're as good as I am"; or a Gentile, speaking to a Jew, "You Jews are a fine race. . . ." Such testimonials are often received by the listeners as patronizing gestures; so are the frequent statements that begin, "Why, some of my best friends . . ."[4]

Humor is found in all societies, and ethnic humor, understandably, strongly marks American social life. But one of the major problems associated with ethnic humor is that, on hearing a joke or story about his own or another group, the listener is often unsure whether the teller accepts or rejects the stereotypical characters and characteristics described. "Pat and Mike" stories about Irish-Americans, "Abie and Izzie" jokes, and those about "Rastus" and "Mandy-Lou" are cases in point. Closely related are the caricatures of minority-group life and the exaggerations of speech mannerisms of Negroes, Jews, Italians, and others. Akin to such expressions as "Yas 'um" and "Oy veh" are the burlesques once portrayed on the stage in minstrel shows, on radio and television ("Amos 'n' Andy," "Beulah," "Luigi"), and in comic strips and stories such as "Little Black Sambo." Negroes as "pickaninnies," Jews as shrewd "Shylocks," Italians as organ grinders and gangsters, and Irishmen as stupid police officers are such characterizations. Of course, not all caricatures are unfavorable. "The" black is often portrayed as a great dancer, "the" Italian as a great singer. But stereotypes have a tendency to remain stereotypes and to be resented, even when they seem favorable to the group described. "Why should they expect me to be able to dance?' asked a black man being interviewed. "All Italians aren't Carusos!"[5]

Members of minority groups often affect accents and tell jokes and stories among themselves seemingly at their own expense. Among Jews it is not uncommon to hear stories that describe the conflict between the desire for acceptance and the ties to the Jewish community.[6] Blacks frequently joke about their low status, the difficulty of advancement, the special significance of "soul," and the white man's image of their lives.[7] Some stories are tinged with the bitterness of self-abasement; others stress the virtues of marginality. Such intragroup humor has subtle social and psychological functions, including the reinforcement of group identity. The fact remains, however, that to laugh at yourself is very different from listening to an outsider tell stories about you or the members of your group.

In recent years, in an attempt to deal more forthrightly with ethnic stereotypes, a number of television programs have been introduced—or reintroduced in new guise. In addition to a sort of revival of the old classic "Abie's Irish Rose" (now called "Bridget Loves Bernie") and of several programs starring blacks in conventional middle-class roles (for example, "Julia"), there is "All in the Family." This controversial show, based on an

English program called "Till Death Do Us Part," pulls few punches. It (purposely) deals directly with contemporary issues —the role of women, sexual deviance, and, especially, ethnic interaction.

In 1972 "All in the Family" was America's most popular television program. Millions of people put aside other things to watch Archie Bunker, the bumbling white Protestant bigot who doesn't trust anybody regardless of race, creed, or color. They got to know his wife, Edith, the "dingbat"; his son-in-law, Mike, a Polish-American sociology student, the "liberal meathead" (a double insult); and his friends—and enemies. The program is filled with epithets used in direct reference to minorities: "spic," "greaser," "jigaboos," "hebe," "a-rab," and the like. Because it has been long assumed that those so labeled see such expressions as an extreme form of derogation, many critics, including the author of *Gentleman's Agreement*, Laura Hobson, argue that "All in the Family" serves to legitimize the use of such terms. (If it does nothing else, there is little question that it does teach many Americans—and others who see the show—many ethnophaulisms they never knew.) Moreover, and more important, Hobson argues that Archie Bunker makes bigotry somehow respectable.[8] Others disagree. Those who support the program contend that it is a healthy thing in that it is good to laugh at oneself.

The few studies that have been conducted for the Columbia Broadcasting System, the network that produces the show, indicate that most of those maligned by Archie Bunker appear to *like* the program[9]—one reason may be that the minority individuals portrayed usually come out on top (and even Archie seems to learn something each time). Some of those who identify themselves with Archie Bunker say that he reminds them of what they used to be like. Undoubtedly other "Joes" realize it is *they* who are being most discriminated against. And, in a sense, they are right. The lesson is clear. Derogation need not be limited to attacks on minorities—though, most often, it is they who do bear the brunt.

Erdman Palmore, on the basis of a careful study of ethno-phaulisms, concludes that:

All racial and ethnic groups use ethnophaulisms. The greater the number of ethnophaulisms used against a group, the greater the prejudice. When the out-group is a different race, most ethno-phaulisms express and support the stereotypes of highly visible physical differences. When the out-group is the same general racial type, most ethnophaulisms express and support stereotypes of highly visible cultural differences. The derivations of most ethno-phaulisms express some negative stereotypes.[10]

Since ethnophaulisms appear to be essential to the support and spread of ethnocentrism, they provide one indication of the relationship between ideas and action. As noted in Chapter Four, the conative dimension of prejudice is that aspect of the attitude construct concerned with predispositions for behavior. There is little question that referring to people in particular derogatory ways or portraying them in terms of negative stereo-types or caricatures heightens one's sense of animus and, if supported by appropriate norms, allows—even encourages— the acting out of one's predispositions.

Palmore notes that ethnophaulisms are used by some mem-bers of all groups at one time or another. Thus not only do certain whites have favorite expressions for blacks ("spades," "niggers," "jungle bunnies") but blacks have their own terms for whites, words like "whitey," "Mr. Charlie," "gray," "the Man," and some with seemingly obscure origins such as "honky." "Honky" was originally "Hunky," used to describe Hungarians (Bohemians were "Bohunks"). Today the term refers to all whites, regardless of national origin. Another ethnophaul-ism used by some blacks is "Ofay," pig Latin for "foe"—which tells much about imagery and at least something about action.

The use of derogatory language, of defamation, of carefully chosen ethnophaulisms, is often of a piece, particularly in the hands of racist demagogues. Throughout history name-calling, trumped-up charges, distortions of social roles, and guilt by association have been used by those wishing to find scapegoats and to teach others to use them.

The Roman historian Tacitus explained this practice as well as anyone. Describing the burning of Rome, an act that most historians (and many Romans) attributed to Nero himself, Tacitus wrote:

> Heaven could not stifle scandal or dispel the belief that the fire had taken place by order. Therefore, to scotch the rumour, Nero substituted as culprits, and punished with the utmost refinements of cruelty, a class of men, loathed for their vices, whom the crowd styled Christians.[11]

It should be noted, however, that Tacitus himself was ambivalent about the Christians, if not about their alleged deed. Thus he further wrote:

> Christus, the founder of the name, had undergone the death penalty in the reign of Tiberius, by sentence of the procurator Pontius Pilatus, and *the pernicious superstition* was checked for a moment, only to break out once more, not merely in Judaea, the home of the disease, but in the capital itself, where all things horrible or shameful in the world collect and find vogue. First, then, the confessed members of the sect were arrested; next, on their disclosures, vast numbers were convicted, not so much on the count of arson as for hatred of the human race.[12]

The practice of using demagoguery is very old. Many examples are to be found during the Crusades, the Middle Ages, the periods of colonization, and throughout the nineteenth century. In various times and places different groups have been the targets for defamation and other forms of discrimination. Jews, however, hold the dubious distinction of having been the most persistently vilified throughout many centuries—in ancient Palestine, in Iberia, in both Czarist and Soviet Russia, in various European countries, and most particularly in Nazi Germany. It was in Germany during the 1930's that anti-Semitic propaganda was refined to an "art" under the direction of Joseph Goebbels and through the pen of Julius Streicher. This kind of "art" (and the characterization of Jews as parasites, money-grubbers, imperialists) did not disappear with the end of the Nazi regime. In the Soviet Union, similar caricatures appear, with one notable difference. Some of the Soviet propaganda portrays Jews as *Nazis,* a curious juxtaposition but one that clearly serves the needs of the demagogues who present it.

Our own country has not been immune to this sort of anti-Semitic hatred. In the early days of World War II several social scientists conducted a study of anti-Semitic demagoguery in the United States. In the volume *Prophets of Deceit* they described the mind and ideology of the hatemonger. This book provides many examples of the sort of message being delivered by such anti-Semites as Gerald L. K. Smith and Father Coughlin. Here are samples:

When will the plain, ordinary, sincere, sheeplike peoples of America awaken to the fact that their common affairs are being arranged and run for them by aliens, Communists, crackpots, refugees, renegades, Socialists, termites, and traitors? These alien enemies of America. . . .

• • •

Hitler and Hitlerism are the creatures of Jewry and Judaism. The merciless programs of abuse which certain Jews and their satellites work upon people who are not in full agreement with them create terrible reactions.

• • •

We are going to take this government out of the hands of these city-slickers and give it back to the people that still believe that 2 and 2 is 4, that God is in his heaven and the Bible is the Word . . . .[13]

Recently Seymour Martin Lipset and Earl Raab published a political history of right-wing activities. In *The Politics of Unreason* they describe in detail the activities and mentalities of such nativistic movements as the Anti-Masonic League, the American Protective Association of the 1890s, the Ku Klux Klan in its various incarnations, the Coughlinites of the 1930s, the McCarthyites of the 1950s, and the followers of George Wallace and other reactionary leaders in the 1960s.[14]

Summing up their views of those who listen to the demagogues and join the movements, Lipset suggests that:

The adherents of extremist movements have typically felt deprived—either they have never gained their due share or they are losing their portion of power and status. We might call these two groups the "never-hads" and the "once-hads." These deprived groups are not necessarily extremist, but *extremism usually draws its strength from them.*[15]

When the demagogue speaks, somebody listens.

While in the past the "once-hads," especially, felt outraged by the thought of newcomers and outsiders getting what they believed to be legitimately theirs, in recent years the "never-hads" seem to be particularly incensed by what they see as people demanding privileges that, they claim, they never had. Much anti-black sentiment, especially by "white ethnics," is couched in these terms. But many southern whites and middle Americans also are attracted by the appeals of those who blame the blacks not only for their alleged personal failings but for wreaking changes throughout society. Some hark back to the turbulent days of the Klan when "nigger-baiting" words were spoken from a stump or written in The Fiery Cross. Others have a more contemporary view, linking black demands with communist conspiracies. (One of the favorite charges of the radical right in the late 1950s and early 1960s was that Daisy Bates, the president of the NAACP in Little Rock, Arkansas, who helped to bring about school integration there, and others like her, were fronting for "commies."[16])

Used by demagogues, ethnophaulisms serve well as vehicles for venting the wrath of the bigot, for stirring up latent prejudices, for fomenting hate, and for calling people to take action against their "foes." Name-calling is a widely used and highly effective form of discrimination.

Denial

Discrimination, of course, consists of more than ethnic labels, humorous anecdotes, embittered oratory, and defamation. Words are inflammatory and, as the Nazi propagandist Joseph Goebbels demonstrated diabolically, they can have far-reaching effects. As noted previously, the doggerel about "sticks and stones" denies the fact that name-calling does hurt. Still, there are more direct means used to break one's bones (and one's spirit). Most discriminatory behavior involves establishing and maintaining some measure of physical and social distance from minorities, either by avoiding contact as much as possible or by "keeping them in their place." *Avoidance* and *segregation* are two effective techniques of institutionalized discrimination. And, in many ways, they are related.

Discrimination often involves the practice of eschewing face-to-face relations with members of this or that minority group. Fundamental lessons in avoidance are learned early in life when children are taught by their parents or playmates, sometimes intentionally, often inadvertently, about groups with which they should—or should not—associate. In adulthood these lessons manifest themselves in a variety of devices used to prevent or minimize contact with group members socially defined as being "of low repute," "unpleasant," or even "untouchable." The diversity of avoidance taboos is well known.

One method of avoidance is the economic boycott. In the not so distant past, stores, restaurants, and conveyances known to be owned or operated by or, more often, frequented by certain minority-group members on an equal basis with those in the dominant group were boycotted as a protest against their integrated policies. Fear of this kind of protest led quite a few department store owners (many of whom were themselves fair-weather liberals) to refrain from desegregating certain facilities such as lunch counters. In turn they often became the targets of civil-rights groups seeking a redress of grievances. Two techniques were used in challenge: one was the sit-in, which forced proprietors to bring in police and, ultimately, to seek adjudication in the courts; the other was a counterboycott to discourage members of the minority from using other facilities in the targeted stores. Further examples of boycotting as a weapon *against* discrimination are discussed in Chapter Six.

Discriminatory boycotts have also been used in public

places such as playgrounds, parks, and beaches abandoned by those who used them in protest against new integrated policies. Frequently leading to a self-fulfilling situation, a common pattern is for certain groups to withdraw from participation or utilization of such facilities as others move in. Ultimately what is most feared takes place. The minority takes over and the initial boycotters say, "We told you so!"

In some cases such boycotting is seen as a worthwhile inconvenience ("You can always go farther up the coast to another beach") or a necessary evil ("Nobody in his right mind would go *there*!"). But the beginning of an end of segregated schools created a setting for a somewhat more permanent pattern. In the urban centers of the North and in many parts of the South, white parents have responded to the threat of integrated schooling by sending their children to private schools or by establishing such schools where they had not existed previously—sometimes with the tacit support of local and state authorities. The implementation of bussing to achieve greater racial balance has intensified the use of the boycott. In city after city their newspapers note what the *Washington Post* headlined on December 20, 1972: "8000 Boycott Prince George's Classrooms" (in protest against court-ordered desegregation).[17]

The most widespread method of avoidance is that of movement away from neighborhoods into which minority-group members are entering. Thus, for many decades, the ecological history of large American cities has been marked by the invasion of residential areas by ethnic and racial minorities, by resistance of earlier inhabitants, by attempts to frighten or cajole people to sell out in response to the perceived threat, and by the eventual abandonment of the block or neighborhood and the succession of the newcomers.[18] Today, with the increasing influx of southern blacks into northern and west coast cities, once all-white areas are rapidly turning into black neighborhoods. Not infrequently the exodus of whites is prompted by the panic of those residents who will not accept black neighbors under any circumstances. (A similar pattern exists when the incoming group is Puerto Rican or Mexican-American or American Indian or, as we shall see, even a particular type of "white.") While the process of changing neighborhoods is far from uniform and the time sequence is highly variable— depending upon such factors as the size of the incoming group, the nature of residential mobility already under way, and the extent of prejudice—many move simply because of the threat of invasion.[19]

A theme runs through all the methods employed for maintaining distances by avoidance. They involve *action or movement on the part of the dominant group rather than the minority*. To do something about "them" means, in these cases, doing something to one's self, one's family, or one's group.

Although related, segregation differs from avoidance. In segregation, instead of doing something to one's self or group, action is directed *against* others. A variety of devices is used to set up and maintain barriers between one's own group and those considered unworthy of normal social interaction. Segregation involves restrictive and exclusionary policies established to keep minorities out of private clubs, certain vocations, schools and colleges, churches, and neighborhoods, and, in many instances, to place and hold them in particular areas such as reservations, barrios, and ghettos.

Segregation has sometimes evolved on a voluntary basis as did the famous ghetto of Cologne, Germany, where the Jews of the thirteenth century sought and obtained permission to set up their own community within the city walls.[20] Most segregation, however, is not voluntary, as suggested by the term itself and by its definition as a "form of isolation which places limits or restrictions upon contact, communication, and social relations."[21] With several notable exceptions—for example, the communities of Hasidic Jews, the Amish, and the Mennonites— most of the segregation practiced in the United States is of an involuntary nature. The castelike restrictions that apply to American blacks are the most obvious examples.

Involuntary segregation usually involves both spatial and social barriers because social distance is most easily maintained through physical distance. American Indians, in the past, have been forcibly restricted to reservations, as the native blacks of the Union of South Africa are being restricted today. Jews have been barred from purchasing homes in certain urban and suburban neighborhoods. Mexican-Americans have had to live in certain parts of several cities in the southwestern cities as blacks and others have been denied easy escape from Harlems, large and small. Clearly, this physical separation serves to limit the interaction with members of other groups. Residential segregation accounts for many other patterns of separation—even when these are unenforceable by law, as in the case of education where school districts tend to follow neighborhood patterns.

Among the various devices used to maintain discriminatory housing patterns are restrictive covenants, neighborhood pressures, and "gentlemen's agreements." In some parts of the country one can still find deeds to property with provisions such as the following:

. . . and, furthermore, no lot shall be sold or leased to, or occupied by, any person excepting of the Caucasian race.

* * *

Provided further, that the grantee shall not sell to Negroes or permit use or occupation by them, except as domestic servants.

* * *

. . . shall not permit occupation by Negroes, Hindus, Syrians, Greeks, or any corporation controlled by same.[22]

Perhaps the most infamous of neighborhood restrictive policies in recent years was the "point system" established for admittance to residence in exclusive Grosse Pointe, Michigan. There, all prospective residents had to be screened and evaluated on the basis of race, religion, education, occupation, accent, "swarthiness," and similar invidious criteria, and were allotted points for each "favorable" attribute. Only high scorers were allowed to purchase property. The Grosse Pointe pattern is an extreme example of an established, though declining, practice in many communities in the United States.[23]

Housing is not the only area where restrictive regulations,

formal and informal, official and sub rosa, prevent outsiders from entering the circle of the dominant group. City clubs and country clubs, sororities and fraternities, lodges and service organizations, have required applicants or initiates to be "members of the Christian faith," or to "believe in Jesus Christ," or to be "white Caucasian." Not long ago there were Greek-letter college fraternities that went so far as to exclude Greeks.[24]

Admission to some private schools and colleges has also been limited by quota systems under which only certain percentages of the members of specified groups are considered eligible—irrespective of academic abilities. Since the 1940s, anti-discrimination legislation has prohibited colleges and universities in some states (and those receiving federal support) from requesting photographs, indications of religious preference or affiliation, or information about national origin from applicants. Still, such restrictions have been circumvented through the implementation of area quotas. By accepting only a certain percentage of city-dwellers or easterners, for example, schools are able to limit the number of Jewish students. (In the past, blacks and other nonwhites have been discriminated against in a variety of ways. Under new directives from the Department of Health, Education and Welfare—brought about by forceful civil-rights agitation—institutions of higher learning are being required to establish "plans of affirmative action," involving the setting of minima that, as we shall see in Chapter Seven, some liberals attack as "reverse discrimination.")

In spite of the increasing salience of performance standards in occupational life, some business corporations (especially, smaller, family-controlled firms), professional organizations, and many labor unions disqualify members of minority groups from employment or membership, severely hampering their opportunities to pursue occupations for which they are trained. The timeworn practice of hiring minorities last and firing them first still holds in many industries.

The following statements from an official government document, "The Social and Economic Status of the Black Population in the United States, 1971," reveals the legacy of discrimi-

nation and the effects of segregation in this country. It begins
on a note of optimism and then . . .

THE SOCIAL AND ECONOMIC STATUS OF THE BLACK POPULATION IN THE UNITED STATES, 1971

Introduction

In the 1960s significant advances were made by the black population in many fields—notably, income, health, education, employment, and voter participation. The current statistics indicate continued progress in some areas of life, while other areas remained
unchanged. Overall, however, in 1972, blacks still lag behind whites
in most social and economic areas, although the differentials have
narrowed over the years.

Income

The median income in 1971 was about $6,400 for black families
and about $10,670 for white families, providing a black to white
median income ratio of 60 percent. In 1971, the relative position of
black to white family income was the same as in 1970. However,
this 1971 ratio represented a significant improvement over the ratio
of 54 percent in 1964, the first date for which corresponding survey
data on blacks were available. . . .

The proportion of families of Negro and other races in the
$10,000 and over income category increased during the 1960s. By
1970, approximately 28 percent were at this income level, compared
to the 11 percent in 1960, taking into account changes in prices. The
proportion with relatively high incomes was still far below that of
white families, as about half of the white families had incomes of
$10,000 or more in 1970.

Significant gains in achieving income parity with whites have
been made by only a very small segment of black families. These
were young husband-wife families residing in the North and West
in which both the husband and wife worked. Among these families,
the ratio of black to white income was about 104 percent in 1970
compared to 85 percent in 1959. In the South, for the comparable
group of black families, the median income was 75 percent of
whites, an increase over the 56 percent in 1959. The working wife
was an important factor in explaining the narrowing of the income
differential between young black and white families. Where only
the husband worked, the income differential in the North and West
remained at about 75 percent in 1970, whereas in the South, the
ratio of 63 percent was up from the 52 percent in 1959.

Among the young husband-wife families, black wives were more likely than white wives to have participated in the employed labor force and as year-round workers in 1970. Nationally, about 68 percent of the young black wives contributed to the family income by working, compared to 56 percent for young white wives. In the North and West, a larger percentage of young black wives worked year round. These black wives earned approximately 30 percent more and also made a larger contribution to the family income than did their white counterparts. For the North and West, the ratio of young wives' earnings to the family income was 35 percent for blacks and 27 percent for whites.

There were 7.4 million blacks below the poverty or low-income level in 1971, comprising about 32 percent of the black population in the country. In 1959, the proportion of blacks who were below the low-income level was much higher, 55 percent. From 1959 to 1971, the proportion of whites below the low-income level declined from 18 percent to about 10 percent. Although Negroes made up about 11 percent of all persons, they comprised approximately three-tenths of all people below the low-income level.

Family heads with low educational attainment are more likely to be below the low-income level. This is true regardless of race or sex of head.

The majority of both black and white men who were heads of low-income families worked at some time during 1970. About one-fourth of the men, black and white, who were heads of low-income families had a full-time job the year round.

Black families below the low-income level were more likely than the comparable group of white families to have received public assistance income, but less likely to have received Social Security benefits.

Employment

There were over 9 million persons of Negro and other races in the civilian labor force in 1971, and of that number, over 8 million were employed.

After declining for several years, the jobless rate began to rise in 1970 and continued to rise during 1971. In 1971, the rates averaged 9.9 percent for Negro and other races and 5.4 percent for whites. The ratio of jobless rate for Negro and other races to that of whites was unchanged from the 1970 differential of 1.8:1. During the 1960s this ratio averaged about 2.1:1.

Historically, blacks have been overrepresented in most lower paying, less-skilled jobs and underrepresented in the better paying, high-skilled jobs. This is still true, but the 1970 census data show that blacks made some advances and were more equally represented in the major occupation groups. In 1970, black workers constituted 10 percent of the employed population, but only 5 percent of the professional workers, 3 percent of managers and administrators, and 6 percent of the craftsmen, as contrasted to 17 percent of service workers, about 20 percent of laborers, and about 50 percent of all private household workers. With the exception of the categories service workers and private household workers, these 1970 figures represent an improvement over those for 1960.

The upward movement on the occupational ladder by workers of Negro and other races is exhibited also in the occupational data for the last 11 years. Those employed in the better paying white collar, craftsmen, and operatives occupations increased significantly over the period—from about 3 million in 1960 to about 5 million in 1971. In 1971 Negro and other races constituted about 8 percent of employees in the better paying jobs compared to approximately 6 percent in 1960.

In 1969, there were 163,000 black-owned firms which represented only 2 percent of all enterprises, and which received less than one-half of one percent of the gross receipts. The highest proportion of black-owned firms were in the transportation and other public utilities industries.

Education

Since 1965 (the earliest year that survey data on blacks were available) there has been a notable increase in school attendance among young black adults at the college level. In 1971, 18 percent of the young blacks, 18 to 24 years old, were enrolled in college compared to about 10 percent in 1965. There was no significant change in the proportion of whites attending college during this period.

Among family members 18 to 24 years old enrolled in college in 1970, 12 percent of the blacks were from families whose incomes were under $3,000, as compared with only about 2 percent of the whites in the comparable group.

Gains also have been noted in the proportions of blacks completing high school. By 1971, about three-fifths of young adult black men and women, 25 to 29 years old, completed high school. The high school dropout rate for young blacks, 14 to 19 years old, declined from 14.6 percent in 1970 to 11.1 percent in 1971. Still, the dropout rate for the blacks remained higher than that for the comparable group of whites—7.4 percent in both 1970 and 1971.

In 1970, both black and white men who were school dropouts were more apt than high school graduates to be unemployed or not in the labor force. This situation is more pronounced among blacks. Half of the black men, 16 to 21 years old, who were neither enrolled in school, nor high school graduates, were either unemployed or not in the labor force. About 34 percent of the comparable group of white men were in this category.

In 1970 less than half of the black undergraduate students were enrolled in institutions which were predominantly minority. [N.B. Minority population includes black, American Indian, Japanese, Chinese, and Spanish-American students.] But, in the South, where the majority of the black colleges and students are located, 65 percent of the black undergraduate students still attend institutions which are predominantly black.

Housing

Crowding—sometimes measured by the index of "persons per room"—was much greater in Negro occupied housing units than in white occupied housing units. In 1970, 20 percent of black households lived in units with 1.01 or more persons per room compared to 7 percent of white households. Renter-occupied housing was more crowded than owner-occupied units for both black and white households.

The smallest percentage of overcrowding in Negro households— both owner- and renter-occupied—occurred inside central cities of metropolitan areas, in 1970.

Between 1960 and 1970, the proportion of blacks living in homes they owned increased from 38 percent to 42 percent. In 1970 the rate of owner occupancy was highest for Negro households in the South, 47 percent.

Negro households were less likely to have most major appliances or an automobile available than white households in 1970.

Family Composition

In 1972, 66 percent of families of Negro and other races were headed by a husband with his wife present. Approximately 88 percent of white families had both spouses present. In 1970, at the upper income level ($15,000 and over), about 94 percent of black families were headed by a man, about the same proportion as that for white families. At the lower end of the scale, the proportion of black families with incomes under $3,000 headed by a man was 40 percent compared to 72 percent for whites.

By 1971, about two-thirds of children of Negro and other races were living with both parents, continuing the decline which had occurred between 1960 and 1970. The comparable proportion for white families was 90 percent.

In spite of the sharp decline in both black and white fertility during the 1960s, the total fertility rate of 3.13 children per black woman in 1968 remained substantially higher than that of 2.37 for white women.

Between 1960 and 1971, the average number of children ever born declined markedly among black women, 20 to 24 years old, reflecting the decline in the birth rate during the 1960s.

Though the infant mortality rate for Negro and other races (31.4 per 1,000 live births) was much higher than that for whites (17.4) in 1970, these rates have dropped sharply during the last three decades. In 1968, the maternal mortality rate for mothers of Negro and other races and white mothers was very low—below 1.0 per 1,000 live births. . . .[25]

The categorical disparities manifest in one area of life after another are related to institutionalized patterns of discrimination, which have made it almost impossible for blacks (and, in many instances, other nonwhites) to run an equal race. They know it—and so, as numerous studies have shown, do political policy-makers (or they would if they would study their own reports). This last point was made abundantly clear when, in the wake of the urban riots that erupted in city after city during the summers of 1966 and 1967, a Presidential Commission was invited to investigate their causes. Asked to find out why these outbreaks had taken place and what could be done to prevent them in the future, a group of leading citizens headed by then Governor Otto Kerner of Illinois carried out an extensive study of twenty-four disorders in twenty-three different American cities. A year later the report was published. In one version, Tom Wicker, columnist for *The New York Times,* wrote a special introduction in which he focused on the central issue that constantly confronted the commissioners and the investigative staff. "In the end," wrote Wicker, "not without dispute and travail and misgiving, in the clash and spark of human conflict and human pride, against the pressures of time and ignorance, they produced not so much a report on the riots as a report on America—*one nation divided.*"[26]

Wicker based his conclusion on his assessment of the report, which included the following summary statements about the explosive mixture that contributed to the potential for upheaval:

Pervasive discrimination and segregation in employment, education and housing, which have resulted in the continuing exclusion of great numbers of Negroes from the benefits of economic progress.

• • •

Black in-migration and white exodus, which have produced massive and growing concentrations of impoverished Negroes in our major cities, creating a growing crisis of deteriorating facilities and services and unmet human needs.

• • •

The black ghettos where segregation and poverty converge on the young to destroy opportunity and enforce failure. Crime, drug addiction, dependency on welfare, and bitterness and resentment against society in general and white society in particular are the result.[27]

Pathology for many nonwhites is directly related to the patterns of life they are forced to adopt. Upheaval may be construed as a desperate cry for help; it may also be viewed as one of the few healthy alternatives to despair in a sick society. Whichever view one takes (and there is considerable controversy over this fundamental question), there is little question that the barriers erected to keep nonwhites in their place have done more than isolate large numbers of people.

Segregation and poverty have created in the racial ghetto a destructive environment totally unknown to most white Americans. What white Americans have never fully understood—but what the Negro can never forget—is that white society is deeply implicated in the ghetto. White institutions created it, white institutions maintain it, and white society condones it.[28]

Practices of segregation, such as those reported by the Kerner Commission, are easier to observe than the more subtle patterns of social separation. Yet these are of equal, if not more, sociological significance. In many communities, where direct physical contact between whites and nonwhites is far more numerous than in the riot cities, and where spatial separation is not nearly as pronounced, local customs serve to insulate the groups from one another. Pre-World War II studies of Negro-white relations in the United States provide numerous examples of southern "etiquette" which enhanced the separation of the races. Some of the practices described by Gunnar Myrdal almost three decades ago are still to be found:

> In *content* the serious conversation should be about those business interests which are shared (as when a white employer instructs his Negro employee or when there is a matter to be discussed concerning the welfare of the Negro community) or it should be polite but formal inquiry into personal affairs. There can generally be no serious discussion.

· · ·

> The conversation is even more regimented in *form* than in content. The Negro is expected to address the white person by the title of "Mr." or "Miss." . . . From his side, the white man addresses the Negro by his first name, no matter if they hardly know each other or by the epithets "boy," "uncle," "elder," "aunty," or the like.[29]

Here we see a direct linkage between derogation and denial. The main function of racial etiquette is to remind blacks, in their day-to-day contacts with whites, of their place in the social hierarchy, which persistently demeans them and weakens their willingness to resist. Such institutionalized intimidation, with respect to its psychological consequences, is one of the cruelest forms of discrimination.

Aggression

Intimidation is sometimes subtle. Most of the time it is blatant. ("Just try stepping out of line!") Violence or the threat of violence has long been used to keep racial and ethnic minorities mindful of their subordinate status. Tied to both derogation and denial, there are many forms of aggressive action in which individuals or groups participate, ranging from the jeering at and threatening of little children to gang fights or organized violence and mob aggression. The lexicon of racial conflict is filled with words related to violent aggression: "lynch," "pogrom," "genocide," and hundreds of others—and examples of their use are not hard to find.

A Puerto Rican is brutally beaten for trespassing on white "turf" . . .

A synagogue is symbolically smeared with swastikas and the slogan "Hate Jews."

A black man is lynched for having looked "that way" at a white woman.

Thousands of Indians are exterminated to make the country safe—and profitable—for white men.

Six million Jews are murdered by the Third Reich in the name of racial purity.

"Violence," Gordon Allport has written, "is always an outgrowth of milder states of mind. Although most barking does not lead to biting, yet there is never a bite without previous barking."[30] Led by the demagogue, the ardent segregationist, and the fanatic patriot, solid and respectable citizens have done unspeakable violence to their enemies.

Even in our society of "law and order" the social conditions for mob violence still exist, as does the violence itself. Not long ago many southern blacks lived in terror of the lynch mob. Their anxiety was well justified for, according to the records of the NAACP, there were 5,112 lynchings between 1882 and 1939 (3,657 of the victims were black).[31] In the past, lynchings occurred mainly in those areas where the practice of segregation was maintained by the harshest forms of intimidation. Some social scientists have interpreted lynching as a means of venting frustrations against a convenient scapegoat. For example, it was argued that the falling price of cotton portended an upsurge in the number of lynchings in the South. Whether one can make a causal reference from the correlation, the wide use of lynching indicates a tacit acceptance of such activity as a legitimate way to maintain the castelike social system. The facts—that lynchings were often not prevented even when known of by the authorities and that when culprits were known and apprehended they were seldom punished to a degree commensurate with the crime—give ample evidence to support the contention that such behavior was condoned by those in official positions of authority.[32]

While the number of lynchings remained relatively negligible from the end of World War II to the mid-1960s, in those same years vigilantes sometimes took the law into their own hands, meting out "cracker barrel justice." The desire to fight against changes in the status quo saw a rebirth of mob aggressiveness in the South. In the 1950s, black parents attempting to send their children to schools desegregated by court decision in Clinton, Little Rock, New Orleans, and more than a score of other southern cities were met with angry crowds of white demonstrators who burned crosses, threatened them, and severely beat them. All too frequently the local authorities failed to provide adequate protection for the Negro citizens. In some cities, once law and order were established or reestablished—sometimes with the aid of federal troops—segregation was maintained by whites who withdrew their children from public schools.[33]

Sit-in demonstrators who sought equal service in restaurants, kneel-in demonstrators desiring to attend integrated church services, wade-in demonstrators wishing to swim in areas restricted to whites, read-in demonstrators wanting to take books from segregated libraries, and "freedom riders" challenging the policy of segregated interstate transportation and separate terminal facilities met with similar outbursts of aggression and violence. In the spring of 1961, for example, a busload of freedom riders was greeted by an angry mob in Anniston, Alabama, who threw rocks, smashed windows, and eventually burned the bus. Another group that had gone to Birmingham was attacked by white men armed with clubs, and several riders were brutally beaten.

In the early fall of 1962 an especially ugly incident in the long fight for desegregation occurred at Oxford, Mississippi, when, aided by several hundred U.S. marshals and 24,000 soldiers, James Meredith was forcibly admitted to the university under a court order restraining the school from denying him

admission. His presence on the campus triggered a series of riots that took several hours to quell. By the time order was restored by the imposition of virtual martial law, two adults had been killed and over one hundred people injured.

Only two weeks earlier, four black churches in rural Georgia were burned to the ground. All but one were being used for registering new voters. On September 17, 1962, the Student Nonviolent Coordinating Committee sent the following telegram to President Kennedy:

Another church burned this morning. Four churches burned in the past month, reminiscent of Nazi burning of synagogues. Imperative you investigate and apprehend arsonists. Halt the outrageous terror of peaceful American citizens. The national shame must be ended.[34]

The President's own violent death a little over one year later indicated that terror remained rampant in our society. And we were to see more and more senseless killing—much of it related to racial tensions—in the years to come.

The annals of civil-rights martyrdom are filled with names of young black and white civil-rights workers gunned down by those who could not tolerate the changes in the status quo that they represented: among them Herbert Lee, Medgar Evers, Mickey Schwerner, Andrew Goodman, James Chancy, and the Nobel prize-winner Rev. Martin Luther King, the "apostle of nonviolence." In addition to the sensational killing of these men (and many others), hundreds of other acts of violence continued to be perpetrated in big cities and rural towns. Crops were burned, workers were fired, women and children were threatened. Even policemen, sworn to uphold the law, sometimes ran amuck, venting their wrath on unarmed protesters and innocent bystanders. The whole world reeled at the image of young blacks being attacked by police dogs in Birmingham and elsewhere in the South.

A headline in the December 12, 1972, issue of *The New York Times,* "City Unit Sees Violence Pattern by Whites Against Minorities," starkly reminds us that vigilantism still exists. The article described a recent study conducted by the City Commission on Human Rights that revealed eleven cases in which homes owned by blacks or Puerto Ricans in New York City had been set afire or vandalized and instances of arson in churches and attacks on school buses. Blaming white gangs, the Commission wrote:

We can no longer maintain the myth that violence and pathology of Southern racism is totally absent in the North. These occurrences, while unconnected, nonetheless suggest an ominous trend that could mean that continued integration in the North will be resisted as forcefully and violently as in the South.[35]

These recent events in the United States are painful reminders to many of the heinous forms of violence of Nazi Germany. The trial of Adolf Eichmann, his conviction and execution in Israel for crimes against the Jews and against humanity, remind us that genocide was a national policy of a sovereign state a mere thirty years ago. Over 9 million Jews lived in Europe before World War II. Nazi leaders were determined to eradicate this group and nearly succeeded.

Forced to wear identifying badges with the word JEW, driven from homes and families, herded into concentration camps, used as forced labor, experimented upon, and ultimately shot down or liquidated in gas chambers, the Jews of Europe suffered the most repressive of all fates that can befall a human group: extermination.

The word "genocide" itself emerged during the war trials at Nuremberg, where it was defined as "a denial of the right of existence of entire human groups in the same way as homicide is the denial of the right to live for individual human beings." Although the term is newly coined, the practice of genocide is very old. It was known in biblical times when Menahem smote Tiphsah;[36] it was practiced by the British when they destroyed the Tasmanians in the "triumph of 'civilization' over 'savagery' ";[37] a version was used in early America when settlers offered bounty for the scalps and sometimes the heads of Indians[38] and when Lord Jeffrey Amherst distributed smallpox-laden blankets to the indigenous peoples.

As we have seen, in recent times violence has raged in our society—much of it based on racial hatred—and although the word is frequently used by militant critics, there is no evidence that genocidal policies are being advocated or carried out by agencies of the United States government *within the borders of the society.* The prolonged situation in Vietnam has been quite another matter and many contend that what was done there falls clearly under the definition set forth at Nuremberg.

Conclusion

These cases of discrimination have been cited not to indicate how inconsiderate and brutal man can be to his fellows (though such might be purpose enough), but rather to describe briefly the varying degrees of discrimination—*derogation, denial,* and *aggression.* Each, except *mass* murder, is a contemporary example of discrimination in the United States and an expression of both unwitting and willful behavior to which too many Americans, including fair-weather liberals, subscribe.

We have examined some formal and informal policies of those with majority status and some ways in which they seek to maintain it. Little attention has been paid to the reactions of those discriminated against. The following chapter examines the impact of discriminatory treatment and some sociological implications of minority status.

NOTES

1. Robin M. Williams, Jr., *The Reduction of Intergroup Tensions* (New York: Social Science Research Council, 1947), p. 39.
2. See, for example, Gordon W. Allport, *The Nature of Prejudice* (Cambridge: Addison-Wesley, 1954), esp. pp. 14-15 and 49-51; and Ernest Works, "Types of Discrimination," *Phylon* (Fall, 1969), 223-233.
3. Richard Wright, *Black Boy* (New York: Harper & Row, 1945), esp. pp. 128-129 and 163-170.
4. A good summary of the language of prejudice is to be found in John P. Dean and Alex Rosen, *A Manual of Intergroup Relations* (University of Chicago Press, 1955), Chap. 2. This chapter was written in collaboration with Robert B. Johnson and the ideas expressed are largely based on Johnson's unpublished Ph.D. dissertation, "The Nature of the Minority Community" (Ithaca: Cornell University, 1954).
5. *Ibid.,* p. 15.
6. Bernard Rosenberg and Gilbert Shapiro, "Marginality and Jewish Humor," *Midstream,* 4 (Spring, 1958), pp. 70-80.
7. See, for example, Russell Middleton and John Morland, "Humor in Negro and White Subcultures: A Study of Jokes Among University Students," *American Sociological Review,* 24 (February

1959), 61-69. See also John H. Burma, "Humor as a Technique in Race Conflict," *American Sociological Review*, 11 (December 1946), 710-715; Milton L. Barron, "A Content Analysis of Intergroup Humor," *American Sociological Review*, 15 (February 1950), 88-94.

8. Laura Hobson, *The New York Times*, September 12, 1971, Section II, p. 1 and continuation. See also Robert Alter, "Defaming the Jews," *Commentary*, 45 (January 1973), pp. 77-83.

9. Some research has been conducted by Joseph T. Klapper, Director, Office of Social Research, Columbia Broadcasting System. One paper, a study of viewers of the first four programs, was presented at the annual meeting of the Society for the Study of Social Problems, August 29, 1971.

10. Erdman Palmore, "Ethnophaulisms and Ethnocentrism," *American Journal of Sociology*, 67 (January 1962), 442-445.

11. *The Annals of Tacitus*, Clifford H. Moore (tr.) (Cambridge: Harvard University Press, 1937), Vol. IV, Book XV, 44, p. 285.

12. *Ibid.*, pp. 285-287. Italics supplied.

13. These phrases are part of a composite speech made up of actual statements by American demagogues; they serve as introduction to the study by Leo Lowenthal and Norbert Guterman, *Prophets of Deceit* (New York: Harper & Row, 1949), pp. 1-2. Current examples of inflammatory writings are *Common Sense, America's Newspaper Against Communism*, published in Union, N.J., and *The American Nationalist*, published in Inglewood, Calif. The support given to such publications is analyzed in an article by Hans H. Toch, Steven E. Deutsch, and Donald M. Wilkins, "The Wrath of the Bigot: An Analysis of Protest Mail," *Journalism Quarterly*, 37 (Spring, 1960), 173-185, 266.

14. See Seymour Martin Lipset and Earl Raab, *The Politics of Unreason* (New York: Harper and Row, 1969).

15. Seymour Martin Lipset, "Prejudice and Politics in America," in Charles Y. Glock and Ellen Siegelman (eds.), *Prejudice U.S.A.* (New York: Praeger, 1969), p. 18. Italics supplied.

16. See, for example, *Common Sense*, September 15, 1958, p. 1.

17. *Washington Post*, December 20, 1972, p. C1.

18. See, for example, Charles Abrams, *Forbidden Neighbors* (New York: Harper & Row, 1955); and Oscar Handlin, *The Newcomers: Negroes and Puerto Ricans in a Changing Metropolis* (Cambridge: Harvard University Press, 1959).

19. Two summaries of the problems of "race and housing" are Morton Grodzins, *The Metropolitan Area as a Racial Problem* (University of Pittsburgh Press, 1958); and Eunice and George Grier,

The Impact of Race on Neighborhoods in the Metropolitan Setting (Washington, D.C.: Washington Center for Metropolitan Studies, 1961).

20. See, for example, Louis Wirth, *The Ghetto* (University of Chicago Press, 1956), pp. 18-19.

21. Brewton Berry, *Race and Ethnic Relations*, 2nd ed. (Boston: Houghton Mifflin, 1958), p. 273.

22. Allport lists these and other examples of restrictive covenants, *op. cit.*, p. 53.

23. See Benjamin R. Epstein and Arnold Forster, *Some of My Best Friends* . . . (New York: Farrar, Straus and Cudahy, 1962), esp. pp. 106-139.

24. This practice has lessened in recent years, largely as a result of college administration action. See Epstein and Forster, *ibid.*, pp. 165-167. See also Alfred McClung Lee, *Fraternities Without Brotherhood* (Boston: Beacon, 1955); and, "A Study of Religious Discrimination by Social Clubs," *Rights*, 4 (January 1962), 83-96.

25. *The Social and Economic Status of the Black Population in the United States*, 1971, Current Population Reports, Series p-23, No. 42, Washington, D.C.: U.S. Government Printing Office, 1971, pp. 1-7.

26. Tom Wicker, Introduction, *Report of the National Advisory Commission on Civil Disorders* (New York: Bantam Books, 1968), p. xi.

27. *Report of the National Advisory Commission on Civil Disorders* (New York: Bantam Books, 1968), p. 10.

28. *Ibid.*, p. 2.

29. Gunnar Myrdal, *An American Dilemma* (New York: Harper & Row, 1944), pp. 610-612. See also John Howard Griffin, *Black Like Me* (Boston: Houghton Mifflin, 1961).

30. Allport, *op. cit.*, p. 57.

31. As reported in George E. Simpson and J. Milton Yinger, *Racial and Cultural Minorities*, rev. ed. (New York: Harper & Row, 1958), p. 515.

32. See Allport, *op. cit.*, pp. 61-62.

33. For descriptions of several instances of school desegregation crises, see the following *Field Reports on Desegregation in the South*, written by social scientists and published in New York by the Anti-Defamation League of B'nai B'rith: A report on Beaumont, Texas, "College Desegregation Without Popular Consent," by Warren Breed; a report on Sturgis, Kentucky, "A Tentative Description and Analysis of the School Desegregation Crisis," by Roscoe Giffin; on Mansfield, Texas, "A Report on the Crisis Situation Resulting from Efforts to Desegregate the School

System," by John Howard Griffin and Theodore Freedman; and, on Clinton, Tennessee, "A Tentative Description and Analysis of the School Desegregation Crisis," by Anna Holden, Bonita Valien, and Preston Valien.

34. Reprinted in *The New York Times*, September 18, 1962, p. 27.
35. *The New York Times*, December 12, 1972, pp. 1, 54.
36. II Kings 15:16.
37. G. P. Murdock, *Our Primitive Contemporaries* (New York: Macmillan, 1934), p. 18.
38. See Berry, *op. cit.*, pp. 187-194. See also Alain Locke and Bernhard Stern, *When Peoples Meet* (New York: Progressive Education Association, 1942), pp. 165-170.

IN THE MINORITY

The View from Outside

Henry James, the American novelist, spent twenty years of his life, from 1883 to 1904, away from his native land. Between his departure and return the country had undergone profound changes, most noticeably in the quality of urban life. When he left, it was English (or Anglo-American) in style and in sound. When he returned to New York the modest city had been transformed into a bustling metropolis, and homogeneity no longer marked the character of the social structure.

The old streets of the city had become warrens of poor immigrants, Little Italies and Little Jerusalems—polyglot enclaves even more strange than the shanty towns of the Irish who had come during James' youth, already signaling the beginning of the end of Protestant preeminence and Anglo conformity.

James was especially moved by the Jews he observed on the lower East Side of New York City. His firsthand account of impressions gleaned from a visit to "that outpost of Jerusalem" was vivid as well as pointed. He likened the Jews to squirrels and monkeys. He was awed and repulsed by the crowded conditions in which they lived, enchanted and dismayed by their exotic ways and lively manners. He drank deeply of the summer-city scene and then departed, as if from a voyage to the moon. (One is tempted to say as if from "abroad" for, more surely than not, he would have found

London or Edinburgh or Paris less foreign than the Lower East Side of his own New York.)

If Henry James were to come back to life and visit Rutgers Street today, he might have a haunting sense of déjà vu. To be sure, the "squirrels" and "monkeys" he would now observe scampering up and down the fire escapes of the tenements would be even darker than the swarthy "Orientals" he saw seventy years ago. The argot of the street would be marked by a Spanish accent or soft-southern English and jive talk rather than the babble of Yiddish. And the kitchen odors would be of paella and plantain or chit'lin's and collard greens rather than the soups and pickled herrings of the Israelites. Still, it would strike him that, once again, his fair New York was "swarming" (a favorite word) with alien elements.

Pushing this fantasy a bit further, James, if he listened carefully, might hear some outlandish proposals: demands for group rights and recognition, schemes for resisting the untenable choice of either completely conforming to the ways of the dominant society (his society) or continuing to be excluded. He might hear rumblings about slumlords who overcharge, politicians who take bribes, teachers who make fun of those who have difficulty with the language. He might even hear of plots to organize against the bosses, plans for greater community control within the ghetto, notions of developing local political organizations or bloc power.

There are many parallels to what was going on in James' New York at the turn of the century and in Nathan Glazer and Daniel Patrick Moynihan's New York of recent years (as described in their well-known volume, *Beyond the Melting Pot*).[1] There are differences, too. To understand these, one must briefly examine the nature of minority status as it affected (and continues to affect) the various groups of white immigrants, who, for whatever reason, chose to come to these shores from Europe; and as it affected other nonwhite peoples like American Indians, black Americans, Asians, and many Latin-Americans.

Minority Status

For most groups migration to America has been followed by successive stages of contact, competition, and some form of accommodation. For some (such as the Protestant groups from northern Europe) accommodation was followed by gradual assimilation into the dominant society, leaving but a vestige of ethnic difference. For others (including many Africans, Latin-Americans, Orientals, and Jews) the process stopped short of full assimilation. In spite of the facts that there has been no major immigration since the early 1920s and that Puerto Rican migrants are the only new group entering the country, clearly identifiable minority communities continue to exist.

Minority status is sometimes "given," often it is inherited. It may stem simply from the ascription of a differentiating label to a category of individuals who share certain social or physical traits, or both, deemed inferior to those of the majority—for example, persons with dark skin, atheists, women, or, in some circles perhaps, "intellectuals." Statistical aggregates such as these are not social groups in the sociological sense of the term. They do, however, possess the potentialities for becoming groups or collectivities, especially when they are categorically singled out for differential treatment.

Minority status is often ascribed to those social groups who have a history of patterned interaction, shared or similar beliefs and values, a sense of ingroup solidarity, and who are *also* relegated to subordinate positions in the prestige hierarchy.[2] The two words *subordinate positions* are central, for all sociological minorities—no matter how tightly knit—share the fact that they have only limited control over their destinies.

In 1945, sociologist Louis Wirth spelled out the concept of minority group in some detail and, implicitly, noted its relation to the concept of power. Stressing both its internal characteristics and the relation of the subordinate group to the wider society, Wirth wrote:

. . . A minority must be distinguishable from the dominant group by physical or cultural marks. In the absence of such identifying characteristics it blends into the rest of the population in the course of time.

. . .

Minorities objectively occupy a disadvantageous position in the society. As contrasted with the dominant group they are debarred from certain opportunities—economic, social and political.

. . .

The members of minority groups are held in lower esteem and may even be objects of contempt, hatred, ridicule and violence.

. . .

They are generally socially isolated and frequently spatially separated.

. . .

They suffer from more than the ordinary amount of social and economic insecurity.[3]

Because of these attributes, Wirth felt that "minorities tend to develop a set of attitudes, forms of behavior, and other subjective characteristics which tend further to set them apart."[4]

In an earlier study I have noted that while Wirth was greatly concerned about the deleterious effect of the inferior status position of particular ethnic groups, he and others, such as E. K. Francis, stressed the fact that most ethnic groups, including many "minorities," frequently shared a positive sense of unity or "we-feeling," an ideology (however vague and unreflective it may be), and an interdependence of fate (whether based upon religious or political or cultural or racial characteristics). Moreover, ethnic-group ties are maintained as long as individuals feel bound to the community, "a community dependent as much upon the idea of communality as on actual proximity; a community one can 'feel' if not 'touch.' "[5]

One of the arguments that persists among students of racial and ethnic relations concerns the extent to which minority status is injurious to the individuals who occupy such a position and the benefits, if any, of ascribed separateness. This debate is most clearly joined in discussions of *marginality*, the concept that refers to those who appear to be on the edges of the dominant society.

Ethnicity and Marginality

More than a few sociologists have suggested that those whose group identity is determined in part by external pressure, who are categorically excluded from opportunities for equal status, who are barred from assimilation and thus must live on the periphery of the dominant society, are "marginal men . . . whom fate has condemned to live in two societies and in two not merely different but antagonistic cultures."[6]

Perhaps the clearest articulation of this viewpoint was offered by the sociologist W. E. B. Du Bois in 1897 when he spoke of his people, black Americans, in the following way:

After the Egyptian and Indian, the Greek and Roman, the Teuton and Mongolian, the Negro is a sort of seventh son, born with a veil, and gifted with second sight in this American world,—a world which yields him not true self-consciousness, but only lets him see himself through the revelation of the other world. It is a peculiar sensation, this double-consciousness, this sense of always looking at one's self through the eyes of others, of measuring one's soul by the tape of a world that looks on in amused contempt and pity. . . .[7]

Max Weber, Georg Simmel, Werner Sombart, and Thorstein Veblen all described the ambiguous role of the "stranger." Usually referring to Jews, their discussions were not far from the sort of dilemma described by Du Bois.

Robert E. Park gave a new label to this phenomenon, calling it *marginality*. Park suggested that members of many racial and ethnic groups suffer from the ambivalence of values created by their longing for the old and their desire to participate in the new. Park and Everett Stonequist, author of *The Marginal Man*, described such persons as "cultural hybrids."[8] One of the results of their marginality, it was suggested, was personal maladjustment.

Critics of the Park-Stonequist thesis have argued that belonging to a minority group in and of itself does not necessarily predispose one to inner strain, personal disorientation, psychic and neurotic difficulties, or various types of deviant behavior such as crime.[9] Most sociologists, however, agree that *status inconsistency*, whether involving ethnic status or not, is a persistent problem, and that personal stability depends, in large measure, on the sense of security the individual member feels within the community.[10] Who one thinks he is and where one feels he belongs are crucial matters.

Minority status repeatedly has been found to intensify already existing group identity or to create it where it had not existed prior to discrimination. Forced to live in particular areas and to associate with one another, members of minority groups frequently come to view themselves as a community, to feel a keen sense of responsibility for one another, and to build institutions that contribute to the protection of individuals and to further the sense of fellow feeling.[11] Such a development suggests that the concept of marginal *man* is too narrow; it may even be inappropriate for vast numbers of minority-group members.

Thus, in one of the many attempts to reformulate the marginal man notion, Milton M. Goldberg, relying in large measure on the work of the anthropologist Alexander Goldenweiser and his idea of "marginal cultural areas," suggested that:

If (1) the so-called "marginal" individual is conditioned to his existence on the borders of two cultures from birth, if (2) he shares the existence and conditioning process with a large number of individuals in his primary groups, if (3) his years of early growth, maturation, and even adulthood find him participating in institutional activities manned largely by other "marginal" individuals like himself, and finally, if (4) his marginal position results in no major blockages or frustrations of his learned expectations and desires, then he is not a true "marginal" individual in the defined sense, but is a participant member of a *marginal* culture, every bit as real and complete to him as is the nonmarginal culture to the nonmarginal man.[12]

Contrary to the views of Park and Stonequist, Goldberg (and those sharing his conception) does not see most minority-group members as maladjusted products of cultural ambivalence, but as adjusted participants in a *marginal culture*, itself a product of accommodation to differential treatment. This interpretation is consistent with our own conviction that members of American minority communities manifest certain common characteristics normal to groups with similar marginal experiences, including certain traits that outsiders sometimes define as pathological.

While minority communities may differ from one another in racial and ethnic composition, their levels of socioeconomic status, patterns of social mobility, and local customs—those retained and those newly created—they tend to possess a transmitted remembrance of how the community developed. Everyone, of course, is "ethnocentric" in some degree. Moreover, spokesmen for almost every group engage in "the creative distortion of history" to emphasize their group's historical legacy and to underscore its unique contributions.[13] Thus references are frequently made to the first members of the group to arrive and the conditions under which they came, how they were received and how they fared, the discrimination they encountered and how they coped with it, the grounds on which the community was established in this country, and the deeds of important leaders.

Many minorities have their own territorial bases, sometimes

marked by physical boundaries ("the other side of the tracks," "down by the riverside," "in the hollow"), sometimes by psychological or social walls that set them apart from the larger community. In his novel *A Walker in the City*, Alfred Kazin explains:

We were the end of the line. We were the children of the immigrants who had camped at the city's back door, New York's rawest, remotest, cheapest ghetto, enclosed on one side by the Canarsie flats and on the other by the hallowed middle-class districts that showed the way to New York. "New York" was what we put last on our address, but first in thinking of the others around us. *They* were New York, the Gentiles . . . ; we were Brownsville—*Brunzvil*, as the old folks said. . . .[14]

Today Brownsville is predominantly black and those who now write of their estrangement often describe Kazin's people, the Jews, as the *they* who represent the Establishment![15]

When separated from the dominant society, minorities frequently develop their own social institutions, replete with norms deemed appropriate to the local situation. Some of these run counter to the ways of the larger community and are viewed as deviant, mysterious, dangerous or simply un-American. One thinks of the ways various people "use" time (for example, the *mañana* spirit of Spanish-surnamed Americans), worship (the practices of Orthodox Jews, Pentecostalists, Zen Buddhists), and relax (perhaps through various sorts of gambling and gaming activities), to say nothing of the myriad differences in ways of perceiving themselves, each other, and the society in which they live.

The last point was most poignantly expressed through the researches and reports of the late Oscar Lewis. Here is a short excerpt from his famous essay in which his Puerto Rican respondents compare life in New York with that on the home island. The passage begins with Lewis asking, "Have you ever been in New York, Hector?"

"Yes, yes, I've been to New York."
"And what did you think of life there?"

"New York! I want no part of it! Man, do you know what it's like? You get up in a rush, have breakfast in a rush, get to work in a rush, go home in a rush, even shit in a rush. That's life in New York! Not for me! Never again! Not unless I was crazy.

"Look, I'll explain. The ways things are in New York, you'll get nothing there. But nothing! It's different in Puerto Rico. Here, if you're hungry, you come to me and say, 'Man, I'm broke, I've had nothing to eat.' And I'd say, 'Ay, Bendito! Poor thing!' And I'd give you some food. No matter what, you wouldn't have to go to bed hungry. Here in Puerto Rico you can make out. But in New York, if you don't have a nickel, or twenty cents, you're worthless, and that's for sure. You don't count. You get swallowed by a horse."[16]

But even such seeming rejection of the harshness of urban life is coped with by hundreds of thousands of Puerto Ricans and others who feel the centripetal attraction of places like New York. While often disillusioned by what they find, many stay and attempt to survive. They do so in part by modifying old ways (or by instituting new ones, engaging in a process that has been called "ethnogenesis").[17]

The street culture of Spanish Harlem, the tight-knit social organization of Chinatowns in San Francisco and Seattle, New York and Boston, the ubiquity of storefront churches in poor, black areas, the twang of western music in Chicago neighborhood bars, the raft of ethnic newspapers found on the stands of every large city, all indicate that many Americans carry on by retaining or reviving that which they once knew. Others, as noted, develop new patterns and organizations such as juvenile gangs (like the "Mexican Marauders"), athletic clubs (the "Jewish Marvels"), ethnically based patriotic organizations ("Polish-American Veterans"), religious societies ("African Methodist Episcopal Church"), social agencies (the "Catholic Youth Organization"), schools (such as those offering Chinese, Hebrew, and Greek to relevant groups), and many kinds of businesses—some set up specifically to serve the minority community or, at the least, to benefit from desires for particular foods and special services.

Many members of minority groups make their living and spend much of their money within the ethnic community itself.

Some, including those who have become quite successful, find themselves in what Norbert Wiley calls an "ethnic mobility trap."[18] Having chosen to make his way within the confines of the ethnic enclave, the individual may lock himself in with a skill or a specialty that is difficult to transfer to the wider world. Norbert Wiley begins his discussion of this phenomenon by reminding the readers of William Foote Whyte's famous study, *Street Corner Society,* a detailed description and analysis of a working-class Italian area in the north side of Boston. There, Whyte noted, two avenues of socialization led to two sorts of "opportunity ceilings." If one was a "corner boy" one could aspire to work in local (ethnic) politics or to a high position in the rackets; if one was a "college boy" he was groomed for professional and managerial positions. Many, frustrated by the seeming remoteness of middle-class jobs, opted for following the line of least resistance. Some of them even became big men in the local community, but they were nothing on the outside.[19]

Many members of minority groups fall somewhere between the "corner boys" and the "college boys." While some spend their lives inside the enclave and some break away completely, a common pattern is to make one's living away from the neighborhood. It is in the workaday world that one tends to have the greatest amount of interaction with members of other groups and with representatives of the wider society. Of course, when night falls, "The WASPs return to their nests—and the others return to their own." Ethnic nests vary, of course, from old law tenements to high rise apartments to ranch homes in what some sociologists call a "gilded ghetto."[20]

On-the-job participation is frequently quite formal and segmentalized, with each person playing his appropriate role. The minority-group member is often seen as an "ambassador of his people" by those with whom he has contact.[21] Because exposure is frequently limited to outstanding figures (such as athletes, entertainers, professionals—for example, the Jewish doctor), to workers, or servants, and rarely involves intimate or informal exchanges, individuals in the dominant group tend to have distorted images of minority peoples and of their personal existence. Their views are frequently a combination of hunches (based on limited observation) and prejudices (which they have learned through contact with other prejudiced people).

The pattern is frequently asymmetrical, however, for minorities are continually exposed to the values and norms of the dominant group through public schooling, mass media, employment, advertising, and just living. They inevitably learn the ways of the dominant group even though they may not accept them all.

Although it is not unusual to hear blanket indictments of the entire Establishment, members of minority groups learn fairly early in life that the dominant group itself is highly differentiated in various ways. They are surprised when they find that so many of those beyond the confines of their communities are unaware that they, too, have their own hierarchies, interest groups, leaders and followers, successful members and ne'er-do-wells, poets and preachers, artisans and laborers, professionals and provocateurs.

Like most communities in complex societies, minority enclaves consist of differentiated clusters of subgroupings, varying in socioeconomic status, occupational interest, and political proclivity.[22] Certain ethnic groups, to be sure, put more stress on one activity than on another and certain occupations hold greater prestige than others. One thinks of the role of the priesthood in a French-Canadian village, of law and politics in an Irish community, teaching and the professions for Jews, or of business and science for the parents of Chinatown's children. While not every French-Canadian child aspires to be a priest nor every Irish-American wishes to be a "pol," there is no question that many members of their communities get a certain amount of satisfaction (or what is more precisely stated in Yiddish, *naches*) from seeing one of their own people become successful, especially in those areas toward which they feel particularly partial for sentimental, ideological, or practical reasons.

Even where there are relatively parallel systems of social stratification, there is no assurance that persons considered to be upper class by members of their own group would be accorded the same status by outsiders; nor does it mean that the respected members of a given minority would be held in the same esteem by those in the dominant group. Consider a well-known historical example: As the Irish and Italians moved into the political arena in cities once dominated by Yankee interests many Brahmins moved aside. In time the latter began to define politics as dirty business more suited to the "saloon culture" of the newcomers than to their drawing rooms and clubs. Today, many an American is highly suspect of those who decide to pursue a career in politics.[23] This discrepancy between the views of the members of dominant and minority groups serves to intensify the most pervasive attribute of any minority community: group identification.

Group identification is revealed in intragroup attitudes and actions; it is reflected in expressions of intergroup behavior or those involving minority reaction to majority treatment. In the former category is the positive feeling of pride and the negative attitude of self-hatred.

Pride

Pride in one's ethnic or racial identity may be illustrated in the fellow feeling that predisposes many young blacks to identify with brothers and sisters they have never met. When introduced they may go through an elaborate handshake, signifying to one another that they are together. Members of other groups perform similar rituals to indicate their sense of identification and their group-based pride.

In the author's study of small-town Jews and their Christian neighbors, each Jewish respondent was asked what first came to mind when he or she read the following newspaper headline: MISCHA GOLDBERG LAUDED FOR CONCERT PERFORMANCE. The most frequent response emphasized pride in seeing a fellow Jew receive recognition. Many respondents echoed the sentiment expressed by one of them who said, "I'm glad when it's one of ours who does well, it makes *me* feel good." When the same individuals were then asked their reactions to a second headline—MAX COHEN INDICTED FOR FRAUD—the characteristic responses were vexation, embarrassment, and anger. "It's bad for us when a Jew gets in trouble."[24]

In similar fashion many Mexican-Americans are delighted when the champion of the farm laborer is named Chavez or the golfer of the year is named Trevino, but upset when the accused in a celebrated mass murder is named Corona. Greeks, even Democrats, are apt to have a special concern about Spiro Agnew; many Italians feel the same about John Volpe, Frank Sinatra, and Sophia Loren—just as many Irish-Americans do about the Kennedys.

Two factors are operating here: a sense of interdependence of fate with others with whom one is identified; a vicarious connection with those in the limelight—or under the gun. In both cases minority-group members often see themselves as part of a whole community: of those they know intimately *and* those they know only by sight or sign or name. The group identity of blacks, or of Jews, or of Mexican-Americans (or of others similarly situated) is expressed in innumerable ways. Perhaps it is best expressed through the immediate response to the question many ask themselves about a stranger they are meeting for the first time: "Is he a 'brother'?" "Is he a *landsmann*?" "Is he a *compadre*?" "Is he a *paisano*?" Social intercourse is apt to be shaped by this definitive beginning.

Self-Hatred

It has been hypothesized that "the greater the pressure of prejudice and discrimination, the greater is likely to be the feeling of interdependence of fate within the minority community."[25] While this relationship has been found to apply to many members of minority groups, it does not necessarily hold for all. Some individuals, objects of severe discrimination, may internalize the negative stereotypes held of them by others and, as a result, display little ingroup solidarity. In fact, rather than drawing into the ranks of the minority, they may seek to withdraw from it.

Those with a positive sense of group identity may feel self-conscious at the thought of "one of theirs" getting into trouble since it puts the whole minority in a bad light. Those who possess a low degree of morale stemming from minority status are sometimes so anxious about their subordinate position that they attempt to disavow membership. To such persons the minority community is not a source of pride but may be one of self-hatred. In order to combat their inability to adjust to minority status they may change their names, deny their racial or ethnic origins, alter their physiognomy (which in the case of Jews, was once facetiously called "cutting off your nose to spite your race"), refuse to associate with group members, attempt to pass as a member of the majority group—and still find themselves rejected. Caught between two social worlds—one that they reject, the other that rejects them—they frequently suffer the plight of the original marginal man as described by Du Bois and Park and Stonequist.

Reactions to Discrimination

What sorts of individual and collective action can minority-group members take to deal with or alter their social position in a society such as our own? Or, putting the point in the words of Langston Hughes, "What happens when a dream is deferred?" Hughes' poetic answer is offered first; ours, which follows, is largely an elaboration of his metaphors.

What happens to a dream deferred?

Does it dry up
like a raisin in the sun?
Or fester like a sore—
And then run?
Does it stink like rotten meat?
Or crust and sugar over—
like a syrupy sweet?

Maybe it just sags
like a heavy load.

Or does it explode?[26]

Many attempts have been made by sociologists to describe

the responses of minority-group members to their social situation. While, to be sure, various minorities suffer greater or lesser discrimination, which is sometimes related to the degree of closeness to the values and norms of the dominant group, nonetheless within most minorities in the United States there are those who "want in" and are willing to do anything to obtain "entry," there are those who simply want to be left alone, there are those who want what they feel they are rightly entitled to. Thus, as George Simpson and Milton Yinger suggest, most discussions of minority responses consider at least the following models: those who favor "acceptance," those who seek "accommodation," and those who are "aggressive."[27] (They may be aggressively for reform to get themselves in; they may be aggressively for radicalization to get themselves out or to form something entirely new.)

Our position is slightly different. While taking into consideration these three models it is suggested here that reactions to minority status are most fully understood when *two* questions are posed. Answers to the questions reveal at least four types of reaction that, as shall be shown, may be further broken down and, in some ways, represent points on a spectrum through which some individuals may pass at various stages of their lives. The questions are these: (1) Does the minority-group member accept or reject the image of subordinate status imposed on him by the majority? (2) Is he willing to play a humble role as expected of him by those in positions of power?

Table 4 presents the four possible types of reaction suggested here: submission, withdrawal, separation, integration. (The first two incorporate what Simpson and Yinger call "ac-

Table 4   Four Types of Reaction to Discrimination
by Members of Minority Groups

	Dominant Image of Minority Member's "Inferior Status"	
Segregated Role:	Accepted	Rejected
Accepted	1. Submission	3. Separation
Rejected	2. Withdrawal	4. Integration

ceptance"—at least on one axis; the latter two only partially parallel the categories of "accommodation" and "aggression" for, as noted below, *both* may involve the processes of détente and militant action to achieve certain defined goals.)

Before examining these types it should be reiterated that in the concrete case all of these reaction patterns are possible, and a given individual may manifest two or more of them at different times or in different circumstances. Since it is the largest minority group in the United States at present, illustrations of these types will be drawn from the experiences of black Americans.

Submission

Malcolm X once said that "the worst crime the white man has committed is to teach us to hate ourselves." There is little question that one of the first things many black Americans learn is their "place" and the roles they are expected to play in the white man's world. They learn "to be Negro" (or, in currently popular terms "to be black"). In 1929 A. L. Holsey wrote,

At fifteen I was fully conscious of the racial difference, and while I was sullen and resentful in my soul, I was beaten and knew it. I knew then that I could never aspire to be President of the United States, nor governor of my state, nor mayor of my city; I knew that I could only sit in the peanut gallery at our theater and could only ride on the back seat of the electric car and in the Jim Crow car on the train. I had bumped into the color line and knew that so far as white people were concerned, I was just another nigger.[28]

Recognizing one's fate as "just another nigger" among whites has led many blacks to accept their inferior status and to play the segregated roles socially assigned to them. American folklore is filled with stories of "Uncle Tom" and "Aunt Jemima," "good niggers" who knew the score and could play the tune as well. They bow and scrape, crack jokes, and play dumb to please the white folks. Uncle Toms exist in real life too.

Some black people feel that the best way to live is to accept second-class status and do the white man's bidding. One such individual is described by Richard Wright in his famous autobiography *Black Boy*. Wright tells of a black elevator operator with whom he worked in a Memphis hotel. One day Shorty needed lunch money and told Wright to watch him get it from the first white man who came along. When such a person eventually got into the elevator, Shorty said to him:

"I'm hungry, Mister White Man. I need a quarter for lunch."

The white man ignored him. Shorty, his hands on the controls of the elevator . . .

"I ain't gonna move this damned old elevator till I get a quarter, Mister White Man."

"The hell with you, Shorty," the white man said, ignoring him and chewing on his black cigar.

"I'm hungry, Mister White Man. I'm dying for a quarter," Shorty sang, drooling, drawling, humming his words.

"If you don't take me to my floor, you will die," the white man said, smiling a little for the first time.

"But this black sonofabitch sure needs a quarter," Shorty sang, grimacing, clowning, ignoring the white man's threat.

"Come on, you black bastard, I got to work," the white man said, intrigued by the element of sadism involved, enjoying it.

"It'll cost you twenty-five cents, Mister White Man, just a quarter, just two bits," Shorty moaned.

There was silence. Shorty threw the lever and the elevator went up and stopped about five feet shy of the floor upon which the white man worked.

"Can't go no more, Mister White Man, unless I get my quarter," he said in a tone that sounded like crying.

"What would you do for a quarter?" the white man asked, still gazing off.

"I'll do anything for a quarter," Shorty sang.

"What, for example?" the white man asked.

Shorty giggled, swung around, bent over, and poked out his broad, fleshy ass.

"You can kick me for a quarter," he said looking impishly at the white man out of the corner of his eyes.

The white man laughed softly, jingled some coins in his pocket, took out one and thumped it to the floor. Shorty stooped to pick it up and the white man bared his teeth and swung his foot into Shorty's rump with all the strength of his body. Shorty let out a howling laugh that echoed up and down the elevator shaft.

"Now, open this door, you goddam black sonofabitch," the white man said, smiling with tight lips.

"Yeess, siiiir," Shorty sang; but first he picked up the quarter and put it into his mouth. "This monkey's got the peanuts," he chortled.

He opened the door and the white man stepped out and looked back at Shorty as he went toward his office.

"You're all right, Shorty, you sonofabitch," he said.

"I know it!" Shorty screamed, and then let his voice trail off in a gale of wild laughter.[29]

There are, of course, two possible interpretations of Shorty's acceptance of his role as buffoon. On the one hand, he was manipulating the white man—he got what he wanted; on the other, his behavior served to demonstrate the depth of his submissiveness, for he played his role according to his image of the white man's expectations.

For many minority-group members, acceptance of subordinate status is the only way to eke out a living. The "red cap" with a master's degree and the Puerto Rican waiter with a high school diploma are well-known examples.

Most often, submission to the inferior status imposed by others is a rational acceptance, a seeming necessity for survival. Berry, for example, states that "it is not uncommon for one to conform externally while rejecting the system mentally and emotionally."[30] Yet, there are significant exceptions to this generalization.

Contemporary sociology and cultural anthropology have shown that people can learn to adjust to, and even accept extremely diverse circumstances that seem strange, painful, or evil to those who have received different training. Standards of value by which the desirability of a given status is judged, as well as the status itself, are a product of the society. A whole group may accept what to others seems to be an inferior role. . . .[31]

For some individuals, acceptance of such inferior roles is

simply conformity to the traditions of the community in which they happen to be raised. While whites may learn that they are superior to Negroes as part of a more general socialization experience, some Negroes similarly may accept the standards of racial inequality. Thus, acceptance of inferior status may be seen as a conditioned reaction in a prejudiced society. Today many of their militant children and grandchildren disparagingly refer to such people as "Nee-groes," in contrast to blacks.

Withdrawal

One reaction to discrimination is submission to inferior status; another is the denial of identity. In this case the individual accepts the majority image of his group[32] and—because of self-hatred or expediency—withdraws from the group. In rejecting the segregated role that they are supposed to play, some light-skinned "Negroes" (and other minority-group members such as Jews who wish to be taken for Gentiles, Catholic ethnics who want to be seen as WASPs, Puerto Ricans who claim they are Spanish) attempt to pass into the dominant group. Not infrequently they hold ambivalent attitudes toward themselves and others, and their conflicting allegiances are apt to induce anxiety, which is further provoked by the constant threat of exposure. Thus a fictional character asks himself:

—But what if a lot of people know it already? Or can detect the Negro in me? I hear lots of Southerners claim they can do that. That man goggling at me down the car—can he see I'm part Negro? Has everybody always guessed it?[33]

In 1945, St. Clair Drake and Horace Cayton estimated that each year at least 25,000 persons permanently leave the Negro population to become assimilated into white society.[34] While one suspects that number would be high today, still there are innumerable individuals who pass on a part-time or segmental basis, for example, working as whites by day and returning home to the black community. In this way they avoid the strain of breaking contact completely and turning away from lifelong friends and neighbors.

"Passing," a course open to those who possess no identifying racial or ethnic characteristics or those who can mask them, is the only method of assimilation available to persons who wish to enter an environment that would reject them out of hand if their true identity were to be revealed. In some areas of society, racial identity is relatively unimportant, and individuals can withdraw from the minority community while still being associated with it by others. Black athletes who attend big universities or join the armed forces, black artists who become expatriates or entertainers, others who engage in such illicit activities as gambling and prostitution, frequently find acceptance in the white world because of the special skills or characteristics that they bring to the situation. Many such individuals, while not denying their minority identity, prefer not to be "professional race men"; they may wish to be accepted in spite of—rather than because of—their racial or ethnic background. In most instances assimilation for such exceptional members of minority groups is only partial, for when they step out of their specialized roles they are considered by many Americans as "just another nigger."

Separation

The reaction patterns of both submission and withdrawal used by certain minority-group members presume acceptance of the inferior image held of them by the majority. Yet, accepting their plight as members of a group considered by the majority to be of lower status does not necessarily mean total capitulation to the stigma of second-class citizenship. In recent years, a large percentage of minority-group members have rejected the idea that they are inferior and have attempted either to avoid contact with the enemy camp or to integrate and take their place alongside those in the dominant group. Here we consider the former response pattern.

Many blacks who have attained a moderate amount of security and have risen to relatively high status within their own segregated community are resentful of those who submit to the indignities imposed upon them. Long ago, Hortense Powdermaker reported:

> Those at the top deplore the others' submission to white assumptions of superiority and their recalcitrance to white standards of behavior. They decry the loose morality and the ignorance by which, they feel, the lower class of Negro lends credence to unfair notions about the race.[35]

Although these attitudes are still prevalent in certain circles, a qualification is in order: In rejecting white assumptions of superiority, many blacks accept pervasive white middle-class cultural standards and frequently establish parallel social institutions that mimic the presumed manners and mores of whites, sometimes to the extent of becoming distorted parodies. Such efforts—often exaggerated accounts of the achievements of individuals—have been described as flights of fantasy. The late E. Franklin Frazier, speaking of middle-class urban Negroes, claimed that "their escape into a world of make-believe with its sham 'society' leaves them with a feeling of emptiness and futility which causes them to constantly seek an escape in new delusions."[36]

The extent to which old "Negro" newspapers and magazines (some of which still exist) were imitative of white society was evidenced by the advertisements and articles that appeared in them. *Ebony*, *Jet*, *Tan*, and others used to be filled with pages of ads for skin whiteners and hair straighteners. Furthermore, stories of fancy cotillions and exclusive clubs, of expensive homes and problems with the help, were reported. The pre-eminence of white standards, even among those who by subscribing to such journals supported their own institutions, was manifest.

Discussing the general problem, Maurice Davie once wrote: "Avoidance is thus a protective device, a way of adjusting to ... [segregation] with the least pain and uneasiness. It may be carried to the point of almost complete voluntary segregation."[37]

What might be considered a conventional response to separate treatment, namely, the development of institutions paralleling those of the dominant society, is not uncommon, especially by middle-class members of minorities (the white *nouveaux riches* are little different from the black bourgeoisie). But it is surely not the only reaction pattern of people who reject others' views of their alleged inferiority but see little point in trying to enter their social world.

Some, most often those too poor to emulate middle-class whites or too disgusted to want to, have taken what seem to many to be more drastic measures. They not only seek to maintain separation and a sense of communal integrity, they also foster the rejection of "white" standards. This type of response is frequently an active and sometimes aggressive method of furthering the goals of the group as a group, strengthening its position, and justifying its separate existence. To combat discrimination, exponents of this reaction pattern sometimes adopt a chauvinistic doctrine of their own superiority, even going so far as to play up those very traits that, at another time, they might have attacked others for suggesting made them unique. Rather than paralleling dominant institutions and values they challenge them—often acting out certain stereotypes in the process. Jeremy Larner has addressed himself to this last point when he notes the tendency of certain black nationalists and their spokesmen to engage in a self-indulgent (and, to him, self-deluding) game of mirroring, particularly in playing on three common white themes: "the noble savage" (with its emphasis on creativity, spontaneity, and willingness to fight); "the hipster" (a black Negro to replace Norman Mailer's famous "white Negro," portrayed as a sort of nihilistic superman who is the cock of the walk); and "the black proletarian" (who is part of the vanguard of the revolution to come).[38] Another key concept marking separation is "soul." Recently the Swedish anthropologist Ulf Hannerz made a careful study of a black neighborhood in Washington, D.C. His observations offer one interesting view. He concluded that "soul as solidarity is a reaction to the threat of a split in the community" among those whose lives are circumscribed by the values and norms of mainstream (or wider American) society and those values more specific to ghetto living. Thus Hannerz contends:

> In order to make [the] solidarity encompass even the least privileged, it must be symbolized by those most undiluted forms of black proletarian experience which everybody can claim as his heritage, and to give it a positive valence weakness must be turned into strength. Thus poverty, oppression, and troubled relationships are interpreted as the foundation of an endurance which can only be appreciated by those who have passed the same way.[39]

Others contend that "soul" is simply a label broadly applied to the shared perspective of all blacks, the basis of their "cultural" character.

As shall be shown in the next chapter, at various stages blacks have opted for revitalization through separation, through the exaltation of all that is black and the denigration of all that is white, and, frequently, through making capital of what outsiders (and some high-status insiders) consider to be lower-class cultural traits specific to the black ghetto.

Thus under the general heading of avoidance one must consider the paths of both parallel participation and of ethnic chauvinism.

Integration

Protest is not always manifest in attempts to pull away, to go it alone. As James Baldwin has indicated, however, the appeal for such action is very great.

> The brutality with which Negroes are treated in this country simply cannot be overstated, however unwilling white men may be to hear it. In the beginning . . . a Negro just cannot believe that white people are treating him as they do; he does not know what he has done to merit it. And when he realizes that the treatment accorded him has nothing to do with anything he has done, that the attempt of white people to destroy him—for that is what it is—

is utterly gratuitous, it is not hard for him to think of white people as devils.[40]

Despite such sentiments, and they are increasingly widespread, not all blacks have attempted to solve the problem of inequality by joining the cause of Black Nationalism and rejecting the possibility of eventual integration. In fact, a very large percentage of Afro-Americans, even today, seek equality without any strings. They do not want to be separate and equal or separate and superior. They want what is constitutionally guaranteed and are willing to fight to get it.

Here, again, the integrationists may try one of two routes: The first is essentially integration-at-a-distance, the kind that most other minorities (namely so-called white ethnics) enjoy; the second is full integration or, better stated, amalgamation.

Most of those we call ethnics in this society do live in two distinct, though not necessarily antagonistic, worlds (as pointed out above). One world is that of their kith, kin, and community; the other is the broader society in which they study and work and sometimes play. The former comes closer to possessing what sociologists call a *gemeinschaftlich* character, a sense of total involvement, of real belonging or weness; the latter is more *gesellschaftlich*, that is, marked by secondary relationships, impersonal ties, partial involvement and remoteness. Thus a surprising number of ethnics (white and nonwhite) keep to their own neighborhoods and enjoy their own activities even when the formal barriers are removed. What they want, at least what many want, is the *right* to do as they please. Once they have that free choice they often opt for life with their own "kind." (This helps to explain the confusion that certain white ethnics feel about blacks who resent *their* insistence on community control, a point we shall further discuss in Chapter Eight.)

Now there are some members of minority groups who wish to live in a truly color-blind, ethnically neutral society, a society where no one is judged, considered, or even recognized on the basis of skin color or any other potentially invidious criterion. They differ from those in the "withdrawal" category in Table 4, for they desire not to leave their own group but to abolish the idea of group difference itself. In terms introduced in Chapter Three, they are the true advocates of amalgamation—the legatees of Crèvecoeur and Zangwill—and wish their children to be the best that the crucible can pour out.

In both instances militance may mark the road to emancipation. For whether one wants the right to decide whether or not to integrate at a distance or to foster fusion, he must often work to convince others that it is his choice to make, not theirs. Since both of these responses are well within the value framework of the American ideal, many of the activities of the civil-rights movement were and are oriented toward these goals and many of the important pieces of legislation—including the Civil-Rights Acts of 1964, 1967, and 1968—were testimony to the efficacy of integrationist pressure for many Americans.

Variations on the Themes

There are times when those in the minority find that they cannot really go it alone (seeking separation), nor can they abide the slowness of change as advocated by those whose perseverance is ever tempered by the call for patience and good-will, as in the civil-rights movement. Feeling stifled by recalcitrant institutions and reluctant officials, hampered by powerful opponents and anxious neighbors, some leaders have pressed their followers to push beyond the tolerance limits and have advocated radical tactics designed to force society to give in to their demands, to play not only on sympathy but on fear of disruption, to appeal not merely to charity and righteousness but to countervailing power marshaled by those considered powerless. America has long been witness to such movements: the struggle for women's rights, the labor movement, and the Black Power Revolt. It is the last-named that concerns us here.

In the preceding section we looked at four typical ways

minority peoples, including blacks, have reacted to their treatment. We noted variations within each type, (1) such as unconscious as well as intentional (or calculated) submission; (2) partial or complete withdrawal; (3) avoidance, that is, mimicking the majority but avoiding contact or opting for nationalism and putting emphasis on real, imagined, or created differences; (4) integration and partial (or what was earlier called cultural pluralism) or full integration (or amalgamation). Discounting those in the first two general categories because they accept dominant-group definitions of their group's inferiority, it may be said that responses the third and fourth and their variations are permissible, even expected, within our normative structure. Like them or not, most Americans would acknowledge that people have the right to remain separate as long as they do not make trouble; to seek to integrate as long as they accept the values of others—and it does not cost too much. The trouble appears to begin when the limits are broached. Integrating a park is one thing, a neighborhood is quite another. Of course, as noted in Chapter One, these limits—and the norms that define them—do vary from region to region and from community to community. Still, in general, one can say that when blacks (or Chicanos or Puerto Ricans or American Indians) become nationalistic at least some Americans approve (they may even find it quaint or amusing) so long as they do it in their own area, on their own turf. Likewise, when integrationists press to have the country honor its own ideals, to force the door open through the slow, tedious, and expensive process of litigations, well and good. Liberals applaud; conservatives complain—but generally they go along once a decision is made.

In other words, both "apolitical blackwardness" and "soulless militancy" are tolerable from the majority viewpoint, even if not warmly welcomed. (Numerous public opinion polls bear testimony to this response.) But when chauvinism is joined with direct action (even nonviolent direct action), when pride and protest are linked together, the critical balance is upset and new responses are devised.

The latter situation was invoked by the Black Power movement in the mid-1960s, for reasons discussed in Chapter Seven. In the present context, however, it is instructive to consider what Table 4 (on page 175) would look like if one thinks in terms of *radical responses* to minority status. Table 5 represents this view:

Table 5   Black Power in Relation to Two Typical Reaction Patterns

Separation
      a. "Parallel participation"
      b. "Apolitical blackwardness"   ↓

                                         BLACK
Integration   POWER
      a. "Soul-less militancy"   ↑
      b. "Color-blind fusion"

Of course, black power and similar derivative movements are not historical accidents. They grew out of the mounting realization that unidimensional programs—whether chauvinistic or reformistic—are usually inadequate to meet the basic challenge, the challenge posed by those who have the power to control the lives of others. And the lack of power, as noted at the beginning of this chapter, is a fundamental attribute of minority status.

NOTES

1. Nathan Glazer and Daniel Patrick Moynihan, *Beyond the Melting Pot*, rev. ed. (Cambridge: MIT Press, 1970).
2. For a more thorough discussion of groups and statistical aggregates, see Ely Chinoy, *Society*, rev. ed. (New York: Random House, 1967), pp. 40-43.
3. Louis Wirth, "The Problem of Minority Groups," in Ralph Linton (ed.), *The Science of Man in the World Crisis* (New York: Columbia University Press, 1945, p. 348.
4. *Ibid.*
5. Peter I. Rose, *The Subject Is Race* (New York: Oxford University Press, 1968), p. 71.
6. Robert E. Park, "Human Migration and the Marginal Man,"

American *Journal of Sociology*, 33 (May 1928), 891; see also Everett V. Stonequist, *The Marginal Man* (New York: Scribner, 1937), p. 217.

7. From W. E. B. Du Bois, *The Souls of Black Folk* (1903), reprinted in *These Negro Colonies* (New York: Avon, 1965) p. 215. Italics supplied.

8. See Robert E. Park, *Race and Culture* (New York: Free Press, 1951), p. 354.

9. For example, Golovensky's study of the Jewish community contradicts many of Park's contentions. See David I. Golovensky, "The Marginal Man Concept: An Analysis and Critique," *Social Forces*, 30 (October 1951 to May 1952), 333-339.

10. George E. Simpson and J. Milton Yinger, *Racial and Cultural Minorities: An Analysis of Prejudice and Discrimination*, 4th ed. (New York: Harper & Row, 1972), p. 186.

11. See Kurt Lewin, *Resolving Social Conflict* (New York: Harper & Row, 1941), esp. pp. 145-216; and a recent critique of Lewin's thesis, Jack Rothman, "Minority Group Status, Mental Health and Intergroup Relations: An Appraisal of Kurt Lewin's Thesis," *The Journal of Intergroup Relations*, 3 (Autumn, 1962), 299-310.

12. Milton M. Goldberg, "A Qualification of the Marginal Man Theory," *American Sociological Review*, 6 (February 1941), 52-58.

13. See Chapter Seven of this text.

14. Alfred Kazin, *A Walker in the City* (New York: Grove Press, 1951), p. 12.

15. See, for example, Candice van Ellison, "Introduction," in Allon Schoener (ed.), *Harlem on My Mind* (New York: Random House, 1968). The author's remarks were adapted from Nathan Glazer and Daniel Patrick Moynihan's *Beyond the Melting Pot* (Cambridge: MIT Press, 1963).

16. Oscar Lewis, "In New York You Get Swallowed by a Horse," *Commentary* (November 1964), p. 69.

17. See, for example, L. Singer, "Ethnogenesis and Negro Americans Today," *Social Research,* 29 (Winter, 1962), 419-432.

18. Norbert F. Wiley, "The Ethnic Mobility Trap and Stratification Theory," *Social Problems*, 2 (Fall, 1967), pp. 147-159.

19. *Ibid.;* see also William Foote Whyte, *Street Corner Society* (University of Chicago Press, 1943).

20. See Judith R. Kramer and Seymour Leventman, *Children of the Gilded Ghetto* (New Haven: Yale University Press, 1961). See also Part I, "Jews, Gentiles and the American Dream," in Peter I. Rose (ed.), *The Ghetto and Beyond* (New York: Random House, 1969), pp. 21-97, *passim*.

21. See, for example, Peter I. Rose, "Strangers in Their Midst: A

Sociological Study of Small-Town Jews and Their Neighbors," Ph.D. dissertation, Cornell University, 1959, especially pp. 157-162. Most of the small-town Jews interviewed by the author were keenly aware of the role they were forced to play as "ambassadors to the *goyim.*"

22. Edward A. Suchman, John P. Dean, and Robin M. Williams, Jr., *Desegregation: Some Propositions and Research Suggestions* (New York: The Anti-Defamation League of B'nai B'rith, 1958), p. 67.

23. See, for example, E. Digby Baltzell, *The Protestant Establishment* (New York: Random House, 1964), pp. 329-334.

24. Rose, *op. cit.*

25. Suchman *et al., op. cit.,* p. 198. See also Arnold M. Rose, *The Negro's Morale* (Minneapolis: University of Minnesota Press, 1949), pp. 85-95.

26. Copyright 1951 by Langston Hughes. Reprinted from *Selected Poems,* by Langston Hughes, by permission of Alfred A. Knopf, Inc.

27. Simpson and Yinger, *op. cit.,* pp. 205-233.

28. A. L. Holsey, "Learning How to Be Black," *The American Mercury,* 16 (April 1929), pp. 421-425.

29. Richard Wright, *Black Boy* (New York: Harper & Row, 1945), pp. 198-200. By permission of Harper & Row, Publishers, Inc.

30. Brenton Berry, *Race and Ethnic Relations.* 3rd ed. (Boston: Houghton Mifflin, 1965), p. 483.

31. Simpson and Yinger, *Racial and Cultural Minorities* (New York: Harper & Row, 1958), p. 251.

32. "Individuals may belong to membership-groups which are different from their reference-groups, and thereby manifest positive prejudice toward a social category other than that to which they apparently belong." Robin M. Williams, Jr., "Racial and Cultural Relations," in J. B. Gittler (ed.), *Review of Sociology* (New York: Wiley, 1957), p. 428.

33. Sinclair Lewis, *Kingsblood Royal* (New York: Random House, 1947), p. 69.

34. St. Clair Drake and Horace Cayton, *Black Metropolis* (New York: Harcourt, Brace, 1945), p. 160.

35. Hortense Powdermaker, *After Freedom* (New York: Viking, 1939), p. 357.

36. E. Franklin Frazier, *Black Bourgeoisie* (New York: Free Press, 1957), p. 213.

37. Davie, *op. cit.,* p. 440.

38. Jeremy Larner, "To Speak of Black Violence," *Dissent* (Winter, 1973), pp. 76-78.

39. Ulf Hannerz, *Soulside: Inquiries into Ghetto Culture and Community* (New York: Columbia University Press, 1970), p. 157; also pp. 144-158.
40. James Baldwin, *The Fire Next Time* (New York: Dial Press, 1963), pp. 82-83.

SEVEN

BLACK CONSCIOUSNESS

Red, White, Blue—and Black

History is often written in terms of the images people, or peoples, wish to project. American history, for example, was long recounted as if the English, Scottish, Irish, Welsh Protestants—and a few Dutchmen—were the only ones to have had an impact on the growth and development of the country. Early books and classroom lectures dealt almost exclusively with the "Anglo-American Tradition" or "Our Christian Heritage." Throughout most of the eighteenth and nineteenth centuries, newcomers from northwestern Europe were encouraged to forget about the customs of Germany or Scandinavia and to adapt themselves to eminently superior *American* lifeways. Other immigrants were often considered beyond the pale of social acceptance. In story and song the Irish Catholics, the Poles, the Italians, and the Russian Jews—and to be sure, those who came from China or Japan—were referred to as "unassimilable aliens." Many politicians expressed serious doubts about whether such immigrants would ever have the makings of "real" Americans. Several noted social scientists, to their discredit, endorsed the Dillingham Commission reports and the restrictive legislation of the 1920s.

In time, historians and social scientists adopted a different viewpoint. Pluralism became *au courant* and school children and college students were then told that our differences make us strong, or that America is a multiplicity in a unity, or, as John Dewey once put it, in this country "the hyphen connects

191

instead of separates." It even became fashionable to teach about the Judaeo-Christian heritage and to consider Catholics as Christians, too. Indeed, as if to bear public witness to such a revisionist view, the single Protestant preacher who had always intoned opening prayers at official gatherings was supplanted by a ubiquitous triumvirate: minister, priest, and rabbi, representatives of "our three great religions." (Some sociologists gave expression to this new conception as a "triple melting pot."[1])

In recent years yet another figure has stepped onto the dais— and another culture has been "added" to the heritage. Behavior rises to meet expectations and the behavior of academic historians and social scientists seems to be no exception. Today the bookstores are flooded with a thousand volumes on "the Negro problem." The problem is not new. It is as old as America. But, worried about the future, the past is again being reexamined and, to some extent, rewritten.

The textbooks being prepared for the 1970s indicate that there is much more to black history than the slave blocks, the old plantation, emancipation and the grateful darkies, the Freedmen's Bureau, the Hayes-Tilden Compromise, *Plessy v. Ferguson*, Booker T. Washington, race riots during the two world wars, Marian Anderson, Jackie Robinson, Ralph Bunche, Thurgood Marshall, and the Supreme Court Decision of 1954. Rather, to judge by the advertising copy of the books already under preparation, they will dwell on the role played by black Americans who, "under the most adverse conditions, fought and died to gain their own freedom" and who (paradoxically it seems) "were enlisted in every major battle to save this Republic."

The new texts will continue to tell a story of life in the ante-bellum South, but the readers will learn that things were not so tranquil beneath the mimosa trees, that not all Negroes sought to emulate the ways of their masters, and that none enjoyed decent relations with them ("no matter what the romantics say"). They will also learn that black people did not really move "North to freedom," but exchanged one kind of hell for another.

As more and more new histories appear, a far different picture of Black Americans will emerge. And it will not be limited to the celebration of the martyrdom of Crispus Attucks (the Negro's Colin Kelly) or to, say, the achievements of George Washington Carver (the black Jonas Salk). The new books will include discussions of black soldiers who fought in the Union Army; they will tell of black politicians in the turbulent days of Reconstruction; they will praise the black cowboys who helped to open the West, the black troopers who rode with Teddy Roosevelt, the black workers who toiled along the rail-beds and in the factories and on the farms. Some will go further, too, extolling the virtues of blackness and the solidarity of soul and exposing the pallid character of white culture in contrast to black.

This latest reexamination of American history and the assignment of blacks to an honored place along with other minorities are largely the consequences of the civil-rights movement and the campaign to eliminate segregation. The demand for an entirely new view of the Afro-American, however, is an offshoot of a larger struggle.

Feeling that many of the hard-won victories of the 1950s and 1960s had not made that much difference, angry black spokesmen began challenging a number of basic assumptions of the reform-minded civil-rights advocates. First, they argued, liberal white leaders (whatever their personal goals) could rarely offer much more than palliatives that, often as not, were viewed as programs to keep their cities from erupting rather than being expressly designed for helping poor blacks. Second, they claimed that traditional Negro leaders rarely were much better: They were either out of touch with the people for whom they claimed to speak (as many felt about the late Dr. King) or were too willing to play the Establishment game (as was often said of Roy Wilkins). Arguing that their people had been deluded by whites who had taken up the "burden" and by

Negroes who were trying to lighten it, the new militants wanted to turn them "blackward," wanted them to have an identity that was truly their own. They began their campaign by excoriating white liberals, Uncle Toms, and, especially, "Honkie society." They carried it forward with appeals to Black Nationalism. They may end by making (and perhaps, in some cases, making up) history itself.

Of course, since no group has a monopoly on ethnocentrism, it should not be surprising to find that many of the new views of black history are similar to most paeans to a cloudy past: compilations of vague memories that have become legends, of vague legends that have become memories, of isolated incidents swelled to monumental significance, and a good deal of hard evidence of what actually happened and, for various reasons, has been overlooked or purposely ignored. The history of Afro-Americans, like that of people from Europe, is almost of necessity going to be a potpourri of fancy and fact. What makes it different is that it serves a double function: it helps to strengthen communal ties among blacks and, simultaneously, it teaches other Americans that those who came from Africa also had a noble past and are a proud people.

To tell it like it really was is a difficult and frustrating task. It is difficult because there is so little information that is untainted by the biases and romanticism of those who captured the oral tradition or the written record; it is frustrating because even the sketchy story that does emerge is so terribly ambiguous—ambiguous not with respect to the well-known patterns of oppression, but with respect to the effects of these patterns upon the oppressed. But one thing is fairly clear: much of the old African heritage was replaced by a new orientation. Western ways and southern values were imposed and absorbed and hundreds of thousands of black Africans became "Negroes."

W. E. B. Du Bois once suggested that "there is nothing so indigenous, so made in America, as me." And yet, few Negroes have been able to enjoy the freedoms that most other Americans take for granted. Few ever got away from the stigma attached to the color of their skins. As Du Bois and others repeatedly pointed out, every Negro child has always asked, "Who am I?" "What am I?"

Self, Segregation, and Soul

In the early 1960s, James Baldwin wrote an essay entitled "Nobody Knows My Name."[2] In a sense, it dealt with only half of the problem. White people did not know what to call him and *he did not know either.* Baldwin's people—variously called blacks, colored, Negroes, and blacks, again—had little to look forward to and even less to look back upon, or so it seemed.

Still, saying they had little is not to say they had nothing. There is such a thing as Afro-American culture, shared in some measure by every black person in this country. Like all cultures it is made up of many things—memories and moods and myths. What makes it different is that the memories and moods and even the myths "remembered" are unique: slavery and its aftermath; spiritual uplifting and over-Jordan imagery;[3] continued subjugation by those who claimed and repeatedly tried to prove that white was always right.

Against and, in some ways, in response to these debilitating circumstances there was cultural resilience, marked by richness and romance. The black world had (and has) its cuisine (now called "soul food"), its oldtime religion, its rules of conduct, its lingo, its literature, its sound. Those who now study the black experience in America contend that it has left Negroes with different conceptions of time and space and property—and life. (Today, it is even fashionable in certain liberal circles to celebrate the unique characteristics of Negro people in this country. A mere five years ago such contentions, traditionally made by many segregationists, would have been called racist by the very same liberals—and by many Negro leaders, too.)

Resistance was another matter. Being frozen into the rigidity of a caste-like system and unable to become full partners in the society from which so much of its own customs, beliefs, and values were derived, black people lacked the organizational apparatus characteristic of other minority groups in America—the very groups with which black Americans have long been compared and, perhaps more significantly, with which they have often compared themselves. For years they talked about organizing and fighting their tormentors, but faced with both entrenched institutions and powerful men, they usually had no recourse but to adapt themselves to the system that kept them in servitude. Even acts of defiance often involved playing roles that reflected the stereotypes—feigning illness, acting the fool, slowing down on the job. Except in the isolated cases of such revolts as Gabriel's Insurrection and Nat Turner's Rebellion frontal attacks were rarely attempted.

Segregation kept most Negroes humble, and sometimes their own leaders in their innocence often aided and abetted the Man. Both spoke of their children, both tended their flocks. (Of course, not all white men and not all leaders of Negroes acted in such a manner. But *these* were the most significant role models available for the vast majority of black people, especially in the Old South.)

A parallel may be drawn between the plight of black people in this country and that of mental patients. Some psychiatrists have recently reintroduced the notion of *reality therapy*. Reality therapy is a technique used to shock patients into the realization that, yes, the world is cruel and if they are going to make it, they are going to have to do more than play out the sick role which enlightened doctrine has ascribed to them and which, quite understandably, they have internalized. For years now, few well-educated people have said that blacks are innately inferior; they know better. Rather the conventional wisdom sounds strikingly like that of the old planters and ministers of God. Acting as if "only we know what's good for them," many social workers and school teachers have held to this view to the present day. Disadvantaged black people are viewed and treated as victims or patients in need of care and succor. And many Negroes, in turn, like the inmates of most mental institutions, have long been internalizing the roles ascribed to them and have acted accordingly.

Slaves were not and their descendants are not simple Sambos. But many did and continue to learn to act out the stereotypes others have held of them and many, even in putting the white man down by seeming to play along, came to believe that they were in fact inferior. It was in this context that, as noted previously, the late Malcolm X wrote that "the worst crime the white man has committed is teaching us to hate ourselves."[4]

One can understand the bitterness of those who say there has really been no progress for blacks, only expanded "welfare colonialism." And one should be able to understand why young black radicals choke on that noblest of all words in the lexicon of human relationists: brotherhood. Brotherhood, to too many, has meant: When you become like me, then we'll be as one. They have a point. Time and again blacks have found that there was one more river to cross; white people would offer the boats if the black rowers did not rock them too hard.

This situation presents a terribly difficult choice for a potential leader. Tell your people to remain supplicants in the hope that someday the white man would overcome his prejudices, lower the barriers, and welcome you into his big *white* house; or become a firebrand in the hope that you might force his capitulation. And once having made the decision, where were you left? As one person said: "Dead on the inside or dead all over."

To solve the dilemma of supplication v. rebellion, most efforts to redress the grievances of the past have been channeled into campaigns for integration (not quite supplication and not quite rebellion). Most black people, it seems, have wished to give the impression (and many have believed) that, someday, somehow, color would really be overlooked. And, as noted in Chapter Three, those held in contempt today by the angriest black spokesmen—the white liberals[5]—helped to perpetuate this myth without, for the most part, realizing what they were doing and without having very much personal contact with those they claimed to accept as equals.

The foregoing observations refer to "most" blacks, and

"many" blacks, but not to all. There are those who have "made it"; some by the same techniques used by members of other minority groups, including the exploitation of those whose identity they share; some by becoming athletes and soul singers and jazz musicians performing for both their own people and a wider audience; some—undoubtedly the largest group—by sheer determination to overcome the barriers of segregation, often by entering government service as postmen and clerks, secretaries and soldiers, and, of course, as teachers, and working their way up. Together, these members of what has come to be called the "black bourgeoisie," the "colored entertainers," or the "Negro respectables" represent to white folks (especially middle-class whites) living evidence that black people can succeed if they try hard enough and are willing to thicken their skins against whatever abuses the system and its agents mete out. It is true that many such people have taken pride in their progress and, for all their difficulties, have seemed quite stable, even happy in American society. They have belied the claims that blacks are characteristically lazy or ignorant or walking phallic symbols;[6] and many of them have seemed to be the essence of middle-class respectability: friendly, hardworking, religious, and community-minded.

Many of their children, however, who are now in college think differently. They, and not merely the poor residents of Watts or Harlem, know what Ron Karenga means when he decries, "There are only three kinds of people in this country: white people, black people, and Negroes. Negroes? They are black people that act like white people."[7]

The message is not lost. Those black college students, particularly at northern schools and the larger southern ones, know that part of Karenga's rhetoric is addressed to them and concerns their parents. ("Which side are you on?") Those who have suffered least from the stigma of color are beginning to feel the strain the most. Many are reacting by forming Afro-American organizations on the campus and by going home to Harlem or Hattiesburg to work and teach and organize. Some, to resolve their race/class schizophrenia, have begun to join the ranks of the most militant members of the black community. Stressing both poverty and race, the disorganized "black lumpen" have become their cause. With the poor, they believe, one can put to use some of the direct and fringe benefits of a college education. And for them one can try to offer a new and different view of the Americans who come from Africa.

The Past, the Present, and the Future

The young black militants are, as one said recently, "a new breed of cat." They see themselves as the vanguard of a movement to erase once and forever the stigma imposed by white slave masters and perpetuated by segregationists over the last hundred years. They want everyone—parents and peers, white liberals and conservatives—to know that times have changed and that they are black *men*, not black *boys*. Often using the future as a guide to the past, they have called for a new view of the black experience, one in which the real truth about black people will finally be known.

In response to mounting pressure, colleges and universities (and some public schools) have introduced Afro-American programs and curricular innovations geared to the special needs of black students. From among the welter of proposals and pronouncements requesting (or, more often, demanding) such programs, one message has come across loud and clear: "We will be *Negroes* no more." This mood, its strategy and its rhetorical style, has signaled the end of an old era and the beginning of a new phase in black-white relations in the United States.

The new ideology is a culmination of years of struggle and crisis during which black people were trying to come to grips with their unique problems and their constantly thwarted desires to become full-fledged Americans. Among the various techniques of protest, two types of action were most prevalent from the time of emancipation to its centennial. One centered on black people themselves and was concerned with "uplift": the learning of useful skills, the instilling of pride in self and neighbor and of such puritan virtues as thrift and practicality. The other focused on integration and the gaining of civil rights. In the first instance, the underlying notion seemed to be that black people would show the white man that they were responsible, upright, and talented citizens and that, in time, they would be ready to take their place beside anyone. In the latter, the argument was that the problem was not the Negro's but the white man's and *he* should be made to change. Thus the seeds were sown.

Uplift

The first sustained challenge to Jim Crow laws and the entire system of segregation was to come from highly educated and remarkably well-integrated northern Negroes, men like Monroe Trotter and W. E. B. Du Bois challenged what they saw as the tendency of southern Negroes and, especially, their leaders to acquiesce and accept their second-class status.

A primary target was Booker T. Washington, who, before the turn of the present century, had sought to come to terms with the problem of Negro alienation. Washington, himself born a slave, saw the hope of his people—at least in a southland of deeply rooted segregation—in the development of pride and self-esteem, in the puritan virtues of thrift and practicality, and in the learning of skills of the honest tradesman. His famous speech at Atlanta, Georgia, in 1895 has been branded as a classic in accommodationist thinking.[8] The implication was clear: Black people were not ready to take their place beside whites.

What Washington and others saw, however, was not simply the Uncle Tomism his critics (such as Trotter and Du Bois) claimed. Rather, it was, to some at least, a sort of live-and-let-live pluralism. As Washington himself put it: "In all things that are purely social we can be as separate as the fingers, yet as one in the hand in all things essential to mutual progress."[9] He also said, in the same speech, that "the wisest among my race understand that agitation of questions of social equality is the extremist folly, and that progress in the enjoyment of all the privileges that will come to us must be the result of severe and constant struggle rather than of artificial forcing."[10]

It was Washington's unwillingness to advocate agitation that won for him contempt in the minds of several generations of radical leaders. Yet, he did begin to come to terms with two of the most serious problems plaguing black Americans, acceptance of self and the question of racial solidarity, especially in the economic arena.

At Tuskegee Institute, which he established, Washington sought and in many ways succeeded in implementing his plan for uplift (as it was called). For a time he became the idol of millions of blacks and to this day he remains the symbol for many whites (especially older school teachers) of the responsible and reasonable Negro. Today, few of his black cousins share these sentiments, although, as we shall see, a growing number have reverted to the argument of self-help and, in some instances, even to the very values Washington promulgated.

Washington's famous theme of accommodation turned toward one of separation for some lower-class blacks, especially those in the urban centers. They joined the ranks of the Garvey movement in the 1920s, followed Daddy Grace in the 1930s, and joined the Black Muslims and other separatist sects more recently. All were, in their own way, considerably militant—and in their militancy very different from those who first followed Washington. Yet each, including the Muslims, was—and is—an uplift organization: giving a sense of identity to downtrodden followers, a measure of importance, lessons in proper decorum and, above all, a purpose for living. Thus, it has been argued, "Washington's separatist ideology functioned both as a mechanism of accommodation to American racism and as a device for overcoming it."[11] The latter point was not at all apparent to his critics who saw accommodation and separatism as blind alleys that would merely give support to segregationist sentiment.

The Burden of Responsibility

Washington's most vocal critic was W. E. B. Du Bois, Harvard graduate, professor of sociology at Atlanta University, and cofounder of the then radical Niagara movement, an all-black organization set up explicitly to oppose Washington and his program. Taking an entirely different tack, the radicals argued that the burden of redressing grievances was not the black's but the white's and that the latter should be made to change. (It should be pointed out that on certain issues Du Bois and Washington did agree. Both believed firmly in the idea of racial solidarity. Indeed, Du Bois the integrationist went considerably further than Washington in proposing a Pan-African movement to unite black people everywhere.)

Washington and his followers were able to stop the Niagara movement of 1905 from getting started, but they were unable to do the same with its successor, the National Association for the Advancement of Colored People, founded in 1909, "with the announced goal of fighting for the black man's constitutional rights and the undeclared aim of curbing Booker T. Washington's power."[12]

The NAACP, as it came to be called, was an organization of black and white civil-rights-minded citizens who sought to fight the battle for justice through education, politics, and, especially, litigation. Closely associated with the organization was the Legal Defense and Education Fund, which, supported by the general membership, brought numerous suits against various parties accused of violating the Constitution through adherence to state and local statutes upholding segregation.

The lawyers were skilled and persistent and, in time, one barrier after another was to fall as the Supreme Court ruled in favor of the complainants. The culmination of the legal movement came in 1954 when in a unanimous decision the high court overturned the old *Plessy* ruling and proclaimed that separate could never be equal. Many black and many white integrationists believed that the critical point had been passed and that rapid compliance with the court's mandate for "desegregation with all deliberate speed" would toll the death knell of segregation in the United States. They were wrong.

Alternatives

As far back as the 1920s a number of black intellectuals had begun to question the advisability of following the slow and deliberate course of taking cases up through the courts while, as they saw it, black people were suffering without letup. Some, even then, questioned any piecemeal approach of attacking one institution—for example, the education system—instead of trying to alter the entire social order. Such men as A. Philip Randolph and other socialists branded men like Du Bois as "a handkerchief head," that is, a hat-in-hand Negro. In *The Messenger*, which Randolph edited, the NAACP was attacked as a bourgeois organization and an alternative, a workingman's movement, was advocated. With capitalism defined as the enemy of all poor people, Randolph sought to rally blacks and whites. He did not succeed. As Meier and Rudwick point out, his ideological rhetoric was too much for many blacks to comprehend; his integrationist appeal was too much for many white workers to stomach.[13] (It should be noted that Du Bois shifted increasingly to the left in his later years and became a member of the Communist Party in Ghana where he had gone to live the remainder of his life and where he died at the age of 93. Randolph is still alive and, ironically, is branded by the latest group of militant blacks as "a handkerchief head" for holding to the notion of a unified—black and white—attack on the system.)

Black Zionism

Randolph never reached the urban masses to which he appealed. Marcus Garvey did. The Jamaican founder of the Universal Negro Improvement Association in 1914, Garvey decried the integrationists as naïve for seeking to win concessions from a society that was and would always be racist.

Instead he favored the development of separate institutions in the United States and, in time, a return to Africa, the "Black Zion." He and his followers opposed miscegenation and extolled everything that was black. The attractiveness of this movement was noted by one sociologist as follows:

The Garvey movement was based on good psychology. It made the downtrodden lower class Negro feel like somebody among white people who said they were nobody. It gave the crowd an opportunity to show off in colors, parades, and self-glorification.[14]

For a time the UNIA had great appeal, but neither Garvey nor his followers ever got to Africa. He was eventually denounced by prominent leaders of the black community, barred from bringing his people to Liberia (which was seen as the African Zion), and finally indicted and sentenced to a prison term for using the mails to defraud in selling shares of stock for his "Black Star Ship Line." What had once been an important movement of black nationalism ended when Garvey was deported in 1927 as an undesirable alien.

But Garvey left a rich legacy. In fact, his banner of red, green, and black is, once again, being seen in the United States. Many a young black nationalist now proudly wears a button with the three colors—the first represents life's blood, the second is for hope, and the third is for the color of his skin.

The Civil Rights Movement

In the 1930s new organizations emerged, many of these seeking to find alliances with New Deal agencies that were more favorably inclined to the plight of black citizens than their predecessors had been. Again criticism of the NAACP arose. Young leaders such as Ralph Bunche felt that the organization was not sufficiently radical to deal with the pressing needs created by the depression and the persistence of discrimination throughout the country.

During World War II two movements arose that presaged

what was to come in the following decade. The first was A. Philip Randolph's March on Washington movement, which pressured President Roosevelt into issuing the famous Executive Order 8802, establishing the first federal Fair Employment Practices Commission. As Meier and Rudwick report:

Even without enforcement powers, the FEPC set a precedent for treating fair employment practice as a civil right. The short-lived March on Washington Movement prefigured future trends in three ways: (1) it was an explicitly all-black organization; (2) it based its strategy on mass action by the urban slum dwellers; (3) it concentrated on economic problems.[15]

The second significant movement of the era was the Congress of Racial Equality, the first of several new civil rights organizations that gained prominence by their efforts to accelerate desegregation through nonviolent direct action. CORE began in 1942. James Farmer, then Race Relations Secretary of the Fellowship of Reconciliation, suggested the founding of an organization devoted to the use of "relentless non-cooperation, economic boycotts and civil disobedience," to fight for racial equality. A sit-in at a Chicago restaurant that same year led to the founding of the Chicago Committee on Racial Equality. Out of that organization CORE was born.

In the late 1940s radical-pacifist CORE was sponsoring sit-ins and freedom rides in the North and in Virginia, North Carolina, Kentucky, and Tennessee. And it was CORE which sponsored the integrated bus rides into Alabama in 1961 which ended in the beating of many of the participants. Those trips may have been a turning point, for, in the years to follow, CORE, an organization that had prided itself on its color-blindness, an organization whose membership was for a long time two-thirds white, turned away from the course of integration and toward the building of racial consciousness. In time its founder Farmer was to give way to Floyd McKissick, who, in turn, was followed by the more nationalistic Roy Ennis.

A third new civil rights movement arose from the highly successful bus boycott in Montgomery, Alabama, in 1956. A young minister named Martin Luther King, Jr., founded an organization called the Southern Christian Leadership Conference. Within a few short years he became the leader and the symbol of nonviolent direct action in the United States. From community to community he and his followers, including Rev. Ralph David Abernathy, who was to become his successor, took their nonviolent campaign. People from many parts of the country joined in marches on the bastions of segregation, marches designed to prove black men could walk with pride even in the face of "redneck" opposition. These committed young men and women followed their leader, turned the other cheek, and, all too often, got their skulls cracked open.

In 1960 a fourth movement began at a lunch counter in Greensboro, North Carolina, when a group of black students decided to defy the proprietor who refused to serve them. The sit-ins of young people spread from town to town and, with the backing of the Reverend King, the Student Nonviolent Coordinating Committee was founded to coordinate such activities. Within a year, however, it severed ties with SCLC, claiming that the parent organization was too cautious. Within five years, the meaning of the acronym SNICK (for SNCC) changed from Student Nonviolent Coordinating Committee to Student National Coordinating Committee, eschewing its previous stances of nonviolence and integration. It, too, was a portent.

But, in 1963, before the break was complete, the old guard and the new—including A. Philip Randolph, Roy Wilkins of the NAACP, Whitney Young, Jr., of the Urban League, James Farmer of CORE, Martin Luther King of SCLC, and some but not all of the SNCC leadership—joined forces to lead a massive march on Washington. To many, it was the culmination of years of struggle. To most of those who were there, it was a day of rededication, a day of hope, a day of dreams fulfilled—or about to be.

From the steps of the Lincoln Memorial, in a powerful and impressive voice, Martin Luther King gave his often repeated speech:

I say to you today, my friends, that in spite of the difficulties and frustrations of the moment, I still have a dream. It is a dream deeply rooted in the American dream.

I have a dream that one day this nation will rise up and live out the true meaning of its creed: "We hold these truths to be self-evident: that all men are created equal."

I have a dream that one day on the red hills of Georgia that sons of former slaves and the sons of former slaveowners will be able to sit down together at the table of brotherhood.

I have a dream that one day even the state of Mississippi, a desert state sweltering with the heat of injustice and oppression, will be transformed into an oasis of freedom and justice.

I have a dream that my four little children will one day live in a nation where they will not be judged by the color of their skin but the content of their character . . .

He went on depicting his dream of a new America and ending with the following words:

When we let freedom ring, when we let it ring from every village and every hamlet, from every state and every city, we will be able to speed up that day when all of God's children, black men and white men, Jews and Gentiles, Protestants and Catholics, will be able to join hands and sing in the words of that old Negro spiritual, "Free at last! Free at last! Thank God Almighty, we are free at last!"[16]

Black Power

By the time of emancipation's centennial (and, for some, before), it was quite evident to many outside observers and to many of the movements' workers that neither apolitical black-wardness nor soul-less militancy could turn the tide of racism, so deep did it flow.[17] Since there was little likelihood that they could really go it alone and even less that they could (or would) ever turn white, new black leaders argued that their people must learn (or relearn) both to take pride in themselves and to become political activists. They had to hark to what Frederick Douglass had prescribed a hundred years before the Student Nonviolent Coordinating Committee was born:

Those who profess to favor freedom yet deprecate agitation are men who want crops without plowing up the ground; they want rain without thunder and lightning. They want the ocean without the awful roar of its many waters. . . . Power concedes nothing without demand. It never did and it never will. Find out just what any people will quietly submit to and you have found out the exact measure of injustice and wrong which will be imposed upon them, and these will continue till they are resisted with either words or blows, or with both. The limits of tyrants are prescribed by the endurance of those whom they oppress.[18]

And Black Power did, in fact, begin as a movement of words, impassioned words, exhorting poor sharecroppers to exercise their franchise. But this was not enough. Intimidation and threats raised the ire of the civil rights workers and turned many black pacifists into soldiers while turning away many white allies. The code of Thoreau and Gandhi was being replaced by the law of Hammurabi—much as Frederick Douglass had suggested.

For years, Negro leaders and their white allies had counseled patience and fortitude. Until quite recently their authority went unchallenged, for it was widely felt that the liberal integrationists (black and white) were on the right path. The civil-rights campaign in the late 1950s and the early 1960s and the bills passed by Congress in their wake seemed, to some at least, positive proof of the efficacy of nonviolent direct action. But as many of the victories proved Pyrrhic, as tensions mounted between black field workers who saw radical pacifism as a tactic and whites for whom it was a way of life, as the Vietnam War syphoned off funds that (it was said) would have been earmarked for ghetto reconstruction, and, most of all, as the relative deprivation of black people became more apparent, the climate shifted. The movement went sour and the old coalitions began to break apart.

Unquestionably, the urban riots were also an exacerbating factor. Many whites, who had begun to feel some sense of sympathy with the embattled civil rights workers or who, at least, were talking of "giving Negroes their due," grew increasingly fearful—and hostile—as they saw the flames of Rochester and

Watts and Detroit on their television sets or, in some cases, from their upstairs windows. Charges and countercharges, cries of duplicity on one hand and corruption on the other, shouts of "burn, baby, burn" and "get the honkies" mixed with "send them back to Africa."

Given the disillusionment, the fear, and the persistence of institutionalized segregation, and, especially, given the fact that little was being done to satisfy those poorest blacks whose expectations had suddenly begun to rise, it is not surprising that the hymn "We Shall Overcome" was replaced—literally and figuratively—with the call for "Black Power."

The new mood began to reach out and envelop the unorganized black masses, particularly in the northern ghettos where few meaningful communal institutions existed around which people could rally and where even the oratory of Martin Luther King could not arouse their residents. Moreover, the focus began to shift away from integration and toward the more basic matter of "getting it together."

Half a century ago, E. Franklin Frazier said that "if the masses of Negroes can save their self-respect and remain free of hate, so much the better. But . . . I believe, it would be better for the Negro's soul to be seared with hate than dwarfed by self-abasement. . . ."[19] Again it was being argued that there is a psychosocial need for black people to call the Man to task rather than to accept and internalize second-class status and all that it means. As William H. Grier and Price Cobbs have suggested, there has long been (and remains) among blacks an almost desperate need to find a sense of both positive self-hood and of meaningful people-hood.[20]

To accomplish these goals has meant that black leadership would have to change. Whites had to be eased or pushed out of positions of dominance to make room for those who could more easily identify with, and be identified with, the black masses. And the new leaders had to prove to their followers that *black* was the symbol of "light" at the end of their tunnel.

As the Black Panthers gained notoriety, those in the traditional organizations changed too. SNCC became more militant.

CORE turned away from its original stance of integration in favor of black consciousness. The Urban League and the NAACP sounded more militant even while trying to assuage the anxiety of many white liberals. The Southern Christian Leadership Conference continued fighting its battles for jobs and freedom but also began forming uneasy coalitions with other embattled minority groups. Despite differences in symbol (the clenched fist or the double bar of equality), in slogan, and in style, pride and protest were joined and, for many, it had become a time to be *black*.

The Second Reconstruction

There is a real question as to whether the new turn of events will facilitate the growth of genuine and relevant organizations with power to effect both psychological and political changes in the black communities and to make the need of those communities apparent to the rest of society, or whether the second Reconstruction will end in tragic failure like the first. Those who take the former position are quick to invoke the model offered by other minority groups. They say that, in essence, Black Power is not an attempt to destroy society, but to provide a basis for pride and representation for those lacking it; the same kind of pride and recognition that the English, the Italians, the Irish, the Jews, and other minority groups have had in themselves, using, among other tactics, a similar creative distortion of history. Black Power is also seen as the basis for the formation of institutions that can implement organized actions to aid in the ascent up the ladder. Those who hold this view suggest that the ethnicity that already exists among black people must be strengthened and embellished, and that once again ethnic power must become a factor to reckon with. They say that this is really nothing new—it is "as American as apple pie."

But there are others who argue that the zeal to expose everybody to released rage may well be self-defeating, for few black leaders will be able to translate the language of estrangement into a meaningful remedy that will cure the disease of racism without killing the patient.[21] There appears to be no easy way out of this dilemma. Old techniques have failed because they very rarely reached those who needed help most. New techniques (as advocated by the black militants and others) will fail, it is said, because they will inevitably alienate the very people who are most needed in abetting the transition— concerned liberals in the schoolrooms and universities, on planning boards, in the government, and the like. Simon Lazarus goes so far as to suggest that many well-meaning liberals, ignoring the innuendoes of a genuine separatist rebellion, often tend to give Black Power a familiar pluralistic face and, believing their own propaganda, have begun to offer Black Power (or their version of Black Power) "both to whites on their right and to blacks on their left." He goes on to say that ". . . convinced the black leaders *should* not adopt systematic violence as a tactic, liberals have assumed they *will* not adopt it."[22] The point is well taken, especially in view of the tensions extant in American society, on the campuses, and particularly in the ghettos. But the point should not be exaggerated. The majority of black Americans, including many in the slums, still wish to join the society rather than to turn it upside down. And, for many, Black Power (read "bloc power") is still seen as a way to get in. How long blacks will feel that way is highly speculative. The potential for independence movements to break out of the colonized status, as Robert Blauner suggests, is substantial.[23]

It is becoming more and more difficult to predict what will happen on the racial front in the coming years. A few years ago the past was used as a fairly accurate guide to the future and predictions were usually based on a critical assessment of available information. The latter provided a fairly clear picture that relatively few whites were about to support any efforts to effect changes unless they were pressured into it. In celebrating the passage of the Civil-Rights Acts of 1960, 1964, 1965, and even of 1968, it was easy to forget that these victories were primarily the result of protest marches, boycotts, demonstrations, and threats of disruption. Such activities, it seems, did more to bring about changes in the status quo than all the pious platitudes from segregated pulpits or the admonitions of the specialists in urban affairs and poverty.

The federal government, dedicated to opening New Frontiers and making a Great Society and dedicated to waging war on poverty, became so bogged down in Vietnam that it could offer only monumental legislation and modest programs for carrying it out—programs offered to show good faith but construed by many as being proof of continued tokenism which contributed to the overall "minus-sum game."

Minus-sum games are those, as Aaron Wildavsky explains, in which *every* player leaves the contest worse off than when he entered:

> Promise a lot; deliver a little. . . . Lead people to believe they will be much better off, but let there be no dramatic improvement. . . . Have middle-class civil servants hire upper-class student radicals to use lower-class Negroes as a battering ram against the existing political systems; then complain that people are going around disrupting things and chastise local politicians for not cooperating with those out to do them in. . . . Feel guilty about what has happened to black people; tell them you are surprised they have not revolted before; express shock and dismay when they follow your advice.[24]

Those who warned about the dangers of such games were often told that the problem was being exaggerated or that they were "nervous Nellies" inadvertently disrupting the cause of civil rights by trying to keep everybody's expectations within certain realistic bounds. And now many other voices have been added to those who decry sociologists and political scientists for their reluctance to take more radical stands.

The entry of large numbers of such spokesmen mounting the stumps from Harlem to Watts and the campus lecture halls from Boston to Berkeley, and writing in old Negro papers and the new black ones—has brought about many changes in the black mood and the black movement. The crystal balls are far cloudier ("Whitey doesn't know what we're going to do next"

—and he doesn't) and the emanations from the computers are consequently less reliable. In retrospect, the emergence of the Black Power movement appears to have been an almost inevitable next stage for those who were called "darker brethren" but were treated like hired hands by most Americans. What lies in prospect, however, for black—and indeed, for all Americans—cannot be foreseen. There are no "musts" in human history.

Now that many black Americans themselves are questioning the way their past has been interpreted by generations of scholars, and now that they increasingly claim that no white man can legitimately speak for them, it is difficult for anyone, black or white, to separate fancy from fact. But perhaps this situation itself (as had been predicted by a few observers) is an "inevitability" of the largely shameful historical record.

A genuine dilemma faces historians and sociologists who believe, on the one hand, that there is a powerful psychological need for black Americans to establish a past at which they can look with pride and advocate, on the other hand, the continuing search for the truth about race relations, whatever may be revealed.[25] But one thing seems to be quite clear: As David Riesman has suggested, to understand black narcissism is one thing, while to feed this sentiment in a gesture of white masochism is dangerous for black and white alike.[26] It is, in current vernacular, "to go from one bag into another."[27]

Still, in the gloomy present there are a few hopeful signs. One of them, perhaps the most important, is a growing realization that the grievances of black Americans are legitimate: Their schools are poorer, their neighborhoods are shabbier, their rents are higher, their jobs are scarcer. At least some teachers, community leaders, landlords, and businessmen are coming to recognize that they have a critical role to play in abetting the transition from dependence to independence. They know that the road is rocky and the risks are great. But failure to act now means even greater dangers in the future.

There is also growing (if reluctant) recognition of the necessity of black Americans to assert their own dignity and to achieve full social recognition as members of the national community. This means a willingness to accept the fact that the demand for equality means equal time as well. The black experience must be seen as part and parcel of the American experience, which itself, of course, is filled with tales of heroic achievements, resurrected "fests" from far-off nations, and the echoes of a hundred cultures resounding in what some would claim is an orchestration of rhythms—and blues.

NOTES

1. See Ruby Jo Kennedy Reeves, "Single or Triple Melting Pot: Intermarriage Trends in New Haven, 1870–1940," *American Journal of Sociology,* 49 (January 1944), 331-339; and Will Herberg, *Protestant–Catholic–Jew* (New York: Doubleday, 1955).

2. James Baldwin, *Nobody Knows My Name: More Notes of a Native Son* (New York: Dial Press, 1961).

3. See, for example, James Baldwin, *Go Tell It on the Mountain* (New York: Alfred A. Knopf, 1952).

4. *The Autobiography of Malcolm* X (New York: Grove Press, 1964), pp. 169-190.

5. See, for example, Eldridge Cleaver, *Soul on Ice* (New York: McGraw-Hill, 1968), p. 46.

6. Norman Podhoretz, "My Negro Problem—and Ours," *Commentary* (February 1963), pp. 93-101.

7. This sentiment was expressed by Ron Karenga at a Human Rights Conference at Brotherhood-in-Action, New York City, May 5, 1967. He made similar statements in Los Angeles and elsewhere.

8. Booker T. Washington, "The Atlantic Exposition Address, September-1895," from *Up from Slavery* (New York: Doubleday, Page and Company, 1901), pp. 218-225.

9. As reprinted in August Meier, Elliott Rudwick, and F. L. Broderick (eds.), *Black Protest Thought in the Twentieth Century,* 2nd ed. (Indianapolis: Bobbs-Merrill, 1971), p. 6.

10. *Ibid.*, p. 7.

11. August Meier and Elliott Rudwick, "Radicals and Conservatives: Black Protest in Twentieth-Century America," in Peter I. Rose (ed.), *Old Memories, New Moods* (New York: Atherton, 1970), p. 124.

12. *Ibid.*, p. 125.

13. *Ibid.*, p. 127.

14. Maurice Davie, *Negroes in American Society* (New York: McGraw-Hill, 1949), p. 440.

15. Meier and Rudwick, *op. cit.*, p. 130.

16. Martin Luther King, Jr., "I Have a Dream," *SCLC Newsletter*, 12 (September 1963), pp. 5, 8.

17. See, for example, James Farmer, *Freedom, When?* (New York: Random House, 1965); and Stokely Carmichael and Charles V. Hamilton, *Black Power: The Politics of Liberation in America* (New York: Vintage, 1967).

18. The quotation is from a West Indian emancipation speech delivered by Douglass in 1857. It appears in Carmichael and Hamilton, *op. cit.*, p. x.

19. This is also expressed most poignantly by Richard Wright. See his "Foreword," in St. Clair Drake and Horace Cayton, *Black Metropolis* (New York: Harcourt, Brace, 1945).

20. William H. Grier and Price M. Cobbs, *Black Rage* (New York: Basic Books, 1968), esp. pp. 152-167.

21. See, for example, Lewis M. Killian, *The Impossible Revolution?: Black Power and the American Dream* (New York: Random House, 1968), esp. Chap. 7.

22. Simon Lazarus, "Domesticating Black Power," *New Republic,* June 8, 1968, pp. 37-38.

23. Robert Blauner, "Internal Colonialism and Ghetto Revolt," *Social Problems*, 16 (Spring, 1969), 393-408.

24. Aaron Wildavsky, "Recipe for Violence," *New York*, 1 (May 1968), 28-36.

25. See, for example, Melvin M. Tumin, "In Dispraise of Loyalty," *Social Problems*, 15 (Winter, 1968), 267-279.

26. Personal conversation with David Riesman, Amherst, Massachusetts, May 18, 1968.

27. See Bayard Rustin, "The Failure of Black Separatism," *Harpers,* 240 (January 1970), pp. 25-34.

EIGHT

THE RESURGENCE
OF ETHNICITY

Social Physics

One of the basic laws of physics is that every action has an equal and opposite reaction. The laws of society are not that simple. Yet, it is safe to say that in social physics (a label the founder of sociology, Auguste Comte, wanted to use for his discipline), there are numerous examples of changes provoking reactions. This is certainly the case in the area of racial and ethnic relations and nowhere is this process clearer than in the responses to the increasing flow of immigrants by earlier American settlers and the reaction of minorities to their treatment in this country.

In the earlier chapters we examined these phenomena and sought to put into context the views of various groups and individuals as they experienced life in the United States. In Chapter Seven we focused on the struggle of many blacks in dealing with two basic problems that plague all minority peoples: the problem of identity and the problem of community. We indicated some of the principal sources of opposition that they faced and the ways they sought to deal with their opponents. Most of this opposition came from what Seymour Martin Lipset calls the "once-hads," that is, persons in positions of power who fear or recognize that they are losing it.[1] In the present chapter we will concentrate on reactions to such movements as Black Power by those once removed from the centers of power, the white ethnics. The latter are not all "never-hads," although some of them claim such status, but they are people who in the past have also "enjoyed" subordinate status, even, in many instances, minority status.

Feeding the Backlash

Placing black people in a different light, giving them new models to admire and to emulate, offering the opportunity to say "We're somebodies, too," have certainly helped to change the self conceptions of many black Americans. Richard Wright once wrote, "White man, listen!" Clearly whites are now "listening," and what is heard and seen and felt has affected their attitudes and behavior.

Some whites welcome the fact that the Black Power advocates and Third World allies have seriously challenged the system that they feel kept many in servitude, perpetuated racism, and took a horrendous toll in human costs. Some are delighted that black assertion has resulted in the foreseeable end of old stereotypes and of deference. Some are confused because they thought the struggle was for integration (or, as noted in Chapter Three, for assimilation) and now see that goal thwarted by the changed tactics and strategy advocated by many leaders—they cannot understand why other blacks do not call a halt to the drift apart. Many blacks are similarly confused. Some are frightened because they simply cannot predict what will happen next. ("Do they *really* mean guerrilla warfare?") Many are angry—angry because they feel that they are being asked or told to pay for the damage they believe was caused by others.

There are many indications of the changes to which those in each of the categories described above are responding. All clearly recognize the profound differences between blacks in the days before the latest shift in orientation and after. All had known protest before; they had known about Black Nationalism. But, as discussed in Chapter Seven, they had not seen the issues joined—until recently. Now they hear demands for a general reexamination of American history to put the black experience into a more balanced light, to get rid of stereotypic portrayal of black people, to prove to others—and to themselves—that black is also beautiful. They see a new swagger in the step, a new assurance in the swagger. They see personal changes, both cosmetic and sartorial. "Processed" hair has been replaced by an Afro; clothes associated with whitey or with the ghetto have been replaced by dashikis and other garb from Africa.

The radio blares soul music at prime time. The television networks scramble for more black actors and actresses and present more programs on "The Problem." The black trend is evident elsewhere: on the streets, on the campuses, in Black Studies Departments, in Black Cultural Centers, in political organizations, both local and national. The first Black Political Convention was held in Gary, Indiana in the spring of 1972, foreshadowing the implementation of the McGovern reforms during the Democratic Party's Miami convention the following summer. "Blacks," said one observer, "were suddenly everywhere." They got there, it should be stressed, through hard work, concerted pressure, and sometimes by demanding special and categorical treatment.

These developments, most especially the last, have had a profound effect, sometimes bringing about what appears to be "an equal and opposite reaction." The new ground rules set up in response to black demands, and the demands of other non-white minorities, have significantly changed the basic premise that many liberals fought long to establish and to which many other Americans, especially those of immigrant stock, subscribed: the idea that every individual must be judged on his or her merits "regardless of race, creed, color, or national origin." Group rights or class rights are now being demanded as recompense for past injustices. Equality of placement is being sought to replace equality of opportunity for that placement. That the issue is exceedingly complicated—involving, for example, the serious question of whether an altogether equal race is possible in the face of structurally guaranteed cultural, social, and political handicaps—does not lessen the important fact that the rules of the game have been changed. And this change, at bottom, is where much of the current backlash is focused.

Affirmative Action and Quotas

Commenting on this change of strategy and, in turn, of policy —as it is responded to by sympathetic power brokers or vulnerable governmental agencies or frightened managers, principals, union leaders, politicians, and college admission boards— Daniel Boorstin recently published a facetious essay. Citing college admission boards, Boorstin suggests that if the current trend were to be followed to its logical conclusion, the I.Q. and other such tests would be abandoned as criteria for academic admission and would be replaced by an "E.Q.," an Ethnic Quotient.[2] This would mean that students and eventually teachers and their subject matter would have to be apportioned strictly according to background. There would be so many blacks and so many whites; so many Jews and so many Catholics—these to be further subdivided according to whether they were children or grandchildren of Italians or Irishmen, Slavs or Slovaks. (Fractional men, as Vance Bourjaily once called people like himself,[3] would prove difficult to judge. What, for example, would one do with an application from a modern-day Fiorello La Guardia, that half-Italian, half-Jewish Protestant mayor of New York? Boorstin offers an answer: give him so many points for each of his traits in proportion to their representativeness in the overall population and make sure, of course, that his curriculum is balanced in similar fashion!)

What Boorstin lampooned a few years ago has become a very real issue and it goes far beyond the campus. Indeed many of the strongest advocates of *affirmative action*, the phrase used to denote weighting the balance in favor of the minority applicant, are finding it increasingly difficult to implement their new policies without exacerbating resistance by those who feel that special treatment and open enrollment and the establishment of minima are designed only for certain segments of the population . . . which, for obvious reasons, they are. And even if what some call benign quotas are applied across the board, certain groups will have to lose. Many Jews, for example, are especially sensitive to this issue—they are currently "overrepresented" in university teaching, law, and medicine, professions in which, ironically, not long ago they were often limited by *numerus clausus* that specified how many Jews would be permitted to enter. (To gain admission to college or university they frequently had to have higher qualifications than other applicants.) Now they fear that in forcing institutions of higher learning to accept at least a minimum percentage of the members of all groups in the overall population, their own numbers would be severely cut. Many see this trend as racism in reverse. And some have brought suit. In the Spring of 1973 complaints were filed against several schools and universities (including the School of Education, University of Massachusetts and University of Washington Law School) for discriminating against "non-minority" applicants.

Jews are not the only ones uneasy about the pressure to right recognized wrongs by accepting a change in the ground rules for "making it" into the university, onto public school faculties, or entering a profession, or getting a job. Others feel the pinch too. While, at the present time, many tend to be more worried about jobs and neighborhoods than *numerus clausus* in college placement, even here, not a few white working-class parents have begun to ask why their children cannot obtain special scholarships to elite schools for which, like many blacks and Puerto Ricans and other nonwhites, they are admittedly "equally unqualified"—at least according to traditional criteria.

There are, as Ralph Levine has so poignantly related, numerous poor and working-class whites who have spent their own lives struggling to get out and keep out of poverty, to survive in the urban jungle, to give something more than they were given to their children. Though he got out, Levine's mother never did. Like many others she was "left behind in Brooklyn."[5]

Looking Backward

We will remember that like nonwhite minorities, Jewish and Catholic ethnics also have had to deal with special problems in this society. Ralph Levine's mother—and Vance Bourjaily's for that matter—were among the wretched refuse Emma Lazarus described in her famous poem cited earlier.[6] As noted in Chapter Two, these people were not always welcomed with equanimity. And many Americans, far from sympathetic, agreed with the sentiments of Madison Grant, who in his racist tract *The Passing of the Great Race* (1916) wrote:

These new immigrants were no longer exclusively members of the Nordic race as were the earlier ones who came of their own impulse to improve their social conditions. The transportation lines advertised America as a land flowing with milk and honey and the European governments took the opportunity to unload upon careless, wealthy and hospitable America the sweepings of their jails and asylums. The result was that the new immigration . . . contained a large and increasing number of the weak, the broken and the mentally crippled of all races drawn from the lowest stratum of the Mediterranean basin and the Balkans, together with hordes of the wretched, submerged populations of the Polish Ghettos. Our jails, insane asylums and alms-houses are filled with this human flotsam and the whole tone of American life, social, moral and political has been lowered and vulgarized by them.[7]

Thus the newcomers found that many were hostile to them. They suffered from discrimination, often based upon erroneous notions about their mysterious ways or their allegedly undemocratic tendencies. Even after the Immigration Laws of 1921 and 1924 had closed the Golden Door (largely in response to widespread antiforeign sentiment), the prejudices remained. "Old stock Americans have become restless," announced a Ku Klux Klan pamphlet in 1924, ". . . They are dissatisfied with the denaturalizing forces at work in the country. There is something wrong and the American people know there is something wrong, and they are talking among themselves as to where the trouble is."[8] The tract continued:

They know the arrogant claims of the Papacy to temporal power and that the Romish church is not in sympathy with American ideals and institutions. They know that Rome is in politics, and that she often drives the thin edge of her wedge with a muffled hammer; they have seen the results of her activities in other lands.

• • •

These old stock Americans are coming to believe that Jews dominate the economic life of the nation, while the Catholics are determined to dominate the political and religious life. And they have apprehensions that the vast alien immigration is at the root an attack upon Protestant religion with its freedom of conscience, and is therefore a menace to American liberties. . . .[9]

And even those who were themselves anathema to the Klan sometimes echoed their anti-Catholic sentiments. The black educator Booker T. Washington is reported to have considered Sicilian sulfur miners deserving of their fate as human beasts of toil—"They are superstitious Catholics who eat garlic."[10] According to Everett and Helen Hughes, "Mr. Washington passed upon them the judgment of a middle-class American Protestant; quite naturally so, for that is what he was."[11]

We are again reminded that the European immigrants were often victims of discrimination and subjects of prejudicial thoughts and sentiments that set them apart from the "WASPs" and sometimes, as one wag once put it, from certain "BASPs" (Black Anglo-Saxon Protestants) as well.

On Being an Ethnic

Hegel once said that "the eyes of others are the mirrors in which we learn our identities." A student of the author once put it even more pointedly: "I am," she said, "what others think I am." For many decades the eyes of others looked down not only upon blacks and Chicanos and the American

Indians, but also upon Jews and Irish and those other ethnics to whom Michael Novak sardonically refers as "PIGS": Poles, Italians, Greeks, and Slavs.[12]

Novak claims to speak for many children and grandchildren of eastern and southern Europe whose relatives left the Old Country to seek a better life in the new and often found it. They also found that they were outsiders and, in many ways, were to remain so despite the fervor of their patriotism and their willingness to prove it. They were, to many, "peasants," looked down upon not only by WASPs who saw them as socially religiously, even racially inferior, but also by more than a few intellectuals of varying backgrounds themselves who depicted them as unwashed, uneducated, uncouth—in general, culturally inferior.

The legacy of this kind of attitude still lingers; sometimes it is expressed in far from subtle terms. To Novak and many of those about whom he writes, there is more than a kernel of truth in Spiro Agnew's remark about that "effete corps of impudent snobs." The latter are the kind of people about whom Ralph Levine writes:

Those who appear most willing to sacrifice time and effort in a "good" cause, whatever the cause, prove invariably to be those who can retreat to upper middle class sanctuary and rejoin the "establishment" whenever the need arises. Such [individuals] seem either unable or unwilling to recognize a simple truth; that people considerably lower (although not the lowest) in the class structure, lack a similar sense of mastery and freedom, but rather are fighting desperately to achieve the sense of economic and social security which these [people] accept as their birthright.[13]

David Riesman summed up this sentiment when he wrote that some intellectuals "espouse a snobbery of topic which makes the interests of the semi-educated wholly alien to them—*more alien than the interests of the lower class.*"[14]

Riesman's words are italicized here because they underscore one of the main points made by those who look with some skepticism at the seemingly selective sensitivity of some of those intellectuals who write about America in general and intergroup relations in particular. White as well as black, they often appear to be unaware of differences in ethnic values, class-based orientations, and political concerns, especially of those who have not so long ago left the ghettos themselves. At least some pundits seem to share this myopia.

While many white ethnics have been more sympathetic to black aspirations than the current controversy might suggest, they have been primarily concerned with their own survival and success, concerns shared by most other Americans. What other Americans, at least those in the middle class who lived in better neighborhoods or suburban communities, did not share with many ethnics was the proximity to the black ghettos, a situation that, in time, was to place the latter in a difficult double-bind. They often found themselves forced to choose between moving or leaving what were, in effect, their urban villages. They had to face the fact that others in similar situations had become victims themselves in places where old neighborhoods, even stable slums, deteriorated into disaster areas marked by anomie and despair, by internal confusion and pent-up frustration, where the old-timers found themselves ready targets and convenient scapegoats for the newcomers.[15]

In pub and parlor the ethnics remonstrated about "the squeeze," about the insensitivity of the people uptown. They also complained about those whom they saw as threats to their safety and security. But even what was said was voiced within the confines of the community itself—"How can you say that, Harry, people won't understand?"

In recent years, however, after decades of public silence, spokesmen for increasing numbers of angry, frightened, frustrated, and seemingly abandoned people have begun to express their feelings. They have done it by supporting conservative candidates for political office both locally and nationally, by organizing neighborhood associations which some observers saw as northern equivalents of white citizens' councils, by playing on the growing resentment that others were feeling. Not only did all Americans hear what was being said, they began to read about

the sentiments in a spate of articles and books on ethnic Americans.[16]

Common themes run through many of these writings: The earlier immigrants faced great difficulties and obstacles, but they accepted the challenges and internalized the values of the wider society, values that were often quite alien to their own heritages. They knew camaraderie with kin and countrymen, their own people who understood them, respected them, and stood by them when others failed to do so. Indeed many had become more pridefully Irish or Polish or Italian or Greek than they had been "back home."[17] They knew what it meant to be helped by others in similar straits and how to use certain public institutions to advantage—especially the schools, political machines, and, eventually, the civil service. But what they also knew, and this is perhaps the most persistent theme, was that one could not ask for special favors because of background or by pleading "special conditions."

Given these sentiments, it is not surprising that many white ethnics reacted with astonishment at the seeming capitulation being made to demands by blacks and other nonwhites for group rights and privileges. "Nobody ever gave us that kind of treatment," they began saying. "Who in hell do they think they are?" "Why can't they be like us?" A growing resolve to get their own share arose. A sense of righteous indignation at being put down by those above them to satisfy the demands from below became more and more apparent, and more and more annoying. Many argued that they were loyal, decent, hard-working, God-fearing, and patriotic Americans who had had nothing to do with slavery or with segregation but were being forced to pay for the sins of other peoples' fathers.

The Challenge of the "Unmeltables"

The current scene provides many examples for the feeling of being had by others by members of white ethnic groups. Let one illustration suffice. In San Francisco a new word entered into the glossary of bureaucratic newspeak in the early part of the 1970s, "deselection." To meet new government guide-lines, certain school supervisors were removed from their positions and placed elsewhere in the system, to be replaced by members of "minorities"—that is, in this case, such nonwhites as black, Mexican, Japanese, and Chinese Americans. In the first month of the program many administrators, all white, were deselected. The merits of this new system are debatable and one can argue that somebody has to begin to pay. But the furor created is also quite understandable.

Episodes of this kind have encouraged one group after another to assume a position of *defensive pluralism* in which they reassert their old ties, stress their own earlier depriva-tions, and demand their own hearings and their own affirmative action plans. This development has already resulted in demands for Irish Studies, Jewish Studies, Polish Studies, and so on.

Thus there is a gnawing sense of frustration and bitterness among many Americans who have been, at best, only moder-ately successful and have received no special aid. They feel that the authorities are too willing to buy urban peace at their expense. They resent what Michael Lerner aptly calls the "respectable bigotry" of those who seem to love the poor (often at a distance) and champion the underdog but condemn the average white ethnic or middle American for his complacency, his ignorance, his lack of compassion, even for living in a "ticky-tacky" house and liking it; those who proclaim support for the Blackstone Rangers but have no sympathy for their victims, black as well as white.[18] And they are equally impatient with the "radical chic" displayed by many celebrities who appear to kowtow to militants, especially when the latter, in their view, are satisfying their own needs to appear magnanimous at relatively little cost to themselves. The comments of a steelworker, Mike Fitzgerald of Cicero, Illinois, reported by Studs Terkel, are illustrative:

Terkel: Does anger get you, bitterness?
Fitzgerald: No, not really. Somebody has to do it. If my kid ever goes to college, I just want him to realize that when I tell him somebody has to do it, I just want him to have a little bit of respect, to realize that his dad is one of those somebodies. This is why even on (muses)—yes, I guess, sure—on the black thing . . . (Sighs heavily) I can't really hate the colored fella that's working with me all day. The black intellectual I got no respect for. The white intellectual I got no use for. I got no use for the black militant who's gonna scream about 300 years of slavery to me while I'm busting my back. You know what I mean? I have one answer for that guy, Go see Rockefeller. See Harriman. See the people who've got the money. Don't bother me. We're in the same cotton field. So just don't bug me. . . .

It's very funny. It's always the rich white people who are screaming about racism. They're pretty well safe from the backlash. You ever notice it's always; go get the Klansman, go get the Hunkies, go get that Polack. But don't touch me, baby, 'cause my name is Prince John Lindsay. Park Avenue, Lake Shore Drive. They're never gonna get at 'em, baby, uh-uh.[19]

People like Mike Fitzgerald feel and express a backlash sentiment most strongly, old ethnics who, for a time, had begun to move up and away from seeing themselves solely in terms of their hyphenation. Since such people were often the first to be affected by the new policies, we have begun to witness a forceful reassertion of ethnicity in many white communities, even at the expense of class-based allegiances. As Glazer and Moynihan have recently noted:

> . . . ethnic identities have taken over some of the task of self-definition and in definition by others that occupational identities, particularly working-class identities, have generally played. The status of the worker has been downgraded; as a result, apparently, the status of being an ethnic, a member of an ethnic group, has been upgraded. . . . *Today, it may be better to be an Italian than a worker. Twenty years ago, it was the other way around.*[20]

The New Pluralism

Andrew Greeley recently has written that "the new consciousness of ethnicity [among white ethnics] is in part based on the fact that the blacks have legitimated cultural pluralism as it has perhaps never been legitimated before."[21] And this legitimation, we would add, has significantly altered a number of other aspects of American life. Not least is the fact that, once again, the issue of assimilation v. pluralism is being hotly debated in the universities, in the journals of opinion, in government circles, and, in some communities, in the streets.

There are those like Andrew Greeley and Murray Friedman who, despite certain misgivings, believe that the resurgence of ethnicity is highly functional for our society—because, in the end, America must remain what it has always been: a tissue of primordial ties.[22] Some writers, such as Peter Schrag and Michael Novak, go further. They argue that not only will blacks benefit from their newfound sense of consciousness but so too will the white ethnics, those who have suffered far too long under the cultural hegemony of "the WASP Establishment."[23]

Still other observers contend that reality is simply catching up with the dreamers, especially those who see everything in class terms. Thus, Irving Levine and Judith Herman write that there has not been much important change, save for the fact that the strains and divisions that have always existed are now being acknowledged by both social scientists and ethnics themselves:[24]

> In most of the cities where the white working class is ethnic—in the Northeast and Midwest particularly—common origin is reflected in distinctive neighborhoods. People tend to live near one another according to ethnic background, even "unto the fourth generation." For some, the choice is a conscious one, influenced by the presence of such institutions as the church. For others, the ethnic neighborhood is a convenience, maintaining some features of the extended family, lost (but yearned for) in more heterogeneous neighborhoods.
>
> Even suburbanization has not diminished the intensity of many ethnic neighborhoods. In many cases, what looks like an economics-based blue-collar suburb is in reality a community consisting of several ethnic enclaves. For instance, Long Beach, a Long Island town, has been described as "three worlds," Italian, Black, and Jewish—though to the outsider it may seem a "typical lower income suburban community."[25]

But, before accepting these views, we should note two—quite different—disclaimers, both dealing less with the substances of the analysis and more with the sympathy expressed for the tendency to advocate further mobilization or separation along ethnic lines. The first is that alluded to by both Glazer and Moynihan and Levine and Herman, that is, the extent to which ethnicity may become a mask to hide greater differences based upon social class.[26] Several sociologists believe that too much attention is given to ethnic feelings and too little to the sense of alienation of all who are relatively powerless in the context of the larger society. Their argument is that fostering ethnicity—of blacks or whites—serves mainly to keep them from uniting into a coalition of opponents to a repressive system. Foremost in the ranks of those who take this stand is the venerable socialist Bayard Rustin, who opposes both black nationalism and white ethnicity. Rustin wants the people to have power and believes that they will not achieve it by putting their special ethnic interests above more basic social and economic needs.[27]

The second critique comes from those liberal integrationists who have stood firm against the winds of change and have challenged the black militants and the new pluralists alike, for somewhat different reasons than those of Bayard Rustin. Most notable among those is Harold Isaacs who condemns what he sees as a "retribalization."[28] Reviewing Murray Friedman's volume *Overcoming Middle Class Rage*, which seeks to explain backlash politics and ethnic insularity, Isaacs writes:

> The two themes—on the Middle American as a harassed man and as an ethnic—are presented . . . as if they harmonize. They are in fact tunes beaten out by separate drummers who march down quite different roads. In effect, the appeal here to the Middle American is to depolarize on social issues and to repolarize ethnically.[29]

Referring to the older pluralists, particularly Horace Kallen and Randolph Bourne and their imagery of symphonic harmony, Isaacs warns against too high expectations. Modern symphonies often sound cacophonous! Thus: "This [repolarization along ethnic lines] may make beautiful music in the heads of some of these composers, but it has to be played out loud to hear what it actually sounds like."[30]

In the years to come, Americans will find out how it sounds —and, more important, what the new pluralism will mean.

NOTES

1. Seymour Martin Lipset, "Prejudice and Politics in the American Past and Present," in Charles Y. Glock and Ellen Siegelman (eds.), *Prejudice U.S.A.* (New York: Praeger, 1969), pp. 17-69.
2. Daniel Boorstin, "Ethnic Proportionalism: The 'E.Q.' and Its Uses," from *The Sociology of the Absurd* (New York: Simon and Schuster, 1970), pp. 25-35. See also Martin Mayer, "Higher Education for All? The Case of Open Admissions," *Commentary*, 45 (February 1973), pp. 37-47; and, "An Exchange on Open Admissions," *Commentary*, 45 (May 1973), pp. 4-24.
3. Vance Bourjaily, *Confessions of a Spent Youth* (New York: Dial

Press, 1952). See, especially, the chapter, "The Fractional Man."

4. See, for example, Pierre van den Berghe, "The Benign Quota: Panacea or Pandora's Box?," *The American Sociologist*, 6 (June 1971). Murray N. Rothbard, "The Quota System, In Short, Must Be Repudiated," *Intellectual Digest* (February 1973), 78, 80. See also Earl Raab, "Quotas by Any Other Name," *Commentary* (January 1972), 41-45; Bart Barnes, "Reverse Bias Alleged in College Hiring," *The Washington Post,* March 5, 1973.

5. Ralph Levine, "Left Behind in Brooklyn," in Peter I. Rose (ed.), *Nation of Nations* (New York: Random House, 1972), pp. 335-346.

6. Emma Lazarus, "The New Colossus," in *Poems* (Boston: Houghton Mifflin, 1889), pp. 202-203.

7. Madison Grant, *The Passing of the Great Race* (New York: Scribner, 1916). (Quoted from the 3rd ed., published in 1944, pp. 88-92, *passim.*)

8. *The Fiery Cross*, February 8, 1924.

9. *Ibid.*

10. The statement attributed to Washington was made by his friend and associate Robert E. Park. See Everett and Helen Hughes, *Where Peoples Meet* (New York: The Free Press, 1952), p. 10.

11. *Ibid.*

12. Michael Novak, *The Rise of the Unmeltable Ethnics* (New York: Macmillan, 1971).

13. Levine, *op. cit.*, p. 342.

14. As cited in Novak, *op. cit.*, p. 149.

15. See, for example Winston Moore, Charles P. Livermore, and George F. Galland, Jr., "Woodlawn: The Zone of Destruction," *The Public Interest* (Winter, 1973), 41-59; Norman Podhoretz, "My Negro Problem—and Ours," *Commentary,* 35 (February 1963), pp. 93-101; and Paul Wilkes, "As the Blacks Move In, the Ethnics Move Out," *The New York Times Magazine*, January 24, 1971, pp. 9-11, 48-50, 57.

16. See, for example, Ben Halpern, "The Ethnic Revolt," *Midstream,* January 1971, 3-16.

17. Nathan Glazer and Daniel Patrick Moynihan have pointed out that, in many ways, the American ethnic groups are a *new* social form, having no counterpart anywhere. See *Beyond the Melting Pot* (Cambridge: MIT Press, Second Edition, 1970), p. 16.

18. Michael Lerner, "Respectable Bigotry," *The American Scholar,* 38 (Autumn, 1969).

19. Studs Terkel, "A Steelworker Speaks," *Dissent* (Winter, 1972), pp. 12-13.

20. Glazer and Moynihan, *op. cit.,* pp. xxxiv-xxxv.

21. Andrew Greeley, *Why Can't They Be Like Us?* (New York:, Dutton, 1971), pp. 13-19.
22. Greeley, *op. cit.,* and Murray Friedman, ed., *Overcoming Middle Class Rage* (Philadelphia: Westminster, 1971).
23. See Peter Schrag, *Out of Place in America* (New York: Random House, 1970); and Michael Novak, *op. cit.*
24. Irving M. Levine and Judith Herman, "The Life of White Ethnics," *Dissent* (Winter, 1972), 286-294.
25. *Ibid.*, p. 290. The reference is to Bob Wyrick, "The Three Worlds of Long Beach," *Newsday*, October 18, 1969, p. 6w.
26. See Dennis H. Wrong, "How Important Is Social Class," *Dissent* (Winter, 1972), 278-285.
27. See, for example, Bayard Rustin, " 'Black Power' and Coalition Politics," *Commentary*, 42 (September 1966), 35-40; and "The Failure of Black Separatism," *Harpers,* 240 (January 1970), pp. 25-34.
28. Harold Isaacs, "The New Pluralists," *Commentary*, 53 (March 1972), pp. 75-79. See also Robert Alter, "A Fever of Ethnicity," *Commentary,* 53 (June 1972), pp. 68-73.
29. *Ibid.*, p. 75.
30. *Ibid.*

SELECTED BIBLIOGRAPHY

Close to one hundred and fifty books are listed here. Included are histories, textbooks, studies, essays, anthologies, and works of fiction. These volumes are a fraction of the many sources available to those who wish to study racial and ethnic relations in the United States—or any of its aspects—more closely. They are presented here to represent the breadth of work in the field and the variety of approaches used to explore racial and ethnic relations in the United States.

— Abrams, Charles. *Forbidden Neighbors.* New York: Harper & Row, 1955.
   One of a number of studies of discrimination in housing.

— Adorno, T. W., et al. *The Authoritarian Personality.* New York: Harper & Row, 1950.
   A study of prejudice and personality. The "F Scale" and others are introduced and used here.

— Allport, Gordon W. *The Nature of Prejudice.* Cambridge: Addison-Wesley, 1954.
   One of the most comprehensive and best known texts on the social psychology of prejudice.

— Asch, Sholem. *East River.* New York: Putnam, 1946.
   Ghetto life in New York during the early part of this century is the subject of this work.

Baldwin, James. *The Fire Next Time.* New York: Dial Press, 1963.

A prophetic essay about white oppression and black response.

———. *Go Tell It on the Mountain*. New York: Alfred A. Knopf, 1952.

Baldwin's first novel. A story based on his early life as a preacher's son living in Harlem.

———. *Nobody Knows My Name: More Notes of a Native Son*. New York: Dial Press, 1961.

Essays on *his* black experience by the famous novelist.

Baltzell, E. Digby. *The Protestant Establishment*. New York: Random House, 1964.

A study of the caste-line of privilege maintained by certain members of society which keeps others from access to power. Baltzell's special concern is with anti-Semitism.

Banton, Michael. *Race Relations*. New York: Basic Books, 1967.

Written by an English anthropologist, this volume offers a series of approaches to the study of race relations. It includes analyses of the American scene.

Bellow, Saul. *Mister Sammler's Planet*. New York: Viking, 1970.

A novel about a European-Jewish refugee in America and his attempts to understand racial conflict in the 1960s.

Berry, Brewton. *Race and Ethnic Relations*. 3rd ed. Boston: Houghton Mifflin, 1965.

A general introduction to the sociology of the subject.

Bettelheim, Bruno, and Morris Janowitz. *Social Change and Prejudice*. New York: Free Press, 1965.

Two books in one, the authors include the full text of their earlier study "The Dynamics of Prejudice" and a reassessment of that study two decades later.

Blalock, Hubert M., Jr. *Toward a Theory of Minority-Group Relations*. New York: Wiley, 1967.

An attempt to systematize theory in the study of racial and ethnic relations. Special attention to socio-economic factors, competition, and power.

Blauner, Robert M. *Racial Oppression in America*. New York: Harper & Row, 1972.

A series of essays in which the author presents his view of the United States as a racist society.

Bloom, Leonard, and Ruth Riemer. *Removal and Return.* Berkeley: University of California Press, 1949.

A study of the relocation of Japanese Americans during World War II and of their experiences after being released from internment camps.

Bogue, Donald. *The Population of the United States.* Glencoe: Free Press, 1959.

A demographer looks at American society and reports his facts, figures, and impressions.

Burma, John, ed. *Mexican-Americans in the United States.* New York: Schenkman, 1970.

A collection of readings.

Carmichael, Stokely, and Charles V. Hamilton. *Black Power: The Politics of Liberation.* New York: Vintage, 1967.

The former director of the Student Non-Violent Coordinating Committee and a political scientist examine the meaning of Black Power and the role it could play in American society.

Christie, Richard, and Marie Jahoda, eds. *Studies in Scope and Method of "The Authoritarian Personality."* Glencoe: The Free Press, 1954.

An examination and critique of the studies of "The Authoritarian Personality."

Cox, Oliver C. *Caste, Class and Race: A Study of Social Dynamics.* New York: Doubleday, 1948.

An examination of the economic basis of prejudice and racial oppression.

Cronin, E. D. *Black Moses.* Madison: University of Wisconsin Press, 1957.

A biography of Marcus Garvey and commentary on his Universal Negro Improvement Association.

Cruse, Harold. *The Crisis of the Negro Intellectual.* New York: William Morrow, 1967.

A cultural history and commentary on black writing, politics, and artistic involvement.

Cullen, Countee. *Color.* New York: Harper, 1925.

A book of poems on black life by a great black poet.

Dean, John P., and Alex Rosen, *A Manual of Intergroup Relations.* Chicago: The University of Chicago Press, 1955.

A short book on prejudice, discrimination and suggested ways for resolving intergroup tensions.

Di Donato, Pietro. *Christ in Concrete.* New York: Bobbs Merrill, 1939.

A poignant story about Italians in the building trades in the 1930s.

Dissent. Winter, 1972.

The entire issue is devoted to the working class. Of particular interest are papers on class and ethnicity.

Dixon, Vernon J., and Badi Foster, eds. *Beyond Black and White.* Boston: Little, Brown, 1971.

A collection of papers on the conflict between black and white Americans and a discussion of the concept of a di-unital approach to help to understand, then deal with it.

Dollard, John. *Caste and Class in a Southern Town.* New Haven: Yale University Press, 1937.

The famous study which examines the bases for prejudice in a southern community. Noted for the combination of Marxian and Freudian perspectives.

————, et al. *Frustration and Aggression.* New Haven: Yale University Press, 1939.

Psychological determinants of behavior are considered in this series of essays.

Drake, St. Clair, and Horace Cayton. *Black Metropolis.* New York: Harcourt, Brace, 1945.

A study of the black community of Chicago.

Du Bois, W. E. B. *The Souls of Black Folks, 1903.* (Reprinted in many editions.)

A classic portrait of Negro life by a great sociologist and famous black leader.

Duran, Livie Isauro, and H. Russell Bernard, eds. *Introduction to Chicano Studies.* New York: Macmillan, 1973.

A reader on the past, present, and future status of Mexican-Americans.

Ellis, John Tracy. *American Catholicism*. Chicago: University of Chicago Press, 1956.

Ellis discusses Catholics in colonial America during the nineteenth century (with particular emphasis on mass immigration and Protestant reaction) and in more recent times.

Ellison, Ralph. *Invisible Man*. New York: Random House, 1962.

A symbolic novel about the black man's search for identity in America. Available in paperback.

Essien-Udom, E. U. *Black Nationalism*. Chicago: University of Chicago, 1962.

An African's assessment of the Black Muslim movement and its appeal.

Farmer, James. *Freedom, When?*. New York: Random House, 1966.

The co-founder of the Congress of Racial Equality looks back at his and others' experiences in the civil rights movement.

Franklin, John Hope. *From Slavery to Freedom*, 3rd ed. New York: Knopf, 1967.

A historian's portrayal of the black experience in Africa and the United States.

Frazier, E. Franklin. *Black Bourgeoisie*. Glencoe: Free Press, 1957.

A controversial study of the Negro middle class.

— Freedman, Morris, and Carolyn Banks, eds. *American Mix*. phia: Westminster Press, 1971.

Speeches, stories, essays, and reports by and about America's ethnic minorities.

Friedman, Murray, ed. *Overcoming Middle Class Rage*. Philadelphia: Westminster Press, 1971.

A series of papers dealing with the views and relations of white working- and middle-class Americans to the changes wrought by black consciousness and the Black Power Movement.

Glazer, Nathan. *American Judaism,* rev. ed. Chicago: University of Chicago Press, 1972.

A synoptic review of American Jewish history from the first settlement in 1654.

————. *Remembering the Answers*. New York: Basic Books, 1970a.

Glazer's essays on the student revolt of the 1960s and related matters.

————, and Daniel Patrick Moynihan. *Beyond the Melting Pot*, 2nd ed. Cambridge: MIT Press, 1970.

An examination of New York City's five major minorities: black, Puerto Rican, Jewish, Italian, and Irish. The book is concerned with the meaning of cultural pluralism and the tenacity of identity. The introduction to this revised edition is particularly important for here the authors review the profound changes that occurred in New York —and elsewhere—since 1963, when the first edition was published.

Glock, Charles Y., and Ellen Siegelman, eds. *Prejudice, U.S.A.* New York: Praeger, 1969.

A collection of essays reporting on recent studies of prejudice in America.

Gordon, Milton M. *Assimilation in American Life*. New York: Oxford University Press, 1964.

An analysis of varying patterns of "assimilation" in the United States. Of particular note is Gordon's typology of assimilation and his discussion of the relationship between social class and ethnicity.

Greeley, Andrew M. *That Most Distressful Nation*. New York: Quadrangle Books, 1972.

A study of the Irish in America.

————. *Why Can't They Be Like Us?*. New York: Dutton, 1971.

Reports on research on the attitudes of "white ethnics" to blacks and others and a series of commentaries on the resurgence of ethnicity in recent years.

Grier, William H., and Price M. Cobbs. *Black Rage*. New York: Basic Books, 1968.

Two psychiatrists explore personality problems which, they claim, are attributable to racial oppression.

Grodzins, Morton. *The Metropolitan Area as a Racial Problem.* Pittsburgh: University of Pittsburgh Press, 1958.

A booklet which describes the character of discrimination in the American city of the 1950s.

Handlin, Oscar. *The Newcomers: Negroes and Puerto Ricans in a Changing Metropolis.* Cambridge: Harvard University Press, 1959.

A short volume which compares the history of New York's earlier immigrants with that of southern blacks and Puerto Ricans.

————. *Race and Nationality in American Life.* Garden City: Doubleday, 1957.

A series of historian Handlin's papers on race, racism and American society.

————. *The Uprooted.* Boston: Little, Brown, 1951.

A Pulitzer Prize-winning history, this book is "the epic story of the great migrations that made the American people." Of special interest are Chapters 4, 6, and 7, which deal with the creation of ethnic communities in the United States.

Hannerz, Ulf. *Soulside.* New York: Columbia University Press, 1970.

An ethnographic examination of ghetto culture and communal life in one part of Washington, D.C. by a Swedish anthropologist.

Hansberry, Lorraine. *Raisin in the Sun.* New York: Random House, 1959.

A play about a black family living in Chicago in the 1950s.

Hansen, Marcus Lee. *The Atlantic Migration: 1607–1860.* Cambridge: Harvard University Press, 1940a.

A classic study of immigration. It also won a Pulitzer Prize.

————. *The Immigrant in American History.* Cambridge: Harvard University Press, 1940b.

A series of essays by the Harvard historian. The book includes material that was to have been used in later volumes on immigration.

Haring, Douglas C. *Racial Differences and Human Resemblances*. Syracuse: Syracuse University, 1947.

An anthropologist's view of "race."

Herberg, Will. *Protestant-Catholic-Jew*. New York: Doubleday, 1955.

A study in the sociology of American religion. Herberg contends that the United States is "a triple-melting pot."

Herskovits, Melville. *The Myth of the Negro Past*. New York: Harper & Row, 1941.

The most famous of Herskovits' many examinations of the retention of Africanisms by Black Americans.

Higham, John. *Strangers in the Land*. New Brunswick: Rutgers University Press, 1955.

An examination of American nativism from 1860 to 1925 and an analysis of the forces which led to the enactment of legislation against unrestricted immigration in the 1920s.

Hobson, Laura. *Gentleman's Agreement*. New York: Simon and Schuster, 1947.

A magazine writer poses as a Jew in this best-selling novel about anti-Semitism.

Hsu, Francis L. K. *Challenge of the American Dream*. Belmont, California: Wadsworth, 1971.

A recent study of the Chinese in the United States.

Kallen, Horace M. *Cultural Pluralism and the American Idea*. Philadelphia: University of Pennsylvania Press, 1956.

An elaboration on an idea, "cultural pluralism," about which Kallen first wrote in 1915.

Kennedy, John F. *A Nation of Immigrants*, rev. ed. New York: Harper & Row, 1964.

A posthumously published edition of President Kennedy's brief history of the American people.

Killian, Lewis M. *The Impossible Revolution? Black Power and the American Dream*. New York: Random House, 1968.

A critical study of the civil rights movement, of Black Power, and the future of race relations in America.

————. *White Southerners*. New York: Random House, 1970.

The author views white southerners as an ethnic group and a "quasi" minority in this sociological analysis.

Kitano, Harry H. L. *Japanese Americans*. Englewood Cliffs, N.J.: Prentice-Hall, 1969.

A brief introduction to the experiences of Japanese Americans in the United States with special attention to the World War II period.

Kovel, Joel. *White Racism*. New York: Pantheon, 1970.

One of the first psycho-histories of the phenomenon of institutionalized racism in the United States.

Kramer, Judith K., and Seymour Leventman. *Children of the Gilded Ghetto*. New Haven: Yale University Press, 1961.

A study of second- and third-generation Jews in America.

Kurokawa, Minako, ed. *Minority Responses*. New York: Random House, 1970.

Various reaction patterns are considered here including *submission, withdrawal, separation,* and *revitalization.*

Lee, Alfred McClung. *Fraternities Without Brotherhood*. Boston: Beacon, 1955.

One of the few full-scale reports of discriminatory practices in private organizations on the college campus.

Lee, Rose Hum. *The Chinese in the United States of America.* New York: Oxford University Press, 1960.

A comprehensive study of immigration, settlement, and intergroup relations.

Lerner, Max. *America as a Civilization.* New York: Simon and Schuster, 1958.

An extensive study of American society. Of special interest is Lerner's discussion of "People and Place."

Levy, Mark R., and Michael S. Kramer. *The Ethnic Factor.* New York: Simon and Schuster, 1972.

The results of a comprehensive study of the significant role of minority-group membership in American elections.

Lewin, Kurt, ed. *Resolving Social Conflicts.* New York: Harper & Row, 1948.

A social psychological treatment of racial and ethnic problems.

Liebow, Elliott. *Tally's Corner*. Boston: Little, Brown, 1967.

An anthropologist's portrait of "Negro Streetcorner Men."

Lipset, Seymour Martin, and Earl Raab. *The Politics of Unreason*. New York: Harper & Row, 1969.

A social history of right-wing movements in the United States and a commentary on those to whom such movements appeal. One should pay particular attention to discussions of the "once-hads" and the "never-hads."

Lopreato, Joseph. *Italian Americans*. New York: Random House, 1970.

In this volume, one of a series on "Ethnic Groups in Comparative Perspectives," the author presents an insightful portrait of Italian Americans as a model immigrant group.

Lowenthal, Leo, and Norbert Guterman. *Prophets of Deceit*. New York: Harper & Row, 1949.

An examination of the language of prejudice and the nature of demagoguery.

Lyford, Joseph P. *The Airtight Cage*. New York: Harper & Row, 1966.

A study of New York City's multi-ethnic west side.

Lyman, Stanford M. *The Black American in Sociological Thought*. New York: Capricorn Books, 1972.

In this "sociology of sociology" Lyman examines the way different schools and various notables (including Robert E. Park) portrayed the black American and dealt with his plight.

————. *Chinese Americans*. New York: Random House, 1974.

A penetrating portrait of Chinese Americans from early contacts to the "Yellow Power" movement.

Malamud, Bernard. *The Tenants*. New York: Farrar, Straus, and Giroux, 1971.

The interaction of a black man and a Jew is the subject of this contemporary novel.

Malcolm X. *The Autobiography of Malcolm X*. New York: Grove Press, 1964.

The life story of the black leader and, for a time, Muslim spokesman.

Marden, Charles F., and Gladys Meyer. *Minorities in American Society*, 4th ed. New York: Van Nostrand, 1973.

This is a tightly organized volume detailing facts and figures about various American minorities. Of particular value are examinations of blacks, American Indians, and Mexican Americans in Chapters 5 through 9, 10, and 11, respectively.

Mason, Philip. *Patterns of Dominance*, New York: Oxford University Press, 1970.

An examination of power relations. While there is little material on the United States, the general theoretical position is extremely relevant to the examination of American materials.

Mayer, Kurt B., and Walter Buckley. *Class and Society*, 3rd ed. New York: Random House, 1970.

An introduction to the sociology of social stratification with special attention to the American scene.

Meier, August, Elliott Rudwick, and F. L. Broderick, eds. *Black Protest Thought in the Twentieth Century*, 2nd ed. New York: Bobbs Merrill, 1971.

A collection of essays on civil rights and black nationalism.

Mendelson, Wallace. *Discrimination*. Englewood Cliffs, N.J.: Prentice-Hall, 1962.

A résumé of the first five-year report of the United States Commission on Civil Rights, a commission created by act of Congress in 1957.

Miller, Arthur. *Focus*. New York: Reynal and Hitchcock, 1945.

A novel about American-style factions and anti-Semitism in the 1940s.

Moon, Bucklin, ed. *Primer for White Folks*. Garden City: Doubleday, 1945.

A collection of short stories and articles on the meaning of being black.

Myrdal, Gunnar. *An American Dilemma*. New York: Harper, 1944.

The classic study of black-white relations in the United States. Often criticized but never ignored, Myrdal's discussion of "creed v. deed" is presented here.

Novak, Michael. *The Rise of the Unmeltable Ethnics*. New York: Macmillan, 1971.

A lengthy essay on the place of Poles, Italians, Greeks, Slavs and other "white ethnics" in American society and American consciousness.

O'Connor, Edwin. *The Last Hurrah*. Boston: Little Brown, 1956.

A description of Irish-Americans in politics. The setting is Boston.

Padilla, Elena. *Up from Puerto Rico*. New York: Columbia University Press, 1958.

A view of migration from Puerto Rico and settlement in New York City.

Puzo, Mario. *The Fortunate Pilgrim*. New York: Atheneum, 1964.

A novel about growing up Italian-American in New York City.

Report of the National Advisory Commission on Civil Disorders. New York: Bantam.

This is the famous "Kerner Commission" report on the urban riots of the 1960s and their causes. Includes comparisons of the experiences of white immigrants and blacks.

Rex, John. *Race Relations in Sociological Theory*. New York: Oxford University Press, 1970.

An examination of the treatment of racial and ethnic relations by sociologists. The book ends with a statement about "race relations" as a distinct field of study.

Rose, Arnold M. *The Negroe's Morale*. Minneapolis: University of Minnesota Press, 1949.

A study of self-identification of black Americans largely based on material from the Carnegie Studies in the early 1940s.

Rose, Peter I., ed. *Americans from Africa*. 2 vols. New York: Atherton, 1970.

Volume I, *Slavery and Its Aftermath*, deals with four controversies: the retention of "Africanisms," slavery and personality, family and social structure, and life in the North compared with life in the South.

Volume II, *Old Memories, New Moods,* considers the roots of black protest, the civil rights movement, Black Power, and changing self-images.

————, ed. *The Ghetto and Beyond.* New York: Random House, 1969.

Essays by the editor and others on Jewish life in America. Topics covered include culture, religion, politics, civil rights, and literary expression.

————, ed. *Nation of Nations.* New York: Random House, 1972.

A volume of readings edited to accompany *They and We.* Includes essays, stories, excerpts from autobiographies, and sociological analyses of "the ethnic experience and the racial crisis" in the United States.

————, *The Subject Is Race.* New York: Oxford University Press, 1968.

A summary of the author's study of traditional ideologies and the teaching of race relations. Reports on hundreds of courses taught at American universities in the mid 1960s.

————, Stanley Rothman, and William J. Wilson, eds. *Through Different Eyes.* New York: Oxford University Press, 1974.

Original essays by twenty black and white writers which examine race relations in the United States in the 1970s from varying perspectives.

Roth, Philip. *Goodbye Columbus.* Boston: Houghton Mifflin, 1959.

A prize-winning novella and several short stories about Jewish life in America today.

Schermerhorn, R. A. *These Our People: Minorities in American Culture.* Boston: D.C. Heath, 1949.

Unlike most books on the subject this one includes discussions of Poles, Czechs and Slovaks, Hungarians and Yugoslavs in this country in addition to historical examinations of blacks, Spanish-speaking Americans, Italians, Japanese-Americans and Jews.

————. *Comparative Ethnic Relations.* New York: Random House, 1970.

Working papers on comparative ethnic relations, the author

includes a commentary on the study of prejudice and the character of "victimology."

Schrag, Peter. *Out of Place in America.* New York: Random House, 1970.

A collection of Schrag's previously published essays on various aspects of American social life. Included here is his "Decline of the WASPs."

Senior, Clarence. *Strangers—Then Neighbors.* New York: Freedom Books, 1961.

A brief introduction to the Puerto Rican situation.

Sexton, Patricia. *Spanish Harlem.* New York: Harper & Row, 1965.

An excellent study of the Puerto Rican community in New York City.

Sherif, Muzafer, and Carolyn Sherif. *Groups in Harmony and Tension.* New York: Harper & Row, 1953.

A series of essays on prejudice and a report on several fascinating studies of induced prejudice.

Shibutani, Tamotsu, and Kian M. Kwan. *Ethnic Stratification: A Comparative Approach.* New York: Macmillan, 1965.

A textbook which raises a number of fundamental questions about the relations between peoples. Many sections are relevant for understanding the meaning of "integration."

Silberman, Charles. *Crisis in Black and White.* New York: Random House, 1964.

Anticipating many of the events of the mid- and late 1960s, Charles Silberman offers an examination of the struggle for and barriers to integration. His comments on Saul Alinsky's radical programs are especially significant.

Simpson, George E., and J. Milton Yinger. *Racial and Cultural Minorities.* New York: Harper & Row, 1972.

A widely used near-encyclopedic text which deals with many different aspects of prejudice and discrimination from both a sociological and social psychological perspective.

Sklare, Marshall. *America's Jews.* New York: Random House, 1971.

The entire volume deals with social history and group identity. Emphasis is on five social characteristics: family, community, education, interaction (and intermarriage), and the issue of Zionism.

Smith, Lillian. *Strange Fruit*. New York: Reynal and Hitchcock, 1946.

The theme of this powerful novel is segregation in the deep South.

Stoddard, Ellwyn. *Mexican Americans*. New York: Random House, 1973.

A controversial study which includes historical background and sociological analyses of Mexican Americans.

Stonequist, Everett V. *The Marginal Man*. New York: Scribner's, 1937.

The author applies Robert Park's notion of "marginality" to a variety of racially mixed peoples.

Suchman, Edward A., John P. Dean, and Robin M. Williams, Jr. *Desegregation*. New York: The Anti-Defamation League, 1958.

This book offers some propositions about research suggestions for understanding both the dominant and minority communities.

Sugarman, Tracy. *Stranger at the Gates: A Summer in Mississippi*. New York: Hill and Wang, 1966.

An artist's commentary and sketches of the "Mississippi Summer" of 1964.

Sumner, William Graham. *Folkways*. Boston: Ginn, 1906.

A classic study in the sociology of culture, this book includes Sumner's definitions of "in-groups" and "out-groups" and a discussion of his conception, "ethnocentrism."

Tumin, Melvin M., ed. *Race and Intelligence*. New York: The Anti-Defamation League, 1963.

The editor and several other behavioral scientists discuss the controversy over intelligence testing.

Van den Berghe, Pierre. *Race and Racism*. New York: Wiley, 1967.

The author views the United States as a "herrenvolk

democracy" and explains why in this comparative study of race and racism.

Wagner, Nathaniel, and Marsha J. Have, eds. *Chicanos*. St. Louis: C. V. Mosby, 1971.

Contributed essays on social and psychological problems and perspectives of Mexican-Americans.

Warner, W. Lloyd, and Leo Srole. *The Social Systems of American Ethnic Groups*. New Haven: Yale University Press, 1945.

One of several volumes in the famous "Yankee City Series," this book deals with ethnicity.

Washington, Booker T. *Up From Slavery*. New York: Doubleday, Page and Company, 1901.

The Negro educator's autobiography.

Wax, Murray. *Indian-Americans: Unity and Diversity*. Englewood Cliffs, N.J.: Prentice-Hall, 1971.

One of the best among a growing number of studies of American Indians by sociologists and anthropologists.

Weinstein, Allen, and Frank Otto Gattel, eds. *American Negro Slavery*, rev. ed. New York: Oxford University Press, 1973.

A modern reader which includes articles on slaves, masters, and "the system."

Whyte, William Foote. *Street Corner Society*. Chicago: University of Chicago Press, 1943.

A sociological study of social interaction among the members of a group of men who lived in the Italian section of Boston.

Williams, Robin M., Jr. *The Reduction of Intergroup Tensions*. New York: Social Science Research Council, 1947.

A quarter of a century ago, this little book provided a guide to understanding the dynamics of intergroup conflict in the United States. Most of what was said then still applies.

————. *Strangers Next Door*. Englewood Cliffs, N.J.: Prentice-Hall, 1964.

A summary report on the Cornell Studies of Intergroup Relations conducted in the 1950s. Important chapters document group attitudes and minority reactions.

Wirth, Louis. *The Ghetto*. Chicago: University of Chicago Press, 1956.

A classic study of Jewish life in Europe and the United States with particular attention to responses to discrimination.

Woodward, C. Vann. *The Strange Career of Jim Crow*, rev. ed. New York: Oxford University Press, 1965.

The development of segregation from the withdrawal of federal forces from the South to the mid-1960s, written by the author of *Reunion and Reaction* (1951) and *Origins of the New South* (1951).

Wright, Richard. *Black Boy*. New York: Harper, 1945.

An autobiography of the famous black writer, this book describes the impact of discrimination.

Young, Donald. *American Minority Peoples*. New York: Harper, 1932.

One of the first sociology texts to be devoted exclusively to the topic. Written by the person credited with introducing the concept "minority" into the sociological literature.

Young, Whitney M., Jr. *Beyond Racism: Building an Open Society*. New York: McGraw Hill, 1969.

The late head of the Urban League offers his views on what is needed to reduce prejudice in American society.

Ziegler, Benjamin M., ed. *Immigration: An American Dilemma*. Boston: D. C. Heath, 1953.

A collection of famous papers on the immigration controversy. Includes Horace Kallen's early view of "cultural pluralism."

INDEX

Siegelman, Ellen, 157n, 231n
Silberman, Charles, 94n
Simmel, Georg, 165
Simpson, George, 124–125n, 158n, 175–176, 188n, 189n
Singer, L., 188n
Slavery, 28–31
Slavs, 65, 224
Slovaks, 220
Smith, Gerald L. K., 137
Sombart, Werner, 165
"Soul-less militancy," 186, 207
Southern Christian Leadership Conference (SCLC), 36, 211
Spanish, 11, 26–27, 29, 41, 54–59
Srole, Leo, 19n, 124n
Stampp, Kenneth, 61n, 78
Stern, Bernhard, 159n
Stevens, Alden, 60–61n
Stevenson, Robert Louis, 98, 124n
Stewart, George, 64, 66, 93n
Stoddard, Ellwyn, 62n
Stonequist, Everett V., 165, 166
Streicher, Julius, 136–137
Student Non-Violent Coordinating Committee (SNCC), 153–154, 206, 207, 209
Suchman, Edward A., 189n
Sumner, William Graham, 124n

Takaishi, Shingoro, 12
Terkel, Studs, 228, 232n
Territoriality, 166–167
Thomas, W. I., 12, 108
Thompson, Edgar T., 126n
Thoreau, Henry David, 209
Toch, Hans H., 157n
Tocqueville, Alexis de, 121, 128n
Trotter, Monroe, 200
Truman, Harry S., 35
Tumin, Melvin M., 126n, 216n
Turner, Nat, 196

Unitarians, 28, 90
Universal Negro Improvement Association (UNIA), 203–204

Uplift, 195, 199–201
Urban League, 206, 211

Van den Berghe, Pierre, 22, 60n
Veblen, Thorstein, 165
Violence, 150–155
Von Linne, Carl (Linnaeus), 107
Vorst, Milton, 93n, 94n

Warner, W. Lloyd, 19n, 124n
Warren, Robert Penn, 18n
Washington, Booker T., 192, 200–202, 215n, 223
Washington, George, 67, 82
Wax, Murray, 61n
Weber, Max, 165
White Anglo-Saxon Protestant (WASP), 66, 169, 179, 223–224, 229
"White Negro," 182
Whitman, Walt, 16
Whyte, William Foote, 169, 188n
Wicker, Tom, 158n
Wildavsky, Aaron, 213, 216n
Wiley, Norbert, 169, 188n
Wilkens, Roy, 193, 206
Wilkes, Paul, 232n
Williams, Robin M., 18–19n, 125n, 130, 156n, 189n
Wilner, Daniel, 124n
Wilson, William J., 114, 127n
Wirth, Louis, 19n, 158n, 163–164, 187n
Woodward, C. Vann, 61n
Works, Ernest, 156n
Wright, Richard, 80, 132, 177–178, 189n
Wrong, Dennis, 233n

X, Malcolm, 176, 197, 215n

Yiddish, 47, 161
Yinger, J. Milton, 19n, 124–125n, 158n, 175–176, 188n, 189n
Young, Donald, 14–15, 19n
Young, Whitney, 121, 128n

Zangwill, Israel, 70, 93n, 185
Ziegler, Benjamin M., 61n